to
Kathy, Mac, and Tyler (DML)
and
Peggy (MWD)

RETAILING
CASES AND
APPLICATIONS

Dale M. Lewison
The University of Akron

M. Wayne DeLozier
The University of South Carolina

Published by Charles E. Merrill Publishing Company
A Bell and Howell Company
Columbus, Ohio 43216

This book was set in Century and Clarendon.
Production Editor: Mary Pound
Cover Design Coordination: Will Chenoweth
Text Designer: Ben Shriver

Library of Congress Catalog Card Number: 81-84267
International Standard Book Number: 0-675-09853-X
Printed in the United States of America
1 2 3 4 5 6 7 8 9 10—86 85 84 83 82

Preface

A number of outstanding case writers in the field of retailing have contributed to this casebook. Its strengths lie in the diverse backgrounds of the contributors' writing and consulting experiences. This casebook can supplement any introductory book in retailing.

All cases are realistic business situations. Some cases have more data and information than are necessary to analyze the cases properly. In these instances, students should determine which data are relevant and which data are not. In other cases, more data and information can be useful to students in making their analyses. Library research can help students supplement the case materials in making their analyses. It is the option of the instructors to decide how much external search they wish for students to undertake in preparing each case analysis.

The editors are indebted to all the contributors who helped to make this book possible. Also, we acknowledge the diligent work of Steve Smith and Gary Bauer at Charles E. Merrill Publishing Company.

Dale M. Lewison

M. Wayne DeLozier

Contents

PART 1

The Case Method

Reading 1

USING THE CASE METHOD

IN THE CASE METHOD, you will be presented with a description of some problem confronting an organization. In addition, the case offers facts and opinions about the organization, its markets, and its environment. You must analyze the situation, answer a set of questions regarding the type of action to be taken, evaluate the merits of a set of alternatives, and defend the approach chosen.

As opposed to other educational methods, the case method places intellectual demands on a student that are substantially different and more taxing. The principal objective of the approach is to reduce the amount of time it takes to become skillful in decision making.

Case analysis, if approached properly, places the student in a simulated business environment. There is usually little structure to a business problem, and you must draw on a wide range of experiences and formal educational tools to attack a problem. An analyst usually has limited time and incomplete information in dealing with a case. And, finally, you will want to present your analysis and findings as a complete unit in written and oral forms for evaluation.

Each individual has had a different set of experiences and has been exposed to a different pattern of courses and formal educational experiences. As a result, the alternatives that you evaluate and recommend may vary from those selected by others. There is no one "best" answer to a case. Each analysis and set of recommendations is based on a unique set of perceptions, analytical skills, and effort expended. Each analysis must therefore be appraised with this in mind. That is to say, while there may be no one best answer, there are vast gradations in the quality, completeness, substantiation of claims, and creative content of the analysis and presentation. Remember

Adapted from Denis F. Healy, "Student Guidelines to Using the Case Method," *Consumer Behavior Dynamics: A Casebook*, ed. M. Wayne DeLozier (Columbus, Ohio: Charles E. Merrill Publishing Company, 1977), pp. 1–8.

this as you attack cases and reflect on how your performance has been evaluated.

As you progress and become sophisticated in case analysis, you will find that short cases of a page or two in length can be just as difficult as those of fifteen or twenty pages. Moreover, you will find that the time spent developing a solution will increase as your skill grows. The same can be said for the depth and quality of your work.

Frequently, students complain that they have to spend too much time on casework, or that they cannot find in the textbook how to attack a particular case problem. Others comment that there must be an easier, more structured way to learn how to deal with such problems. Unfortunately, little comfort can be offered on these points. Case analysis takes considerable time, and a special kind of time, at that! One cannot possibly do a respectable job on a case when tired or only partially committed to the problem.

Textbooks are useful in case analysis when used as a tool to supply information about the merits of one analytical approach or decision alternative over another. In a sense, a text is a bag of tools. The selection of which set of tools to use to fix a problem, however, is *up to you*, the analyst, *not the book*. Thus, it is often useful to scan the text after reading a case to glean ideas and to refresh your memory about possible alternatives. However, never depend on the text to do the intellectual work for you. You, not the book, have a brain. So use it!

Finally, in dealing with student objections, it is difficult to suggest an easier route to the acquisition of knowledge at the analytical and integrative level. The case method, by simulating real business situations, offers the student a very efficient method for gaining decision-making skills in a low-risk setting.

With today's high-speed pace of business decision making, one can ill afford to be a novice in this area. Although luck is a decided factor in the successes and failures one experiences in organization life, there is no question that the most successful people are sophisticated analysts and decision makers. The case approach is designed to help you gain these skills early in your career, and at a low total personal cost.

Guidelines on Case Analysis

Although they may vary in length, scope, and degree of difficulty, cases have many things in common and can be approached using a general analytical framework. This section discusses ways to approach a case analysis.

Five main elements to a well-developed case analysis are

1. Identification and specification of the problem
2. Appraisal of the facts and opinions expressed in the case
3. Development of alternative approaches to the case problem
4. Selection and justification of best approach
5. Discussion of implementation schedule and organizational responsibilities

A brief discussion of the contents of each stage of the analysis follows.

Step 1: identification and specification of the problem

Often a beautifully prepared case analysis will be worthless because the analyst failed to identify the basic problem(s) in the case. Instead, attention was directed at a symptom, and analysis dealt with how to make the symptom go away. Just as an elevated body temperature indicates a more fundamental problem, so too in a business case, a decline in sales or profits points to more basic problems. For instance, the underlying trouble may be a breakdown in the organization, a new competitor who has entered the market, or perhaps a target market whose tastes or needs have changed.

Problem definition should constitute the single most important aspect of case preparation. To accomplish this task, one must read and think about the case several times. Next, a list of potential problems should be prepared. Then, the list should be purged of all items symptomatic of more fundamental problems. Finally, the remaining items that truly constitute the problem areas should be organized in terms of degree of importance, or by topical area. A precise, tightly written statement of the case problem(s) should be presented for every case.

Step 2: appraisal of facts or opinions

Every case deals with the behavior and relationships between people and organizations. Moreover, virtually every case contains bits and pieces of fact, information, opinion, and conjecture. It should be apparent, then, that some of the material presented is extraneous, incorrect, or improperly organized. The analyst must be sensitive to the hazards of accepting such information as "gospel."

A useful way to net out the substantive from the spurious is to (a) sift out the interrelationships that exist among the participants, (b) develop a profile of the likely postures, attitudes, and reactions of the key figures in the case, (c) separate the facts from the opinions, (d) arrange the facts in sequence of importance to the case, (e) arrange the opinions in terms of their plausibility or centrality to the case, and (f) present the preceding in outline form as part of the case write-up.

When you weigh alternatives and make a choice, you will draw on a list of facts, opinions, and relationships. Well-developed cases are built on a careful appraisal of the *relevant* facts and upon a cautious and selective interpretation of the opinions and organizational interrelationships uncovered in this step. Never forget that human beings, with all of their biases, prejudices, and perceptual hang-ups, are involved. A business is not a machine.

Moreover, energetic and ambitious students will want to locate additional sources of information concerning the structure and practices of the industry, government legislation and regulatory agencies that affect the industry, current consumer behavior data related to the product or service discussed in the case, and other pertinent information that might be useful.

Step 3: development of alternative approaches

The typical case asks the analyst to propose a course of action to rectify the problem or achieve some objective. The potential action areas may cover a wide range of specific possibilities, but all can be placed under the general headings of organization and the marketing mix.

Organizational changes may include such items as changes in the personnel who staff a particular marketing function, or change in the structure of a particular function (such as a shift from product management to market management). Marketing mix changes involve alterations or changes in emphasis of the product, promotion, pricing, and channel of distribution areas.

For any problem, there may be several organizational and marketing mix combinations that have a reasonable potential for overcoming the problem and for achieving objectives. A well-developed case presentation will normally present not less than three nor more than six alternative action plans. Each alternative should contain a description of the organization scheme and marketing mix combination to be used and comments on the "how" and "why" aspects of the choice.

Step 4: selection and justification of most promising alternative

Ultimately a decision must be made about the direction to take. In "real world" situations, the decision maker operates with incomplete information and often under excrutiatingly painful time pressures. Often, there is lingering doubt about the chosen action and, frequently, information about the impact of a strategy is incomplete, late, confused, or nonexistent.

Case analysts find many of these characteristics in dealing with a case situation and are tempted to avoid making a decision by resorting to excuses about incomplete information and lack of time or experience. These excuses, although understandable, are unacceptable in the real world and so, too, in case analysis. The only justifications for no action is that "no action" is the preferred strategy or that there is a *cost justified* basis for seeking additional information before committing to a strategy. In either of these cases, a well-documented rationale must be presented.

Should additional information be needed to complete a strategy or action plan, the following support information must be contained in the case write-up:

1. Precise statement of the kind of information needed, including dummy displays to show formats
2. Source(s) and expected time and dollar costs to obtain information
3. Discussion of how the information is to be used in shaping a decision
4. Course of action if information is favorable
5. Course of action if information is unfavorable

For each action alternative (strategy) the analyst should list its strengths and weaknesses using a ledger (T account) format. Using this approach and a summary statement, the chosen alternative should be highlighted and justified over the others.

Step 5: implementation of strategy

An important ingredient to all managerial activity is the finesse with which decisions are put into action. Timing, sensitivity to human relations issues, and the ability to concentrate resources to impact on a situation have a great bearing on success or failure of strategies. Thus, implementation considerations are an essential part of the decision-making process.

In this section of the case development, the analyst must plan and make explicit the implementation steps. Consideration should be given to factors such as timing, organizational reaction, competitive reaction, resource requirements and availability, and methods of measuring and tracking performance. Useful questions to ask oneself in developing this area are Who should be involved? When should action be taken? How can performance be measured? What market responses are expected?

Case Presentation

Cases may be presented orally or in writing and may be prepared by individuals or by groups. Throughout your use of the method, you may be asked to prepare and present a case analysis using each mode. This section is devoted to a discussion of the more important aspects of each mode. Hopefully, some time-saving tips can be gleaned from a careful reading. We want to stress that the prime criteria for evaluating the merits of a presentation are the quality of the analysis and the communication power of the presenter. Weakness in either detracts from the other.

Written presentations

In some cases, you are asked to respond to a set of questions; while in others, you may be left to unravel the problems and alternatives without any clues. In either instance, the format for presentation is essentially the same. A good topical outline for written or oral case analysis can be seen in the previously presented discussion of case analysis. For most write-ups, the steps listed could be subheadings. For cases in which questions are specified, a direct answering of the question should be organized using a similar format but tailored somewhat to the situation. Should it be necessary to develop the case, assumptions may be made and must be stated explicitly. The student must be prepared to defend assumptions; otherwise, many problems could be assumed away. Finally, diagrams, tables, charts, and the like should always be considered as a means of improving the communicating power of the presentation.

The analyst should assume one of several postures in developing and presenting the case. For most cases, the appropriate role is that of a line manager responsible for planning and implementing strategy. In other situations, a plausible role might be that of a staff analyst or outside consultant. Regardless of the role assumed, the analyst should not assume the student or the innocent bystander role.

The case write-up should be concise, organized with liberal use of sub-headings, employing outline or list formats, tables, and so forth. A general format for written case development involves statements about these factors:

1. Pertinent facts, opinions, etc., of present situation (includes analysis and presentation)
2. Objectives (desired situation)
3. Problems
4. Alternative approaches to the problem
   (a) Advantages
   (b) Disadvantages
5. Criteria in selecting approach
6. Implementation of selected approach
7. How to monitor progress and measure results
8. Additional research needed
9. Conclusions

Judgment of the quality of your presentation will consider the following dimensions:

1. Appearance, grammar, organization, and form. Clarity of expression, sentence and paragraph structure, and readability.
2. Problem definition and fact identification. Ability to distinguish between problems and symptoms, and between fact and opinion.
3. Alternative selection and evaluation. Completeness, substantiation of decision, creativity of alternative identification and selection, and skill used in critiquing each alternative.
4. Selection and implementation. Precision of strategy statement and completeness of implementation considerations. Weakness in this area is as harmful as weakness in the problem definition area.

Oral presentation

Although written analysis is important in many situations, the ability to explain one's ideas verbally is critical in persuading others. Some students find oral presentations difficult, but they are a good way to learn verbal skills. Portraying ideas persuasively but tactfully is a delicate process, the mastery of which can only be achieved through practice. As a result, much of your work in case analysis will involve the use and development of these skills. Therefore, you may be called on frequently to present either a partial or full case analysis. This exercise normally will be associated with the written development of a case.

An oral presentation requires a slightly different format and set of considerations than does a written one. The principal differences are in the character and environment of the audience. Written presentations typically are analyzed under less distracting conditions than oral ones. In addition, the audience for the oral presentation is likely to be considerably more passive, uninformed, and disinterested than the audience of the written report. Thus, attention to the communication task normally is greater in oral work. Care should be taken to organize your presentation so that the audience is constantly aware of the sequence or direction of your comments and where you are in the sequence. Furthermore, the use of visual aids is essential for an effective oral presentation. Every major presentation should include a judiciously chosen set of aids. Even a more informal individual presentation should contain some visual treatment to capture attention and to clarify a point.

The following aspects of oral presentation are subject to evaluation:

1. Organization of presentation
2. Content (quality and thoroughness)
3. Quality of visual aids
4. Speaking voice (delivery)
5. Courtesy to audience
6. Ability to answer questions
7. Posture, poise
8. Ability to defend position
9. Persuasive impact
10. Mannerisms
11. Practicality of recommendations

Group versus individual presentations

Group and individual work will be treated along the previously listed dimensions, with the further proviso that within any group presentation, each member is expected to make a visible impact on the group output. Group case development is for the more involved cases and may require numerous meetings, division of labor, rewrites, presentation rehearsals, and visual treatments.

Group work is part of the learning process in the case method because it puts the students into a role relationship that more closely parallels the "real world" than does individual work. Without question, group assignments are more demanding than others if for no other reason than the difficulty in scheduling meeting times, extracting commitments from peers, dividing the work, and performing other activities. Every instructor who has assigned group work is confronted with such objections; however, these same problems extend far into the "real" business world where one must contend with them on a daily basis. Most instructors understand the problems associated with the process; but few are willing to eliminate group work from their courses, because of the high learning value of the approach.

Every member of a group should define his or her role with group consensus and with the understanding that peers as well as the instructor will evaluate both the quantity and quality of his or her work. In other words, it is very important that the group task be subdivided and the responsibilities be communicated in writing to each member within the group and to the instructor. Failure to do this task early in the group case development process will detract from the smooth functioning of the group and the evaluation of group performance. Finally, it should be remembered that roles should be traded from case to case to the extent possible. Each individual should have a turn at presenting a portion of the group's findings.

PART 2

The World of Retailing

Case 1

W.T. GRANT COMPANY— THE DEATH OF A GIANT

FOUNDED IN 1906, W.T. Grant, a seventy-year-old variety store chain, had 1,100 stores, 70,000 employees, and $2 billion in annual sales by 1975. The firm had compiled an enviable record. Except for a loss in 1932 at the height of this country's depression, Grant's had reported annual profits for the first sixty-seven years of its existence and had developed into one of the country's largest variety store chains. It had expanded into the suburbs and attempted to become a department store, selling furniture and major appliances on credit.

Then, quite suddenly, W.T. Grant reported the largest loss ever to hit a retailer. At fiscal year-end 1975, Grant's reported a loss of $177.3 million, even with a tax credit of more than $100 million.

History

The Grant Company was founded on a $1,000 investment by its name-sake, William T. Grant, who had been employed previously in the shoe department of a Boston department store. Grant set up his first store in a corner of the Lynn, Massachusetts, Young Men's Christian Association building. A window sign on opening day announced "A new kind of store—a department store with nothing over 25 cents." The founder's merchandising idea was to fill the pricing niche between the then burgeoning "five-and-dimes" like Woolworth's and Kresge's and the department stores whose wares at that time began at about fifty cents. Merchandise moved swiftly and profitably at twenty-five cents since there were no size or fitting problems and no personal selling effort involved. With spartan surroundings and an emphasis on solid quality at bargain prices, the Grant chain, which expanded initially throughout New England, began to move into the mid-Atlantic states. From its beginning, Grant's customer base was lower-middle-class working people. By 1919

This case was prepared by Steven J. Shaw, University of South Carolina.

the chain grew to thirty-three stores. Although its top price rose to $1.00 during the inflationary period of World War I, Grant's remained a working family store with inexpensive, ready-to-wear clothes and low-cost drygood staples, which was the backbone of its daily business.

During the Great Depression, Grant's and other variety store chains expanded and prospered while consumers with reduced incomes turned to the lower-priced retailers. The Depression's severe deflation created a wide variety of new goods under the "top" price, and Grant's quickly became a "junior" department store. With the severe deflationary effects of the Depression, Grant's buyers were able to procure drastically low prices on major items such as all-silk slips, wool bathing suits, rayon bedspreads, and men's shoes and pants. Also, their staple merchandise such as goldfish, lipsticks, brass screws, art lamps, and brassieres were virtual steals.

During the mid-1930's, William T. Grant assumed the position of chairman of the board of W.T. Grant Company and left the day-to-day operations of the business to his managers. After many years of successful operation and wide expansion during the 1940's and 1950's, Mr. Grant retired in 1966 at the age of ninety.

Changing Environment, Changing Strategy

During the 1940's, Grant's removed ceiling prices on its merchandise and slowly began to introduce furniture and appliances into its stores. Also, during this decade the chain began opening stores in the suburbs, shifting from its emphasis on in-town locations. Grant's management recognized the shift of families from downtown to suburbia and decided to follow this trend by locating stores nearer to its customers. Management, however, believed it was important to avoid the large regional centers and preferred the smaller community or strip center locations. Following this basic game plan, management decided in 1962 to embark upon a rapid expansion program. Over the next ten years, Grant's opened 612 new stores, bringing the total to 1,188 with a payroll of 82,500 employees. This rapid expansion, which was financed mostly by external borrowing, was very costly. A total of twenty-seven banks loaned W.T. Grant's $614 million to launch their new suburban stores.

A shift in strategic emphasis

In 1968 under a new president, Richard W. Mayer, Grant's shifted its merchandising emphasis from softgoods to hardgoods. With an eye apparently on Sears and J.C. Penney, Grant's tried to make the transition to a suburban department store at a time when aggressive discount stores like K-Mart and Woolco were making the same move. The Grant stores began stocking refrigerators, television sets, air conditioners, and other big ticket appliances and furniture items. Usually these were produced by nationally known manufacturers such as Westinghouse and Fedders. But management insisted on removing the brand name and marketing these appliances under its own private label, Bradford. Unfortunately, the Bradford label was not well known to consumers. Shoppers were confused by the shift from softgoods to hardgoods. They neither could identify with Grant's as the retailer of variety softgoods it had been nor as the retailer of upgraded, higher-priced hardgoods it was trying to become.

Liberal credit terms

President Mayer, who had moved up the corporate ladder through credit management, went all out to induce customers to buy Grant's big ticket items by offering liberal credit terms. Store employees were given bonuses for signing up new credit card customers. Credit applications were not carefully screened, and by January, 1975, Grant's customers owed the company $600 million. Grant's was now in an untenable financial position of having to borrow money to buy new merchandise while waiting for customers to pay their bills.

Merchandise planning and control

Inadequate merchandise inventory controls led to excessive accumulation of stock in many departments and out-of-stock conditions in others. Indiscriminate, unplanned buying and lack of a sound markdown policy resulted in seasonal merchandise being left on the shelves long after the season had passed and consumers passed it by. By 1975 it was clear the company's problem was one of survival. Some suppliers began selling to Grant's on a C.O.D. basis only. Others stopped shipments in mid-transit.

Final efforts at recovery

Under new management, Grant's petitioned for Chapter XI, a procedure under bankruptcy law that allows a firm to continue operating while formulating a plan to pay its debts. Robert H. Anderson, a highly successful ex-Sears executive, embarked on a program to close unprofitable stores and reduce excess inventory. In the northeastern United States, he cut Grant's down to 359 stores with 24,000 employees. Under Anderson, Grant's dropped its major appliance lines and returned to the merchandising of low-cost softgoods.

But these efforts came too late. In February 1976, creditors moved to have the company declared bankrupt, and the court so ruled. Robert Anderson blamed suppliers for Grant's inability to make the recovery plan work. The merchandise didn't come in, he said, apparently because vendors were afraid of suffering further losses. With liabilities of $1.1 billion, W.T. Grant Company became the largest failure in retailing history.

Questions

1. Identify and discuss the principal reasons Grant's failed.
2. Under what conditions should a retailer stick to marketing nationally advertised brands? What conditions are necessary for private branding to be successful?

3. Since Grant's was trying to transform itself into a merchandiser of expensive shopping and specialty goods, what locational strategy would you have suggested to Grant's? Explain.

4. Several years ago, a major West Coast aircraft manufacturer was saved from bankruptcy by means of a huge government loan and certain guarantees. Discuss the pros and cons of having the U.S. government move in and keep a giant like Grant's from going out of business.

5. What are the relative advantages and disadvantages to a liberal credit policy? How can a retailer control credit?

6. S.S. Kresge (K-Mart) and F.W. Woolworth (Woolco) were variety store chain operations that successfully entered the mass merchandising field as discount stores. Why were they successful while Grant's was unsuccessful at entering the mass merchandising field as a chain department store?

7. What do you believe is the future of variety store retailing in tomorrow's world of retailing?

8. How important is store image? How does a retailer go about changing the image consumers have about his or her store? What problems of store image did Grant's encounter? Are any national chain retailers currently attempting to change their image? (If so, who are they and how are they going about changing their image?)

9. During the late 60's and early 70's what were some of the major changes occurring in the retailing environment (e.g., competition or consumer buyer behavior) that might have been a contributing factor to Grant's failure?

Case 2

AVON PRODUCTS, INC.—FOR WHOM THE BELLES TOLL

OUR GROWTH ONLY EMPHASIZES what energy and fair dealings with everyone can accomplish. We propose first to be fair with our customers by giving them the very best goods that can be made for the money; we propose to be fair and just, even liberal, with those who form the sinew of our business.

As we have grown in the past, so shall we grow in the future; the limit in this business is measured only by the amount of hard work and energy that is put into it. While we have worked faithfully and loyally in this field, yet if we stop and look over the past and then into the future, we can see that the possibilities are growing greater and greater every day; that we have scarcely begun to reach the proper results from the field we have before us. The millions and millions of people in this country of ours today who are not using our goods are the losers, and it is our place and purpose to see that at least they must be made acquainted with the merits of the goods, the honesty with which they are made and delivered direct from the laboratory to the consumer.[1]

With these words, the founder of Avon Products, David H. McConnell, commented on the promise and future of Avon products. Without a doubt, Avon has been a stalwart company in spite of a radically changed and turbulent marketplace. It claims to be the world's largest manufacturer and distributor of cosmetics, toiletries, and costume jewelry.[2] Avon has managed to respond to changing life styles and shifting markets through well-organized and orchestrated managerial systems and marketing approaches.

Commenting on Avon's success, *Forbes* reported that:

Avon's explosive growth took place after World War II, with the growth of disposable income, the spread of suburbanization and the increase in the proportion

Adapted from Denis F. Healy, "Avon Products, Inc.: For Whom the Belles Toll," *Consumer Behavior Dynamics: A Casebook*, ed. M. Wayne DeLozier (Columbus, Ohio: Charles E. Merrill Publishing Company, 1977), pp. 94–104. The material in this case has been obtained from a variety of published sources. The case has been prepared for teaching purposes only and is not intended to be evaluative of industry or company structure or performance.

17

of large families tending to keep women confined to their homes. Prior to this, Avon was just getting by. As recently as 1946, the company's sales were only $17 million—small progress indeed for a company already 60 years old. The economic and sociological trends in the late forties, fifties, and sixties were just right for Avon.[3]

Recent changes in life styles, the emergence of the liberated and career-oriented woman, consumerism, competitive threats, and so on, pose challenges and opportunities to Avon's vitality and growth potential. With the resource base and distribution capabilities of Avon, creative responses are possible and even likely. Historically, Avon's marketing costs have been lower than competitors. And through the use of direct sales representatives and modest advertising, Avon has been able to obtain very high gross margins. But with changing times and costs, Avon realizes that it must consider new alternatives.

Present Operations and Products

Not counting makeup shades, Avon offers 700 products to its markets. In addition to the direct sales of cosmetics, Avon has diversified into the costume jewelry business, the operation of beauty salons, mail order sales of men's and women's apparel under the "Family Fashions" name, and the sale of glass and plastic housewares in Canada under the name "Geni" using the party plan method. Although it is a comparatively recent entrant into the costume jewelry business, it has the distinction of being the world's largest marketer of such products—testimony to the distribution strength of the firm.

The cornerstone of the Avon operation is its worldwide network of 800,000 Avon ladies. This field sales system has evolved over the past ninety years and today involves five levels of management. The senior position is given the title *general manager.*

The general manager is responsible for one of seven branches in the United States and has two regional managers reporting to him or her. Each regional manager assumes responsibility for eight divisional managers. Divisional managers direct eighteen district managers who in turn have recruiting, training, and supervisory responsibilities for about one hundred Avon representatives. Avon ladies are given sales territories of between 100 and 200 households in their own neighborhoods and typically are able to cover 20 to 30 households every two weeks for twenty-six sales campaigns a year.[4]

Company Objectives and Commitments

A company of the size and diversity of Avon justifiably must recognize multiple commitments and must have a series of underlying objectives for its business. In the early 1970's, Avon began to give explicit recognition to the notion of social responsibility. This resulted in a "Statement of Corporate Responsibility," which deals with the consumer, discrimination, and the environment. The written commitment to the consumer says

> We seek to assure complete customer satisfaction by offering quality and safe merchandise through prompt and courteous service, using the most ethical marketing methods. We subscribe to the principle that all consumers should be informed. Therefore, we shall take further steps to communicate to them information about our company and our products, and to encourage their inquiries and comments.[5]

In terms of economic objectives, the following two were considered most significant:

> First—to achieve greater penetration of the United States market, with special emphasis on improving the effectiveness of our field organization. It is our goal through better training and new programs for our District Managers to increase the number of customers served by Representatives and thus expand coverage of the country's households.
>
> Second—to pursue the fine potential in foreign markets, which in total are several times larger than the United States. In so doing, it is our objective to improve the marketing programs and operating efficiency of our international operations and to raise their level of profitability to a point comparable with that of the United States.[6]

The Business Environment and Avon's Position

As with virtually every other company in its industry, the impact of spiraling costs, shortages of raw materials, and the energy crisis has had a damaging effect on Avon. Furthermore, the inflation of the 1970's retarded consumer interest in cosmetic and personal care and related products.

Some speculate that the sensitivity of Avon to business cycle fluctuations is amplified by the character of its customers, who usually are members of blue-collar families. Avon, on the other hand, indicates that the demographic characteristics and trends of its market will help it grow through the early 1980's. In recent times, one of the fastest growing segments of the U.S. female population has been the twenty-five through forty-four age group. This group accounts for 60 percent of total Avon sales. Also, about 60 percent of sales comes from those in the $15,000 to $20,000 income group. About 50 percent of U.S. families are currently in this group.[7]

During the mid-1970's, sales and earnings dropped markedly during the period of high inflation. Avon's rebound occurred, according to *Fortune,* "only after draconian cost controls were imposed." But, as the article continued, "No amount of cost cutting will solve Avon's basic problem—it needs to increase sales."[8] Recent favorable trends in sales productivity through increased advertising, reorganization of the selling organization, and product line revisions have contributed to increased sales.

One of the most pressing and unique challenges confronting the company is the changing life style of its customers and representatives. The same inflationary pressures that precipitated a general decline in sales also has a hidden impact. With increased costs of living, more and more women are finding it necessary to work part- or full-time to supplement the family income. Currently, more than two out of five women of working age are employed. As a result, it has become more difficult to find potential customers at home. In addition, women have become quite mobile and less homebound in the last decade. For those women not working, "tennis fever," volunteer work, and other diversions tend to pull them away from home during the prime selling hours. This forces the Avon representative to work in the evening and Saturday, to be much more active on the phone, to call on women at their place of work, and to use other indirect selling methods.[9] Regarding working women, an Avon executive said, "42 percent of our customers are working women— the same percentage as the national average, and they account for 50 percent of our total U.S. sales."[10]

On the other side of the coin, however, Avon feels it might benefit by having access to a larger potential market of representatives, although many are finding other work more satisfying and profitable.

As if these pressures were not enough, Avon faces a challenge from a growing number of powerful and sophisticated marketers. *Business Week* made the following observations on the competitive situation:

> To add to the challenge, the cosmetics industry itself is changing complexion. Starting ten or fifteen years ago, major outside companies began buying dozens of small independent cosmetics houses. Now, many of the larger houses are being gobbled up. Among the latest: Max Factor (Norton Simon), Helena Rubinstein (Colgate-Palmolive), Elizabeth Arden (Eli Lilly), and Lanvin-Charles of the Ritz (Squibb).
>
> On the door-to-door side of the business, Dart Industries added Vanda Beauty Counselor (along with Tupperware), Bristol Myer bought Luzier cosmetics, and giant General Foods acquired Diviane Woodward cosmetics.[11]

The industry

In 1973, *Forbes* reported that Avon had captured 80 percent to 90 percent of the domestic, direct sales market for cosmetics. There were no competitors with more than 4 percent of the door-to-door market. Moreover, Avon was reported to hold approximately 20 percent of the total U.S. cosmetic market of $5 billion.[12]

Presently, Avon estimates it has about 25 percent of the foreign market.[13] In its mode of distribution, Avon has a virtual monopoly with its most staunch competitor reported to be Mary Kay Cosmetics. Mary Kay was founded in 1963. The firm has somewhat different selling styles and philosophies from Avon. It calls its salespersons "consultants" and uses home demonstrations for groups rather than for individuals. The commission structure is higher than Avon's, and movement to the field manager position is earned by sales performance as a consultant and is retained subsequently by territorial productivity.[14]

The marketplace

There have been dramatic changes in the consumption patterns and life styles of consumers. The influence of rapid inflation, changing orientations to work, and the change in the family unit and leisure activity have challenged the creativity of Avon and others in the industry. Consumers most affected economically and psychically tend to be those in Avon's prime market. The "squeeze on the middle class" is taking its toll by making it more difficult to purchase a single family home, to afford education for one's family, and to purchase discretionary, nondurable items such as those offered by Avon. The prolonged inflationary and unemployment period of the 1970's has caused uncertainty in the minds of all but the most secure consumer. Although the impact of the squeeze is visible mostly in a slowdown of consumer durable purchases, a prolonged period such as this one also has a profound effect on consumer purchasing patterns and attitudes toward nondurable goods.[15]

The Avon Product Line

Cosmetics

The market for cosmetic products is segmented readily into a number of classifications based on age and sex. For Avon, the primary market is women in the eighteen to fifty-five-year-old group. In addition, they have developed a line of products for men, which constitutes between 10 and 15 percent of net sales. For the teens market, Avon offers a line of fragrances called Sweet Honesty, introduced in 1973, which quickly became one of its top three fragrances. Overall the teen market for cosmetics is estimated to purchase over $40 per capita per year. The baby market also is served by Avon through its Clearly Gentle line of ointments and lotions. Also, soaps, shampoos, and hair care products are offered. Finally, there is the black consumer market. In mid-1975, Avon began marketing a line of makeup, Shades of Beauty, designed for and marketed to black consumers.[16] Also available to the black market are hair care and skin care products.

Noncosmetic items

In addition to the door-to-door sales of cosmetics, Avon sells directly to the consumer in two other major product areas, clothing (Family Fashion) using mail-order methods, and housewares (Geni) using the party-plan approach. In its annual report, Avon reported on these areas:

Last year Family Fashions increased its customer base to 575,000 and expanded sales to all fifty states. Other 1975 developments included centralization of all operations in Newport News, Virginia...issuance of our first complete product catalogs...and introduction of a new home furnishings category, such as sheets, bedspreads, and draperies. Family Fashions products are sold by mail order and not through Avon representatives.

Two years after acquisition of Geni Company, about 2,000 Geni representatives now sell plastic and glass housewares through the party plan across Canada. Products include decorative servingware, saladware, thermal containers, and such items as terrariams, cigarette boxes, and bathware. There are some seventy-five products in the line with prices ranging from $1.75 to $15.95. The most popular products are in the $10 to $11 bracket.[17]

For the Family Fashion line, a sales increase of 40 percent was reported representing a 50 percent growth in unit sales with 1.5 million pieces. There were over 600 items in the line.[18]

Another major market served by the representatives is in jewelry and gift items. Avon, after only four years in the business, became the nation's largest distributor of costume jewelry. In the jewelry portion of the business, prices range from $4 to $14 with women's items accounting for most of the business. About fifty new designs, mainly suited to the younger working woman, were introduced in the mid-1970's. The other part of the line, gifts, is principally in the form of decanters.

Questions

1. In what ways have consumer life styles changed? How have these recent changes affected Avon's marketing approach?

2. How should Avon adapt its marketing program to the changing consumer life styles you have identified?

3. Identify the threats and opportunities that the change in consumer life styles has for Avon. Discuss how Avon should minimize the threats and take advantage of the opportunities.

4. Are there particular segments in which life styles are changing more rapidly than others? If so, describe these segments.

Endnotes

1. Taken from "Great Oak" as it appeared on the cover of Avon's *1972 Annual Report* and written by Avon's founder, David H. McConnell, in 1903.
2. Avon Products, Inc., *1975 Annual Report,* p.1.
3. "Avon Products: Is Its Beauty Only Skin Deep?" *Forbes,* July 1, 1973, p. 22.
4. "Troubled Avon," *Business Week,* May 11, 1974, p. 100.
5. "The Avon Commitment," Harvard Business School Case No. 9-375-165, p. 14.
6. *1973 Avon Annual Report,* p. 6.
7. David W. Mitchell, speech before the West Coast Analysts' meeting, June 14, 1976, pp. 4-5.
8. *Fortune,* January 1976, p. 28.
9. "Avon Calling—Is Anyone Home?" *Finance World,* October 30, 1974, p. 37; See also *Business Week,* May 11, 1974, pp. 98-106.
10. Speech delivered before West Coast Analysts' meeting, pp. 5-6.
11. *Business Week,* May 11, 1974, p. 98.
12. *Forbes,* July 1, 1973, p. 20.
13. *1974 Avon Annual Report,* p. 12.
14. *Forbes,* July 1, 1973, p. 20.
15. "The Squeeze on the Middle Class," *Business Week,* March 10, 1975, pp. 52-60.
16. *1974 Avon Annual Report,* p. 12; *1972 Avon Annual Report,* p. 7.
17. *1975 Avon Annual Report,* p. 18.
18. Ibid.

Case 3

McDONALD'S— CURRENT STRATEGIES AND FUTURE PLANS

McDONALD'S is an international chain of restaurants, with more than 5,200 outlets located throughout the world, in all fifty of the United States and twenty-four international markets. The company is the world's largest retail foodservice organization. Its headquarters is located at McDonald's Plaza, Oak Brook, Illinois.

McDonald's is primarily a licensing operation. Approximately 74 percent of the restaurants are licensed to independent, local business-people. The remainder are company owned. The company follows a strategy of building its management staff from within. A McDonald's restaurant typically carries a staff of from fifty to seventy-five people. Many crewpeople are high school and college students working at their first job. Many others are homemakers who work part-time.

The majority of McDonald's restaurant managers come from the crew ranks. These men and women have the opportunity to move up either in the restaurant companies owned by McDonald's licensees or in the corporation itself. Today many former crewpeople work as area supervisors, field consultants, and in the corporation's home and regional offices.

Ownership of a McDonald's restaurant calls for the capability to finance an investment of $250,000 plus a commitment to pay McDonald's rental and services fees amounting to 11.5 percent of gross sales. Before a newcomer can qualify for a McDonald franchise, however, he or she must meet McDonald's rigid franchise requirements. In addition, he or she must work for several weeks in a McDonald store to learn firsthand what is involved in both crew work and store management. If, after the required period of time, the applicant likes the business, he or she is placed on a list of registered applicants waiting for a location.

Despite the demanding financial and internship requirements, there is a year-long waiting list of new applicants. Since experience makes the best

This case was prepared by Steven J. Shaw, University of South Carolina.

operators, the bulk of new licenses are awarded to existing franchises. However, it is company policy to give at least 30 percent of new franchises to qualified newcomers. At least two weeks of final restaurant management training is given to all prospective owners at the company's national training center just before they take over their stores.

McDonald's international management training center

Since 1961 the licensees, managers, and corporate personnel of the McDonald's restaurant chain have studied at a modern training center in Elk Grove Village, Illinois. This school is affectionately referred to as Hamburger University. Built around a college-type format, the training center curriculum includes not only work experience in a McDonald's restaurant, but also an intensive classroom program. Subjects taught range from the day-to-day management of a McDonald's to courses in business management, accounting, marketing, personnel management, and community relations.

The training center has lecture- and classrooms, a complete research library on restaurant management and the food industry, a closed-circuit television studio, film-processing equipment, and a United Nations-type simultaneous translation system for non-English-speaking students. Nearly two thousand trainees a year pass through its doors. Besides its regular campus curriculum, the international training center prepares audiovisual films for use in management and crew training at all stores in the United States and in McDonald's twenty-four international markets.

Product Line

McDonald's first menu was centered around the hamburger. Today the menu has expanded to include not only the original regular hamburger, french fries, and shakes, but also several large sandwiches—the Big Mac, Quarter Pounder, McChicken, and Filet O' Fish—as well as hot apple and cherry pie, cookies, and sundaes. Since 1976, McDonald's restaurants have begun to serve a full breakfast menu, which includes the Egg McMuffin, hot cakes and sausage, scrambled eggs and sausage, hash browns, English muffins, Danish pastry, and juices.

The menu in McDonald's international restaurants, like in the United States, is centered around hamburger sandwiches, french fries, and shakes. In many international markets, however, McDonald's has added menu items that specially meet local eating tastes. For example, wine is served in France, beer in Germany, tea in Britain, chicken croquettes in the Netherlands, and soup in Japan.

Extensive Use of Marketing Research

To identify consumer preferences and opinions, McDonald's annually conducts hundreds of thousands of consumer interviews. In 1978 alone, this number was over 1.8 million. As a result, the company has some of the most current and complete marketing information on consumer eating-out habits. Thanks to market research, the company has been able to respond to its customers' changing needs through such innovations as indoor seating and new types of restaurant locations. Recently many restaurants have begun adding convenient "drive-thru" windows to better serve those McDonald's customers who prefer to remain in their automobiles.

Traditionally McDonald's restaurants were located in suburban areas. In recent years, however, the company has expanded its locations to include small towns, urban centers, shopping malls, interstate highway exit areas, even college campuses. Today McDonald's restaurants serve people not only where they live, but also where they work and play.

McDonald's Television Advertising

McDonald's corporation aired its first national television commercials in 1967. Since that time the company has become one of the largest television advertisers in the United States. In 1978, for example, McDonald's and its licensees spent an estimated $200 million on advertising and promotion, nationally and locally.

One of McDonald's first network advertising themes was "McDonald's is Your Kind of Place." It was followed by "You Deserve a Break Today," introduced in 1970. Since 1975 the theme has been "At McDonald's, We Do It All For You." Traditionally McDonald's advertising was geared to families. Today it also tries to reach senior citizens, single adults, and teenagers.

National television advertising is supported by a voluntary contribution of one percent of gross sales by licensees and company stores that want to take part in the program. Most local restaurant operators value highly the national television advertising opportunity. Recently sponsored special television programs include "The Sound of Music," "Christmas Around the World," and the "Charlie Brown" series.

In addition, operators can contribute a percentage of their gross sales to an advertising co-operative in their local markets. There are currently 170 local McDonald's co-ops throughout the United States. These are serviced by some 100 local advertising agencies.

Public Relations by McDonald Licensees

Participation in civic and charitable activities has been part of the McDonald's tradition since the first restaurant opened in 1955. The local, independent businesspeople who own McDonald's restaurants typically are active in many events, both in their communities and nationwide.

Many of McDonald's national community-involvement programs originated in one market and were then adopted by the licensees on a national scale. McDonald's work in the Fight Against Muscular Dystrophy is a prime example. The initial involvement began in the 1960's when local McDonald's restaurant associations, particularly in New York City, began their work for the charity. Then, in 1971, McDonald's restaurants throughout the country joined together to raise money. These funds, contributed by the restaurants and their customers, are annually presented at the Jerry Lewis Labor Day Telethon Against Muscular Dystrophy. In 1978, the contribution exceeded $1.7 million.

The McDonald's All-American High School Band, which celebrated its twelfth anniversary in 1978, is another local program with strong national support. Each year McDonald's licensees throughout the United States encourage local high schools to nominate their outstanding young musicians; 102 such students, two from each state and the District of Columbia, are chosen to play in the Band, which annually appears in Macy's Thanksgiving Day Parade in New York City and the Tournament of Roses Parade in Pasadena, California.

Most licensees participate in additional "home town" activities. For example, some award annual college scholarships to local students; others sponsor youth athletic teams or organize charity bike-a-thons and walk-a-thons.

Some restaurants help collect Christmas toys for needy children, while others help raise money for high school bands or cooperate with community clean-up and beautification drives.

Local managers and crewpeople often conduct tours of their restaurants, showing the other side of the counter to school children, clubs, and other groups. Many restaurants offer Ronald McDonald Birthday Parties for neighborhood children.

A fleet of Big Mac Coaches—comfortable, customized buses—serves McDonald's restaurants throughout the United States. When not in company use, they are available free to civic and charitable groups.

Some Future Plans

Expansion plans

The company's plans call for the construction of some 300 new units in the United States and perhaps 150 overseas every year for the next five years.[1] This is an ambitious objective. The magnitude of the challenge can be seen when environmental threats are considered. Increasing energy costs, rising beef prices, and higher minimum wages are creating serious problems in the fast-food industry. Also, McDonald's top management estimates that some 6,865 new fast service restaurants were opened in 1978 and this should further intensify the competition.

McDonald's uses selection-of-location techniques that have proven highly successful in the past. Location strategy calls for the following procedures. First, a general picture of the prospective sites is obtained through aerial surveys. For this purpose the company has available five helicopters. Aerial observations and photographs frequently uncover important topographical details that ground travel would not reveal.

Next, sales potential of the sites under study are calculated by computer at the company's Oak Brook division. The computer analysis uses the customary statistics on changes in population, income and competition.

Finally, company officials visit promising areas for personal observations. The locations are closely studied by driving through them. Stops are made at supermarkets, cocktail lounges, and other places where the local people congregate. McDonald's is a people business and these personal observations and contacts are important in finding good locations.[2]

Expansion of breakfast sales

Breakfast menus first introduced in 1976 account for more than 15 percent of company sales. The addition of McDonald's original creation of Egg McMuffin to the usual breakfast items has opened up a whole new area of potential business for McDonald's. Breakfasts are currently being served in all McDonald restaurants. Substantial national television advertising reminds customers of the breakfast opportunity.

New product development

Unlike some competitors, McDonald's is very cautious when it comes to menu expansion. As a result, the company has had very few product failures in its twenty-five-year history. Before introducing a new product, the company tests it extensively in test kitchens and test markets. And these tests frequently last several years. For instance, McDonald's tested chicken for over seven years to develop a chicken recipe that McDonald's could be proud of.

In 1976, an executive chef with rigorous European culinary training was added to the McDonald staff. His task is to study ways to make menus more nutritious, get more fiber into them, and also to help refine recipes for new menu items.

Questions for Discussion

1. Evaluate McDonald's site selection strategy. How does it compare with the strategies of other large retail organizations?

2. In addition to television, what other advertising media would you recommend for McDonald's?

3. What public relations activities does the McDonald's franchise owner use in your home town?

4. If you had the financial backing to finance the $250,000 investment in a McDonald's, would you be interested in obtaining a franchise? Consider the fact that 11.5 percent of gross sales had to be paid continuously regardless of whether the bottom line shows a profit or loss.

5. Do you think the McDonald's approach to new product development is overcautious?

Endnotes

1. "McDonald's Grinds Out Growth," *Dun's Review,* December 1977.
2. Ray Kroc with Robert Anderson, *Grinding It Out: The Making of McDonald's* (Chicago: Henry Regnery Company, 1977), pp. 166–67.

PART **3**

The Retail
Consumer

PARTICIPATIVE PHOTOGRAPHICS—A NEW CONCEPT IN PHOTOGRAPHY

PARTICIPATIVE PHOTOGRAPHICS is a company that represents a new concept in photography. Most photographic businesses sell photographic equipment and/or photographic services—everything from enlarging and special effects to finished photographs. Participative Photographics provides neither. It rents out photographic facilities—cameras, enlargers, darkrooms, studios, and so forth.

When James Humberg founded Participative Photographics in 1972, he was addressing a need felt by many young photographers: a place where they could do their own work before they had enough business to support full-time facilities. The answer was to develop facilities that could be rented as needed.

Humberg located his operation on the floor of a low-rent industrial building in downtown San Francisco. It consisted of a small front office, a gallery, 10 darkrooms for black-and-white photo development (rented at $4 per hour), a darkroom for color development ($5 per hour), a darkroom for developing 8×10 prints ($8 per hour), and 2 studios ($10 per hour). His facilities also included an array of specialized equipment for the advanced photographer.

Between 1972 and 1979, Humberg's business grew slowly—on the average of about 5 percent per year. In 1979, sales totaled $58,000, just barely covering expenses. Humberg had to admit that he was stumped. He knew photography and he knew photographers. There was a big need for his service, but his service was not selling.

Analyzing His Customers

In the fall of 1979, Humberg arranged with a near-by college in San Francisco to have some students study his business and make recommendations.

Source: Maurice I. Mandell and Larry J. Rosenbert, *Marketing*, 2nd ed., © 1981, pp. 237–39. Reprinted by permission of Prentice Hall, Inc., Englewood Cliffs, N.J.

The students spent several days reviewing his past records. Then they interviewed a number of customers and followed up these interviews with a short survey.

Survey Results

	Local Professionals	Out-of-Town Professionals	Beginners/ Students
Average visits (per mo.)	2.2	0.3	1.1
Where heard about facilities:			
Friend or colleague	64%	91%	81%
Advertisement/Yellow Pages	22%	3%	15%
Read about it	12%	5%	2%
Other	2%	1%	2%
Average satisfaction (5 = high)	3.7	4.8	4.1

The students came to the conclusion that Humberg was right about the value of his service. Everyone they interviewed was enthusiastic about it. Nevertheless, they discovered that there were really three distinct customer segments: (1) local professionals, (2) out-of-town professionals; and (3) beginners/students. The survey results revealed differences in the ways these three groups viewed Humberg's operation.

The students pointed out several interesting facts. Local professionals accounted for 42 percent of Participative's customers, but they represented 70 percent of Participative's dollar volume. Out-of-town professionals accounted for 11 percent of Participative's customers, but 4 percent of its dollar volume. Beginners accounted for the remaining 37 percent of customers, but only 26 percent of dollar volume.

In contrast to these findings, the students discovered that out-of-town professionals were the most satisfied with Participative's service and local professionals the least satisfied. Beginners/students occupied the median position.

There also were differences in the way the various groups found out about Participative Photographics. While word-of-mouth communication was most important for all three groups, advertising (mostly in the San Francisco newspapers) and listings in the Yellow Pages were very helpful for local professionals and beginners. Furthermore, the students found that the respondents who indicated that they had read about the service were referring to an article that had appeared in *Popular Photography* describing Humberg's unique operation. The article had appeared a year before and had been followed by a noticeable jump in the number of local professionals using Participative's facilities.

Customer interviews

The customer interviews conducted by the students were classified according to the segment that they represented. The following interviews were typical of the three types of customers.

A local professional: Humberg really has a good thing going. He provides professional facilities for people like me who need them, but can't afford them. My only complaint is that they are expensive. Most of use are living on a shoestring. So $5 an hour doesn't sound like a lot of money for using a color darkroom, or $10 an hour for a studio, but it becomes a lot when you use them as much as I have to—especially when you add it to all the other expenses involved in high-quality photographic work.

An out-of-town professional: My work takes me to lots of different places. I have extensive contacts in each city. And I make a habit of reviewing the photography section of the Yellow Pages periodically to make sure I don't miss anything. Someone in my profession never knows when he'll need a special type of service or a rush order. I heard about Participative Photographics from a friend in town. Once he mentioned it, I remembered seeing its ad in the phone book. But I had thought it was a "hobby shop" operation. As it turns out, I wish I had paid more attention. It is the ideal facility for an out-of-towner like me. I can get immediate turnaround with the quality I need by simply using the facilities and doing my own work.

A beginner: I really like the Participative Photographics concept. I go down to their studios and get professional advice while I work. Mr. Humberg really knows his photography, and he is willing to help out beginners. In fact, some of the photography instructors at school give us lab credit for the time we spend there. What's more, I have met one or two really big names—people whose work I have studied. They were in town and needed to do some work, so they went down to see Mr. Humberg.

Questions

1. Explain the differences in usage rates among the three customer segments.

2. Comment on the different ways in which the customers of Participative Photographics found out about its services. Do these differences suggest a course of action for the company?

3. Discuss the varying degrees of satisfaction experienced by the three consumer segments.

4. Based on your consumer behavior analysis for each of the three segments, evaluate the potential of each as a target for Humberg's marketing efforts.

5. Is Participative Photographics a good name for the businesses?

6. Develop a marketing program for Mr. Humberg.

Case 5

CRAMPTON AUTO SALES, INC.

CRAMPTON AUTO SALES was established by Bill Crampton in 1954 after his return from Korea. Bill learned automotive mechanics in the service and decided to open an automotive service center and dealership after the Korean Conflict.

Bill opened Crampton Auto Sales in his hometown of Atlanta with a used car lot and auto repair service. With the population growth in Atlanta and the surrounding area, Crampton Auto Sales skyrocketed.

Recalling the words of his former Army commander, "Seize the opportunity," Crampton opened a dealership that sold new and used cars while continuing to service all makes of automobiles. With the rising prosperity of Atlanta and the South, Crampton decided to expand operations. During the 1960's he opened dealerships in Birmingham, Augusta, Columbia, Jacksonville, Charleston, and New Orleans.

Recently, Crampton's experienced a decline in new car sales as did other dealers in the automotive industry. Moreover, Crampton noticed a shift in sales from his dealerships to other dealerships selling other new cars. Although many consumers were buying smaller, fuel-economy cars, Crampton believed that his sales were shrinking more rapidly in the intermediate to luxury size cars than those of his competition. Furthermore, dealerships in other parts of the country that sold the same make of car were not experiencing the same rate of decline as Crampton.

At a meeting of the Sales and Marketing Executives International (SMEI) Club in Atlanta, Crampton discussed his situation with Bill Maggard, a marketing professor at Emory University. Maggard told Crampton about a recent article he had read concerning automotive purchasing in the local retail market. The article described a study stating that although advertising by

Adapted from M. Wayne DeLozier and Arch G. Woodside, "Crampton Auto Sales, Inc.," *Consumer Behavior Dynamics: A Casebook,* ed. M. Wayne DeLozier (Columbus, Ohio: Charles E. Merrill Publishing Company, 1977), pp. 41–44.

auto producers created certain images and informational characteristics in the minds of consumers, purchasers at the local level were more influenced by the local dealer's merchandising activities.

Maggard explained to Crampton that within specific classes of automobiles, image projections of quality, styling, and handling were perceived by consumers as "about the same" among models offered by General Motors, Ford, Chrysler, and American Motors Corporation. The difference in local sales primarily was a function of local dealership promotion.

In clarifying his statement, Maggard offered the following examples: "In consumers' minds the Pontiac Catalina, the Buick Lasabre, and the Oldsmobile Delta 88 are perceived as very similar. The Chevrolet Lemans and Malibu, the Buick Century, and the Olds Cutlass also are perceived as similar by consumers. And, the Pontiac Sunbird and Chevy Monza also appear to be alike to many consumers. Once a consumer decides the class of car he wants, local dealerships play a major role in influencing the final purchase decision. The study revealed that the *amount* and *kind* of information dealers conveyed to potential customers directly influenced the customer learning process and, thus, local dealer sales."

Crampton was intrigued and asked Maggard to conduct a study in his market areas to determine the major informational sources for cars that affect his customers' learning behavior.

The Maggard Report

Maggard conceptualized his task as one of determining the prepurchase information-seeking behavior of automobile consumers. He decided to assess the relative importance automobile consumers attach to the variety of personal and impersonal information sources.

TABLE 5-1

Sources of information used by new car purchasers

Information Sources	Weight
Dealer visit[1]	20
Expert opinions[2]	16
Consumer reports	14
Friends' opinions	12
Spouse's opinions	11
Dealer advertising	10
Brochures	8
Manufacturers' advertising	6
News articles	3
TOTAL	100

1. Information from salespeople, service personnel, personal inspection of cars and facilities, etc.
2. Auto repair and service people and others perceived by purchasers as knowledgeable about cars.

Maggard conducted interviews in all seven of Crampton's markets. Three hundred and fifty personal interviews were conducted with recent new car purchasers (i.e., those who had purchased within the past ninety days). Table 5-1 shows the results of the study in terms of the relative weight of importance new car purchasers attach to each of the stated information sources.

Maggard also collected data on what kinds of information new car purchasers sought and the relative importance that each kind of information had in the purchase decision. Table 5-2 summarizes the results.

TABLE 5-2

Information sought and its relative importance in purchasing a new car

Price[1]	11
Dealer service and reputation	28
Warranty	5
Convenience of dealership location	20
Physical product features[2]	22
Options available	14
TOTAL	100

1. Importance of price information after consumer had determined affordable price range.
2. Refers to styling, comfort, handling, horsepower, gas economy, etc.

In writing his report for Crampton, Maggard felt that he needed to provide an interpretation of the data and recommendations for a course of action for Crampton Auto Sales. Moreover, he believed that he should include several behavioral principles related to learning and explain to Crampton how these principles could help market Crampton's cars.

Questions

1. What merchandising strategy decisions are most critical for Crampton Auto Sales?

2. What merchandising problems have been identified by the Maggard report?

3. How would you advise a new car buyer in evaluating automobile brands?

4. What learning principles would you suggest that Crampton use in helping his customers learn about his automobile offerings? How would you implement them?

Case 6

THE NEW CAR DILEMMA

IT WAS THE SUMMER that Stephen and Laura were five and three years old, respectively. While my wife and I were in reasonably good control of the problems attendant with growing children, a crisis was developing. The five-year-old was due to start school in September on a five-day-per-week basis, and the kindergarten nearest our home did not provide transportation.

Our automobile inventory had been one—a four-year-old Pontiac Grand Prix—since Martha's Volkswagen had been stolen several years earlier. The Pontiac replaced the only other car I had ever owned, a 1966 Chevrolet Biscayne, bought as a used car in 1972.

The previous summer Martha had reminded me of the need to buy a second car when transportation to school became necessary. On many occasions after the Volkswagen was stolen, she complained about the inconvenience of being a one-car family. Needs had to be anticipated. If a shopping trip was in order, it had to be done in the evening, on the weekend when stores were crowded, or when she could drive me to work and pick me up in the evening.

Unanticipated needs presented the worst problems. "What if one of the children had an accident and I was without a car?" Martha had asked. "What would I do?"

When the Pontiac required service, everyone was inconvenienced. It was particulary unpleasant for me because I usually drove the car to the university and back home in the late afternoon. Thus, I felt the problem to an even greater degree.

A fairly strong case for a second car was being constructed. I had always agreed with the existence of a need, but felt that we had learned to live with the inconveniences very well. There seemed to be a clear-cut economic advantage to having only the Pontiac. Therefore, I put off serious consideration

Adapted from John F. Willenborg, "The New Car Dilemma," *Consumer Behavior Dynamics: A Casebook*, ed. M. Wayne DeLozier (Columbus, Ohio: Charles E. Merrill Publishing Company, 1977) pp. 262–68.

of the issue as long as possible. After all, the thought of having to draw upon hard-earned savings was not a pleasant one. Nor was the prospect of car payments for one to three years very bright. And when would the Pontiac need to be replaced? It was already nearly four years old.

In January, Christmas-related bills came due and we dipped into our savings account. The inconvenience of the fall semester, with me coming home early to let Martha use the car, or Martha taking me to work and picking me up, was temporarily pushed out of my mind. I reminded her several times that it would be difficult to afford a car in the upcoming months, particularly since my salary at the university ended in June (I was on a nine-month contract).

In April I was forced to cancel two tennis matches because the logistics of the car could not be worked out to accommodate family needs. In May, the Pontiac's water pump had to be replaced for the second time in less than six months.

Just before final exams in late May, Martha remarked one evening that she had stopped in at a Datsun dealership that day and had checked the prices. Martha said she hadn't had time to drive any, though. "Why don't we stop by and drive one on Saturday?" she asked me.

On Saturday, we drove several Datsuns. The kids had a ball in the back seat. (The salesperson didn't think he and the kids would fit in the back seat, so we went out by ourselves.) We shared the opinion that the cars were a bit smallish, but fairly comfortable. My father (who is 6′3″) had always said that he wouldn't buy a car unless he could wear a hat while sitting behind the wheel (it was cold in Iowa and he had sinus trouble). I'm also 6′3″ and had to bend slightly to see out of the front window and to avoid messing my hair. When I mentioned that to Martha, she reminded me that she would usually be driving the little car.

I commented further that the car seemed "tinny" and that all the colors were "garish." She agreed but countered with, "It sure moves out faster than the Pontiac. Would be great in heavy traffic!"

"That's true," I said.

By the time we had finished our test-drive, it was after 5:30 P.M., and we were in the middle of rush-hour traffic. The drive home lasted nearly a half hour. We were both acutely aware of the time and distance involved. "How would you like this trip every time the Datsun needed service?" I asked Martha.

For several weeks, the subject of the new car was not mentioned. One evening in early July, we both were "turned on" by a television commercial for a car that had been selling well since its introduction into the market, the Mercury Capri. Martha and I agreed to get a baby-sitter for the children the next afternoon and look at the Capri and some other small cars.

When we arrived at the Mercury dealership, we looked around the lot (I didn't want to attract the attention of a salesperson, whose presence looking over my shoulder always made me nervous). We saw several cars that seemed to fall into the small-car category, but none of them were very exciting. Finally, we saw a bright red Capri, conspicuously parked directly in front of the showroom. The door was unlocked, so I started to get in, finding that the seat was pushed too far forward to allow me to get past the steering wheel.

After several minutes, I was able to push the seat back far enough to get in. I found myself looking through the upper third of the windshield. My head was flush against the roof, and, if I hunched forward, I could see some distance in front of the car. "Maybe it has a reclining seat back," I speculated.

"Martha, close the door so I can get a feel for the size of this thing." The first time she pushed the door, it didn't close. When I moved my elbow, the door closed on her second try.

When I got out, I said, "No way. Japanese must make this car for Japanese. (I didn't realize the car was not manufactured in Japan.) I don't care how fast it'll get to sixty miles per hour. I couldn't ride in this thing for ten minutes before I'd have to get out and stretch!"

"But it's a beautiful little car. I'd love to drive one," Martha said.

I looked up and saw a salesperson approaching. "Let's go up the street and look at the Dodges and Plymouths. I think their cars have more room. They're generally made 'boxier' and more conservatively."

The Dodge-Plymouth dealer's lot was packed with new cars, in contrast to most other lots we'd passed. There were many cars in the Volare and Omni categories. The colors were not attractive, but there were many from which to choose. We talked to the salesperson, who was confident he could find the color combination we wanted.

"What do you think, Martha?" I said on the way home. We had spent nearly an hour talking to the salesperson, looking at his card file of cars in stock, and trying to get a feel for how much of a reduction he would give us from the sticker price. We drove an Omni within a several block radius of the showroom. "Lots of room in those cars—not bad-looking either. And I think we can really get a great price. Did you ever see more cars in the lot? They really are overstocked."

"Looks pretty good. I agree," Martha said. "But I felt like we were driving in a box. And it had rather poor acceleration, don't you think?"

"Well, it is going to be a second car, you know."

She seemed disappointed. "I'll go by the Chevy place tomorrow. A lot of people are buying Monzas, I hear. Or is it the Chevette? I'll take a look at them on the way home."

The next day, at the site of the largest Chevrolet dealer within one hundred miles (according to their advertisement), I found exactly one Chevette (a big seller), and it was a sort of sherbet orange color that didn't appeal to me at all. There were many Monzas, all seemingly the same drab color. I drove one and asked the salesperson about a comment a friend made to me about a possible defect in the transmission. "Only one chance in a thousand that the defect will show up," he noted.

Despite my feeling that a Chevy was a sound car (my 1966 was a gem), I couldn't get "turned on" by the Monza, and the Chevette was not readily available. And I liked the Dodge Omni better, anyway.

When Martha and I discussed the matter that evening, we wondered about the next step. "What about Fords?" she queried.

"Wouldn't have one if it was given to me," I replied. "The most economical model they make is the Fiesta and I've heard nothing good about them."

"Well, what about a Fairmont or a Granada," Martha asked.

"Okay, but I think we're at a disadvantage with the American cars. The manufacturers are already tooling up for next year's models. We'll have to take what's left and the best ones are already sold. But we can look."

It was ten days or so before I could get motivated to go looking again. We agreed that the Fiesta was too small and, apparently, put together with "bailing wire." The Fairmont was a plain little car, not exciting at all. We weren't impressed overall, but I did drive a Fairmont briefly. It handled nicely in traffic and had pretty good acceleration. But I just couldn't get "turned on" by such a plain-looking car. Granadas, we concluded, were too expensive for what you got.

It was now mid-August and the start of school was less than three weeks away. "What's next?" I wondered.

"How about a Toyota?" Martha asked one night.

"I had thought about that possibility, but the dealership is way over near the Datsun dealer. The prospect of having to take the car over there for service is not pleasant. And I understand they are a bit more expensive than the comparable Datsuns."

Martha then reminded me of a new dealership she had driven by, much more accessible than the original one. It sold only Toyotas (in contrast to the other, which also sold Volvo and Mercedes) and was advertising heavily on the radio. I recalled seeing recently a Toyota Cressida (one of Toyota's more expensive models) and being impressed with it. "Well, what do we have to lose? We can go tomorrow afternoon."

The showroom of the new Toyota dealer (Toyota Town) displayed four cars: a Cressida, two Corollas (one a station wagon), and a Celica (a sporty-type Toyota). We walked around and looked at price stickers for about ten minutes before a salesperson came over and introduced himself as Fred. We asked all the relevant questions about mileage, trunk space, and service. The Corolla got better mileage than the Cressida, but the Cressida had more horsepower and was much classier looking. Additionally the Cressida had a lot of extras for more comfort and had somewhat more interior room. There were more Corollas from which to choose. Obviously, the Cressida cost more (about 30 percent more on the sticker price than the Corollas).

Fred explained that Toyota's model year began in January or February or whenever the cars were ready. So, there would be no problem in obtaining cars during August or September.

While we were test-driving the Cressida, I asked Fred, "What do we really have to pay for a Cressida like the one in the showroom? How much below the sticker price?"

"The sticker price on foreign cars is what you pay. There is very small margin on them. They're not like American-made cars. I might be able to get you fifty bucks off, but that's about it. And demand is very high for Toyotas. We haven't been able to get all the cars we want."

"Come off it, Fred," I said. "You have a new dealership and your competitor (Thom's) has been in business for years. You mean to say you'll let them beat you out of a sale on a price basis?"

"Well, I don't know. You're right to some extent. We are trying to establish ourselves in this market. Just tell me which car you want and I'll see what I can do."

I liked the Cressida I had driven and I think Martha did, too. It seemed to be made better than the Datsuns, roomier than the Capris and Fiestas, and there were quite a few on the lot from which to choose. The price was the big hangup, and I didn't like the Corolla well enough to buy it at the lower price.

Back at the showroom, while Fred went to get some brochures for us, we looked at the cars on the floor again. Martha sat in the Celica. "Sure wish we could buy a sports car like this one," she said.

"But it's not practical for us. Look at the back seat. There's not enough room for one person. The trunk is very small. And we'd be paying for the fancy instrumentation. And this has off-white upholstery. Wouldn't the kids have a time with that!"

On the way home, Martha again remarked that she had liked the Cressida, but that she still thought the sports car was a good idea. She liked Fred. She thought the new dealership probably would treat its customers with great care. But, most of all, she wanted to buy a car and have it over with. I argued that Fred ought to be willing to take less for the Cressida. So I said I would go over to Thom's in the morning and see what they would do pricewise.

The salesperson's name at Thom's was Harold. When I told him we were looking at cars at Toyota Town, he said he could beat any price they offered by $100. He had several Cressidas and one Celica. "How about letting me drive the Celica around the block?" I asked. When I got into the car, I slid the seat back all the way and was surprised that I was very comfortable. And since the seat also reclined, I had plenty of head room when the seat back was lowered a notch. On the highway, the engine did not falter noticeably when I turned on the air conditioning (which had happened on most of the other small cars I'd driven). The car handled well and I began to appreciate the sports-car features.

When I got back, Harold was ready to sell me either the Celica or any Cressida on the lot. I put him off because the ride in the Celica had changed some of my decision criteria: the need for trunk space didn't seem so pressing (we wouldn't travel long distances in it anyway), the back seat was certainly large enough for two small children, and a sports car would have good resale value. "Let me talk it over with my wife," I said.

When I got to the office, I called Fred and told him what Harold had said about the price. Fred was quiet for a minute, then said he didn't know how Harold could do it. But, he said he would do what he could for me. I said that we might come back over in the evening.

I told Martha about the price dealings, but not about my impression of the Celica. That evening, we went to Toyota Town again. While we waited for Fred to return from dinner, we looked at the Cressidas in the lot again and then ended up in the showroom in the Celica with the white upholstery. "Do you think we could get by with a car like this?" I asked.

When she answered enthusiastically in the affirmative, I asked, "What about the lack of trunk space? What about the light upholstery? What about the higher price?'' Her answers corresponded almost exactly with those I had arrived at that afternoon. She agreed that the white upholstery was not practical, but the other points were minor. She looked dumbfounded when I said, ''If we can get a different color with different upholstery and can get Fred to come down further on the price, should we buy the Celica?''

Before she could answer, Fred returned and I asked him about other models. He said he could call around to other dealers and ask, but the Celicas were big sellers and he wasn't optimistic. ''We'll have more cars shipped into Jacksonville about September 1, but we never know what we'll get,'' he said.

I shook my head. ''I don't know, Fred. We like the Celica, but not the white upholstery. I'd like to deal with you, but Thom's is willing to beat your price on either a Cressida or a Celica. Any suggestions?''

He took out a pad and began to figure. ''On the Celica, I can give you this price (about $50 higher than Thom's). But I can't even do that if I have to call around and get a car from another dealer.''

''Fred,'' I said, ''sell me this Celica at the same price that I could get the one at Thom's and I'll take it with the light upholstery.'' Fred didn't look happy, but said he would ask his boss (the same strategy followed by every salesperson I'd ever dealt with).

While he was gone, Martha said I was being ridiculous to quibble over $50. She also pointed out that if we waited for a new shipment at Jacksonville, school would have started, and there would be no guarantee that we'd get the right color anyway. I had already thought of that but didn't want to give in. When Fred returned, he said, ''I got him to take off another $25, but that's rock bottom.'' Now I did have a dilemma. I looked at Martha and her look was unmistakeable. I told Fred that we'd take it.

In the weeks that followed, several things of interest happened. I noticed that the car had received a safety inspection in April. Thus, it had been in the showroom for at least that long before we bought it. I calculated that we had spent $400 more than we had intended, had less trunk space and got poorer mileage than we had been looking for. I saw several gold Celicas with black interiors (the color I had liked) on the road.

An additional concern that I had not expressed to Martha was the energy crisis, with higher gas and oil prices, and the cost involved. ''Gas efficiency,'' I thought, ''should be an important consideration.'' Many thoughts raced through my mind at this critical time of considering whether to purchase or not to purchase—gasoline prices, maintenance, handling, styling, distance to the dealer for repairs, the kid's transportation, my transportation, what my colleagues would think, and many other considerations.

On a more positive side, I noted that a student of mine, who was very soft spoken and clearly conservative, had purchased a new Dodge Omni. I was relieved that I had not pursued that idea further. Later I read that the Celica had won an award as Import Car of the Year for several years in a row. Even more significant was the favorable reaction of some of my colleagues who vowed to me that they were going to talk their wives into letting them buy a sports car next time, too. I didn't describe to them the way in which I had made the decision to buy the sports car.

For Discussion

1. The retailer's problem is often described as developing the right blend of marketing ingredients in terms of offering the right product...in the right place...at the right time...in the right quantities...at the right price...by the right appeal. In the case of John, Martha, Stephen, and Laura and the new car dilemma, what constitutes the right blend of marketing ingredients?

2. Prepare a flowchart describing how the "new car dilemma" was resolved.

3. Does the process described in this case seem to represent one decision with many stages or many different decisions? Describe the major and minor influences on each stage or on each decision.

4. Explain which of the following concepts have applicability to the decision making in this case and describe how they apply: reference group influence, family influences, attitudes, brand loyalty, learning processes, family life cycle, personality, and prepurchase and post-purchase dissonance.

PART **4**

The Retail Environment

Case 7

THE SECOND NATIONAL BANK OF CAPITAL CITY— THE ADOPTION OF SERVICE INNOVATIONS

THE SECOND NATIONAL BANK OF CAPITAL CITY in Columbia, South Carolina, was chartered in 1920 and is now the second largest commercial bank (in total deposits) in the state. The bank's current facilities consist of a central bank and twenty-seven outlets. The central bank serves as the center of banking operations and is located in downtown Columbia (Standard Metropolitan Statistical Area population 341,000), the state's largest city. Second National's statewide facilities consist of a centrally located outlet in each of the state's eighteen principal cities (populations ranging from 32,000 to 280,000).

In its early years, the bank's management philosophies were quite conservative under its now retired founder, J.P. Homestead. While the present board chairman, Arthur B. King, and the current president, Malcom S. Hargrave, have followed a somewhat more aggressive management philosophy, Mr. Homestead's conservative influence is still prevalent in many of the major policy decisions. Several of the bank's top managers feel that it was Mr. Homestead's conservative influence that helped Second National avoid the recent problem of overextending on high-risk loans, which led to the collapse of several banks during the 1973–1975 period, including one in Columbia.

Second National's current operating philosophy was described accurately by one competitor as "progress through discretion." In past years, Second National's management has adopted banking innovations only when there was sufficient evidence that the innovation was in the best interest of the bank and its customers. These policies have created a consumer image of reliability, an image most managers feel is one of the bank's strongest assets. Recently, however, there has been considerable pressure by some of the bank's younger managers to initiate more progressive policies. John F. Peterson, vice-president of marketing and research, feels that the bank's management should be

Adapted from Dale M. Lewison and Roger Cannaday, "The Second National Bank of Capital City: The Adoption of Service Innovations," *Consumer Behavior Dynamics: A Casebook*, ed. M. Wayne DeLozier (Columbus, Ohio: Charles E. Merrill Publishing Company, 1977), pp. 274–86.

more receptive to banking innovations. Mr. Peterson believes that increasing competition, in terms of new competitors and new competitive marketing strategies, will require early adoption of new technologies and approaches if Second National is to maintain or increase its present growth.

The Banking Industry

The trend in recent years has been toward greater competition among commercial banks as well as intensified competition with other financial institutions, such as savings and loan associations, mutual savings banks, and credit unions. From 1950 to 1974, the commercial banks' share of total deposits had dropped from 81.5 percent to 66.5 percent, while savings and loan associations and credit unions had gained and mutual savings banks remained about the same.

A comparison of branching practices among these financial institutions is presented in Table 7-1. The number of commercial banks initially declined, then increased slowly while the number of locations more than doubled from 1.3 to 3.0 locations per institution. This number is held down considerably by the thirteen unit-banking states that allow only one location per institution, and by the nineteen states that allow only limited branching, usually countywide. In the more populous states where statewide branching is allowed, it is not uncommon for one institution to have fifty to one hundred branches. The profit margins of commercial banks have been narrowed significantly in recent years, due in part to the rapid expansion of the number of banking offices.

TABLE 7-1 ━━

Number of selected financial institutions and locations, 1950-1974

Year	Commercial Banks		Savings and Loan Associations	
	Institutions	*Locations*	*Institutions*	*Locations*
1950	14,121	18,966	5,992	N/A
1960	13,471	23,954	6,320	7,931
1970	13,686	35,330	5,669	9,987
1974	14,458	42,890	5,102	13,922

Year	Mutual Savings Banks		Credit Unions	
	Institutions	*Locations*	*Institutions*	*Locations*
1950	529	742	10,591	N/A
1960	514	1,000	20,456	N/A
1970	493	1,580	23,456	N/A
1974	479	2,121	22,889	23,500 (est.)

Sources: Federal Reserve Board, U.S. League of Savings Associations, National Association of Mutual Savings Banks, Credit Union National Association.

The product-service mix

Commercial banks offer a wide array of financial services to individuals, firms, institutions, government, and other types of organizations. These services include storage of funds for safekeeping in interest-bearing accounts (savings accounts), storage of funds in noninterest-bearing accounts (checking accounts) for day-to-day transactions, loans for a variety of purposes, trust services, safe deposit boxes for valuable personal items, traveler's checks and money orders, payroll check and check-cashing services, financial planning, investment counseling, and similar services. While commercial banks offer a wide range of services to both commercial and retail consumers, not all services are offered by all banks. The product-service offering of each bank facility is shown in Table 7-2.

TABLE 7-2

Product-service offering by facility type

Service	Full Service Bank	Limited Service Bank	Automated Teller Machine	Point-of-Sale Terminal
Open accounts	X	X		
Make loans	X			
Cash withdrawals	X	X	X	
Deposits	X	X	X	
Transfers	X	X	X	
Loan payments	X	X	X	
Credit card payments	X	X	X	
Other bill payments	X	X	X	
Determine current balance	X	X	X	
Trust services	X			
Safe deposit boxes	X			
Financial counseling	X			
Cash third party checks	X	X		
Purchase traveler's checks	X	X		
Purchase cashier's checks	X	X		
Purchase money orders	X	X		
Check authorization	X	X		X
Credit card authorization	X	X		X
Debit card authorization (to allow immediate transfer of funds from buyer's to seller's account)	X	X		X

The operating environment

The overall environment in which the banking industry operates is illustrated in Exhibit 7-1. The general state of the economy affects the level of checking and savings deposits, the demand for personal and commercial loans, and the costs of resources. Banking operations are affected by cultural and social factors such as attitudes toward the use of credit, attitudes toward women as customers, pressure for greater social responsibility, and the continuing redistribution of the population into the suburbs.

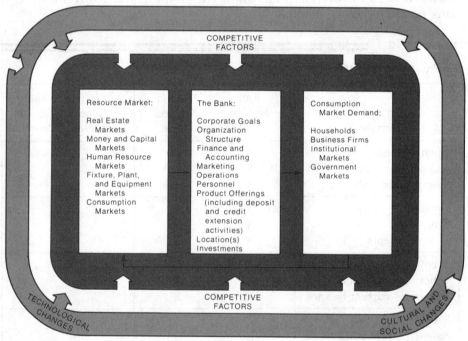

COMPETITIVE FACTORS

Resource Market:	The Bank:	Consumption Market Demand:
Real Estate Markets	Corporate Goals	Households
Money and Capital Markets	Organization Structure	Business Firms
Human Resource Markets	Finance and Accounting	Institutional Markets
Fixture, Plant, and Equipment Markets	Marketing	Government Markets
Consumption Markets	Operations	
	Personnel	
	Product Offerings (including deposit and credit extension activities)	
	Location(s)	
	Investments	

COMPETITIVE FACTORS

TECHNOLOGICAL CHANGES

CULTURAL AND SOCIAL CHANGES

EXHIBIT 7-1

The banking environment

Source: Rex O. Bennett, *Bank Location Analysis* (Washington, D.C.: American Bankers Association, 1975), p. 5.

As a quasi-utility, the banking industry has been subject to a high degree of government control and regulation. Regulatory agencies include the Federal Reserve Board, the Federal Deposit Insurance Corporation, the Comptroller of the Currency, and state banking authorities. As an example, national banks must obtain approval from the Comptroller of the Currency for the location of new branch banks.

Major technological changes affect the competitive environment of the banking industry. Electronic Funds Transfer System (EFTS) is an example. EFTS is an electro-mechanical method of transferring value, partially replacing the method of paper transfer of value (i.e., cash and checks).

One of these EFTS components has been classified as Customer-Bank Communication Terminals (CBCT) by the Comptroller. These terminals may be located on the site of an existing banking office or off-site such as a shopping center. They can be manned (operated by a bank employee) or unmanned (operated by the customer), on-line (connected directly to the bank's central computer) or off-line (self-contained). One type of CBCT is the Automated Teller Machine (ATM), which typically allows customers to make deposits, withdraw cash, pay on loans, and make account transfers. Another type of CBCT is the point-of-sale (POS) terminal, which can be used at checkout counters in supermarkets, department stores, and other business establishments. Retailers use POS for check or credit card authorization and for debit card authorization, which allows immediate transfer of funds from the purchaser's account to the store's account.

In December 1974, the Comptroller ruled that a CBCT is not a branch, partially in response to the Federal Home Loan Bank Board's ruling in January 1974, which allowed off-site CBCTs for savings and loan associations. The Comptroller subsequently suspended his ruling in response to lawsuits in several unit-banking states and is no longer accepting or processing branch applications for CBCTs.

Second National's Current Situation

In recent months there has been considerable discussion among Second National's top management concerning the need for additional banking outlets. The management concensus is that potentially profitable sites exist in the rapidly expanding suburban areas of Columbia. Moreover, they feel there is additional profit potential in several of the state's eighteen other principal cities and smaller cities (10,000 to 30,000 people). Although there is general agreement that expansion is necessary to increase market share, there is considerable disagreement among senior management as to what form the expansion should take.

The need for a decision on the expansion issue has taken on greater importance in recent weeks. Two of Second National's competitors, First Central Brank (the state's largest) and First Farmers' Bank (the fourth largest), have been expanding their service offerings through the use of ATMs in conjunction with their existing branch facilities. Just recently, Mr. Peterson learned that First Farmers' intends to limit further construction of traditional brick-and-mortar branches and embark on an ambitious expansion program of off-site ATMs in shopping centers, employment centers, and other major activity centers. Its expansion program is based on the belief that banking services are primarily convenience goods; therefore, banking facilities should have the greatest possible geographical distribution. Since ATMs are available to customers twenty-four hours per day, seven days a week, the marketing strategy appears to be one of creating greater spatial and time convenience.

Second National's senior management is concerned about a recent report that shows that market share of deposits peaked in 1970 and has declined slowly since then. Management's assumption is that market share of deposits is closely correlated with share of the total number of branches. However, Second National's share of branches continued to increase in 1974 and 1975 while share of deposits decreased. Many of the larger banks in the state experienced a similar trend. The exceptions to this trend were First Central and First Farmers', which experienced substantial growth.

One of the stated goals of Second National is to maximize market shares subject to a rate of return of at least 15 percent. In 1975, the market share fell to 19.5 percent, under 20 percent for the first time since 1967, although the rate of return remained slightly above 15 percent.

In light of the situation, Mr. Hargrave asked Mr. Peterson to develop and evaluate alternative expansion plans that would increase Second National's market share and rate of return. In addition, Mr. Hargrave instructed Mr. Peterson to consider the following issues:

1. Construction of a brick-and-mortar branch costs a minimum of about $250,000, or about five times as much as the cost of an ATM.
2. The chairman of the board has expressed repeatedly the opinion that ATMs cannot be cost-justified in terms of the profits they generate, an opinion shared by some experts.
3. Several of Second National's large commercial accounts have expressed a wide range of views as to the desirability of Electronic Funds Transfer System (EFTS).
4. At the recent conference of the National Association of Bank Managers, several experts expressed strong feelings concerning the problems of fraud, security, and malfunctioning of automated banking equipment.
5. Recent consumer surveys showed considerable mixed reactions to the use of automatic banking equipment.
6. Savings and loan institutions in several states are using ATMs, thereby allowing their customers to use savings accounts much like a checking account. In addition, two states are being allowed by federal agencies and Congress to experiment with negotiable ordering of withdrawal accounts that essentially are interest-paying checking accounts.
7. There is concern among several of our senior bank officials that any radical departure from current modes of operation might have considerable negative effects on the bank's image.
8. Pricing concepts in the banking industry are undergoing significant changes; whereas most banks seek to make each application of each service profitable, some banks will adopt pricing strategies based on the profitability of the total customer and/or a total class of customers.
9. Point-of-sale terminals are used at check-out counters in retail stores and generally are installed with one terminal per check-out counter, or anywhere from one to twenty terminals per store.

In his initial meeting with the bank's Marketing Research Department, Mr. Peterson outlined the major issues of the problem as presented in the previous discussion. He expressed the following opinion:

"Innovative expansion is the key to regaining and increasing the bank's market share. In order for any expansion program to meet the bank's market-share goals, we must develop expansion alternatives incorporating product-service mixes that not only satisfy the needs of our existing customers, but also provide the opportunities for attracting new customers. It is my opinion that the only way to attract large numbers of new customers is to create the image of a modern progressive bank. This type of image requires that our marketing programs be fresh and imaginative. Today's banking customer chooses and continues to patronize a bank for many different reasons; however, all of these reasons are strongly related to today's modern life styles. What I need from this department are innovative alternatives of expansion that are not only conducive to the consumer's modern way of life, but which will be acceptable to the "dated" gentlemen upstairs.

"I believe that our current research files" (the reader should refer to Tables 7–3 through 7–8) "are sufficient for the initial development of these alternatives. We can always collect additional data later that would be more suited to whatever alternative we come up with. If you have any ideas as to what type of additional information might be required, or if there are any specific aspects to the problem you feel should be drawn to my attention, submit them to me in writing by the end of the week. Otherwise, within the next six weeks, I expect from the department recommendations as to the most feasible expansion alternatives. Now, are there any questions?"

Mr. Sidewood: "How many alternatives do you want?"

Mr. Peterson: "I'll leave that up to you."

Mr. Sidewood: "Are there any specific issues you wish us to consider?"

Mr. Peterson: "I think we have at least mentioned in some fashion most of the issues pertinent to the problem. Again, I would think that consumer needs and responses might serve as the focal point in the development of the alternatives. However, that is not to say you should overlook all of the other issues that have been noted. Also, I am sure that there are additional issues that you might consider."

Mr. Sidewood: "One last question. How extensive an area should we consider?"

Mr. Peterson: "The entire state."

Mr. Armstrong: "As a resident of this state for fifty-five years and a banker for twenty-seven, I feel that I know the people of this state and the customers who bank with us. Although we want to think progressively, let us not forget that this state's population is quite conservative. These people are bound in tradition. They follow the habits of their grandparents, their great-grandparents! Why, twenty years ago most people thought the safest place for their money was a hole in the ground. It has taken this long for them to trust dealing with us. How long will it take to get them to trust dealing with a machine?"

Mr. Peterson: "You have a point. But people have changed. We have an influx of people from all parts of the country into this state. They don't have the same life styles."

Mr. Robeson: "As research analyst, I have data that supports both of your contentions. People in this state have been slow to adopt banking in general, and innovative banking practices in particular. However, the composition of the population has changed in the major cities of South Carolina. Companies from Detroit, Chicago, New York, Pennsylvania, and Connecticut, just to name a few, have opened major branches of their businesses here and have relocated many of their personnel as well. Although they represent a small percentage of the state's population, they have learned the advantages of using the new technologies in banking and draw high salaries. Their impact on the habits of other people in the state is difficult to assess.''

Mr. Peterson: "Well, it is true that these people have been exposed to new banking techniques and do adapt to change more rapidly, but they are a minority. I think we should consider educating the rest of the population to the advantages of new banking technology. Just look at the strides First Central and First Farmers' have made.''

Ms. Lucas: "Mr. Peterson, it is true that those banks have increased their market shares, but I agree with Mr. Armstrong. The people of this state are staunch conservatives, and particularly the customers who bank with us. If we try to become 'progressive,' as you call it, we will lose the solid image we have built with our loyal customers and they'll go elsewhere. People are reliable and trustworthy; machines are nothing but metal and electrical circuits.''

Mr. Peterson: "But people of this state are changing, and people from out of state with more progressive views are coming in. We cannot continue to manufacture the horse-drawn carriage! Does anyone have any final comments before we adjourn?''

Mr. Robeson: "If I may make one last comment, let me say once again that I can see both sides to this question. As I view it, we are concerned with several issues. Each must be analyzed. We must consider changing life styles of bank consumers in this state. On the whole, are they changing rapidly enough to accept modern banking techniques in the near future? Secondly, what image do we convey and to whom? Third, can we educate people to accept and use machines? Their prior learning habits may not be easy to change. I don't presently have answers to these questions.''

Mr. Peterson: "You've raised some good questions, Mr. Robeson. I feel there also are other questions we should raise and try to answer before reaching a decision. Let's adjourn and reconvene in two days.''

Questions

1. What behavioral dimensions must be considered in this case? What information should Second National's Marketing and Research Department collect to consider in developing strategic alternatives?

2. Which behavioral concepts come to bear on Second National's strategy decision? Explain.

3. What alternatives do you propose and which alternatives do you choose? What criteria did you use in arriving at your choice?

4. What are the possible effects of your recommended alternatives on the bank's (a) internal operations, (b) promotional programs, (c) product-service mix, and (d) pricing strategy?

TABLE 7-3

Bank patronage reasons: retail and commercial consumers

Patronage Reason / Importance	First	Second	Third	Fourth	Fifth	Sixth	Totals
Location	42%	5%	19%	25%	3%	6%	100%
Hours	34	4	22	20	10	10	100
Services	10	43	15	13	11	8	100
Personnel	7	20	9	17	22	25	100
Reputation	5	7	10	6	21	51	100
Facilities	2	21	25	19	33	0	100
TOTALS	100%	100%	100%	100%	100%	100%	

Source: Statewide Consumer Survey, Marketing Research Department, Second National Bank.

TABLE 7-4

Consumer banking trip behavior: retail and commercial consumers

Shopping Characteristics / Type of Consumer	Retail Consumer	Commercial Consumer
Type of trip: I conduct my banking business in connection with:		
Trips between home and work	32%	10%
Special trips from home	30	8
Special trips from work	17	57
Shopping trips	18	—
Business trips	2	23
Other	1	2
TOTAL	100%	100%
Trip frequency: I visit the bank:		
Less than once a month	1%	—
Once a month	8	—
More than once a month (less than weekly)	21	—
Once a week	51	1%
More than once a week (less than daily)	19	11
Once a day (weekday)	—	69
More than once a day	—	19
TOTAL	100%	100%

TABLE 7-5 ▬▬▬▬▬▬▬▬▬▬▬▬▬▬▬▬▬▬▬▬▬▬▬▬▬▬▬▬▬▬▬▬

Demographic characteristics of automated equipment users and nonusers

Demographic Characteristics	Nonuser	Infrequent User	Frequent User	Total User
Sex				
Male	53.9%	64.0%	64.9%	59.1%
Female	46.1	36.0	35.1	40.9
Age				
21–34	36.8	49.3	54.5	43.4
35–49	47.4	44.0	39.0	43.4
50 and over	15.8	6.7	6.5	13.1
Social class				
Upper-middle	27.6	14.7	33.8	23.7
Lower-middle	38.2	53.3	39.0	45.6
Upper-lower	34.2	32.0	27.3	30.7
Marital status				
Married	86.8	85.3	87.0	86.9
Single	7.9	10.7	9.1	8.4
Widowed, divorced	5.3	4.0	3.9	4.7
Education				
Postgraduate	13.2	13.3	14.3	12.8
College graduate	23.7	32.0	29.9	27.7
Some college	28.9	32.0	28.6	30.3
Subtotal	65.8	77.3	72.8	70.8
High school graduate	25.0	17.3	19.5	22.6
Some high school	6.6	5.3	6.5	5.5
Eighth grade or less	2.6	—	1.3	1.1
Income				
Under $5,000	2.6	4.0	2.6	2.9
$5,000–$7,999	3.9	6.7	2.6	5.1
$8,000–$10,999	21.1	22.7	10.4	17.2
$11,000–$13,999	19.7	24.0	15.6	20.1
$14,000–$17,999	13.2	10.7	18.2	16.1
$18,000 and over	34.2	22.7	44.2	32.8
Refused	5.3	9.3	6.5	5.8

Source: Rex O. Bennett, *Bank Location Analysis* (Washington, D.C.: American Bankers Association, 1975).

TABLE 7-6

Consumer bank selection criteria

Customer Type and Importance Rank / Selection Criteria	Retail Consumers			Commercial Consumers		
	First	Second	Third	First	Second	Third
Recommendation of friends or relatives	3%	4%	8%	—	—	2%
Recommendation of a professional acquaintance	2	6	1	11%	9%	8
Good reputation	4	3	—	9	8	14
Located near where I shop	10	8	3	—	—	10
Located near where I work	11	10	14	16	10	10
Located near where I live	18	16	10	—	1	1
Offers full service	11	13	11	29	22	13
Helpful personnel	8	7	4	6	15	10
Open during the evening hours	5	7	4	11	6	8
Open on Saturdays	7	4	6	4	12	6
Attractive facilities	—	6	3	—	—	—
Convenient automatic services	5	6	12	4	5	11
Interest charges on loans	1	—	1	6	7	9
Interest paid on savings	3	3	3	—	—	1
Availability of credit	—	1	—	4	5	5
Overdraft privileges on checking accounts	3	4	6	—	—	—
Premiums or gifts for new accounts	7	2	9	—	—	—
Convenient parking	1	—	2	—	—	1
Convenient entrance/exit	1	—	3	—	—	1

Source: Statewide Consumer Survey, Marketing Research Department, Second National Bank.

TABLE 7-7

Likelihood of using automated teller equipment

Characteristic	Very Likely	Somewhat Likely	Somewhat Unlikely	Very Unlikely
Age				
18–34	34.1%	21.7%	11.2%	29.2%
35–49	33.2	18.6	11.3	33.2
50–64	19.8	12.5	14.7	49.6
65 and over	10.9	7.8	14.7	51.9
Income				
Under $7,500	15.2	11.0	11.0	51.7
$7,500–$10,000	25.8	20.8	11.9	37.7
$10,000–$15,000	34.8	17.4	12.1	32.6
$15,000–$20,000	34.1	20.3	14.8	26.8
Over $20,000	28.9	12.3	15.8	41.2
Sex				
Male	26.8	16.7	15.0	37.0
Female	28.0	16.2	10.5	40.0

Source: Rex O. Bennett, *Bank Location Analysis* (Washington, D.C.: American Bankers Association, 1975).

TABLE 7-8

Automated teller equipment: advantages vs. disadvantages

Characteristics	Advantages Outweigh	About Equal	Disadvantages Outweigh	Advantages Outweigh plus Equal
Occupation				
White collar	31.6%	38.6%	29.8%	70.2%
Blue collar	25.4	12.8	61.7	38.3
Professional	12.9	45.2	42.0	58.0
Housewife	23.6	31.1	45.3	54.7
Retired	23.5	5.9	70.6	29.4
Other	41.2	35.3	23.5	76.5
Age				
18–23	40.0	40.0	20.0	80.0
24–34	27.5	25.8	46.7	56.3
35–44	16.7	33.3	50.0	50.0
45–55	20.3	29.7	50.0	50.0
56–64	16.7	16.7	66.7	33.3
65 and over	33.4	13.3	53.4	46.6
Income				
Under $5,000	12.5	25.0	62.5	37.5
$5,000–$10,000	32.6	30.2	37.3	62.7
$10,000–$15,000	38.2	21.8	40.0	60.0
$15,000–$20,000	25.0	36.5	38.5	61.5
Over $20,000	29.2	33.3	37.5	62.5
Refused	17.1	31.4	51.4	48.6

Source: Rex O. Bennett, Bank Location Analysis (Washington, D.C.: American Bankers Association, 1975).

Case 8

MULTIPURPOSE STORES, INC.—A RESEARCH PROPOSAL FOR EVALUATING THE RETAIL ENVIRONMENT

MULTIPURPOSE STORES (MPS) is a regional retail chain stores organization which operates six furniture/appliance stores in the state of Arkansas. One of these stores is located in the city of Fayetteville, whose population is approximately 33,000. Fayetteville, which is surrounded by several smaller towns, and Springdale, with a population of 27,000, formed the hub of economic, social, and cultural activity in the area. The economy grew very fast during the 1960s and the twin-city area was declared an SMSA in 1972. Despite the general economic health of the area, the local MPS experienced declining sales during the mid to late 1970s. Early in 1980, MPS management appointed a new manager for the Fayetteville-Sringdale store. He was directed to improve the sales performance of the Fayetteville MPS store.

According to the president of MPS, sales of the Fayetteville store were suffering because of a poor store image. He thought there was some confusion in the minds of both actual and potential customers as to the true identity of the stores. It was hypothesized that such confusion resulted in the loss of sales. MPS president felt that the store was not able to attract many buyers of furniture and appliances because they identified the store with various other items of merchandise including hardware. At the same time, the president felt that the company lacked proper information on which to base any systematic marketing strategy aimed at improving the store's image and sales. The president of MPS and the new store manager agreed that a clear understanding of the overall store image was necessary. A clarification of the

This case was prepared by C.P. Rao and G.E. Kiser, University of Arkansas at Fayetteville. This case was prepared as a basis for class discussion and student analysis. All names of individuals and the company have been disguised. This case was made possible by the cooperation of a business firm that remains anonymous. This case is an updated version of one presented at the ICH-SCRA Case Workshop, New Orleans, November 11–13, 1975. Copyright 1975 by the authors. Permission has been granted by the authors for use in this book. All rights reserved to the contributors.

strengths and weaknesses of the local store would help them to develop an appropriate and creative marketing program.

Within a few months of his appointment, the new store manager decided that his predecessor had projected a "mom-and-pop" type of store image. He also felt that the previous manager gave the impression that he himself was the owner of the store for the store clientele seemed to have been doing business mainly on the basis of their personal relationship with the store manager. He felt that such lack of corporate image was a deterrent to business. On the basis of his discussions and his own intuitive evaluation of the situation, the new store manager concluded that knowing the nature and dimensions of the store's image would greatly help him to improve sales performance. Additionally, he felt that an independent assessment of the MPS store and its environment would give him an unbiased basis for initiating a constructive marketing program. With these dual purposes in mind, he sought the help of a marketing consulting firm in Fayetteville.

The "Image" Study

After discussing the problem with the consultants, it was agreed that a store "image" study would be carried out to achieve the following objectives:

1. Identify the relative importance of various store features that respondents take into account when selecting or patronizing a furniture/appliance store;
2. Identify respondents' relative preferences for the area's furniture/appliance stores;
3. Identify the respondents' evaluation of MPS store in Fayetteville on the basis of those store features mentioned under #1 above;
4. Collect data about the demographic characteristics of the respondents.

A consumer survey would be conducted utilizing a structured questionnaire. (See Exhibit 8-1 for the questionnaire designed to be used in the survey.) It also was agreed that the data should be gathered from a sample of present and past MPS customers as well as from a more general list of consumers. With this purpose in view, the following research plan was developed by the consultants.

1. Approximately one-third of the respondents would be selected from present customers who previously had patronized the MPS stores. Those respondents would be selected randomly from a file of sales tickets issued during the past five years.
2. The remaining two-thirds of the respondents reached would be selected randomly utilizing the area telephone directory. While it was expected that most of these respondents would be potential customers in the sense that they have not patronized the MPS stores, it also was expected that a few of these respondents would already be the patrons of the MPS store.

3. Approximately 20 percent of the sample members in each group would be interviewed personally; data from the remainder would be collected through mailed questionnaires.
4. For considerations of time and cost, it was decided to reach 150 MPS store customers and 300 potential customers.
5. Following the data collection phase, the marketing consultants would submit a written report consisting of the following two parts:
   a) An independent evaluation of the MPS store by the marketing consulting group.
   b) An interpretation of the data gathered in the field research.

EXHIBIT 8-1 ══

Questionnaire proposed by the marketing consultants for use in the proposed store image survey

Please answer the following questions with a check mark and/or a brief remark to express your experience or opinions.

1. Have you purchased any of the following durable items in the last *six months?* Or planning to buy in the next six months? (Please check as many as applicable)

Type of Item	Purchased during the last 6 months		Planning to buy in the next 6 months			
	YES	NO	YES	NO	NOT SURE	NOT PLANNING
Major appliances (Refrigerator, Washing machine, etc.)	___	___	___	___	___	___
T.V., Phonograph, Tape Recorder, etc.	___	___	___	___	___	___
Major furniture item(s) costing more than $100	___	___	___	___	___	___
Minor furniture item(s) costing less than $100	___	___	___	___	___	___

2. Below is a list of desirable features of any furniture-appliance type of store. Please indicate, how important are these features to you in selecting or patronizing such a store for your purchase needs?

(If you consider any feature as highly important please check 7. On the other hand, if the feature describes a least important consideration, please check 1. If your importance rating is in between for any statement, please check the number—2, 3, 4, 5, or 6—which comes closest to expressing your opinion.)

EXHIBIT 8-1 (continued)

High Numbers More Importance—Low Numbers Less Importance

	MOST IMPORTANT						LEAST IMPORTANT
Attractive decor and display	7	6	5	4	3	2	1
Accessibility of store	7	6	5	4	3	2	1
Informative Advertising	7	6	5	4	3	2	1
Courteous Store Personnel	7	6	5	4	3	2	1
Easy Credit	7	6	5	4	3	2	1
Competitive prices	7	6	5	4	3	2	1
Quality merchandise	7	6	5	4	3	2	1
Easy to find part place	7	6	5	4	3	2	1
Wide selection of merchandise	7	6	5	4	3	2	1
Carry well-known brands	7	6	5	4	3	2	1
Well known to our friends	7	6	5	4	3	2	1
Quick delivery service	7	6	5	4	3	2	1
The type of customers patronizing the store	7	6	5	4	3	2	1
Convenient location	7	6	5	4	3	2	1
Well known generally	7	6	5	4	3	2	1

3. Would you please mention as many furniture-appliance type of stores in our town as you can recall in order of your liking for the stores? (If you like store most, please mention first, then the next and so on).

_____   _____

_____   _____

4. How do you consider the Multipurpose Stores in our town? (Please write the word(s) which comes upper most in your mind to fill the blank.)

MULTIPURPOSE STORES mostly sells _____

5. On the following list of features, how do you evaluate the *MULTIPURPOSE STORES* in our town? (If your evaluation is highly favorable please check 7. Alternately, if your evaluation is highly unfavorable please check 1. If your evaluation is in between check 2, 3, 4, 5 or 6 whichever comes closest to expressing your evaluation.)

High Numbers More Favorable—Low Numbers Less Favorable

	HIGHLY FAVORABLE						HIGHLY UNFAVORABLE
Attractive decor and display	7	6	5	4	3	2	1
Accessibility of store	7	6	5	4	3	2	1
Informative advertising	7	6	5	4	3	2	1
Courteous store personnel	7	6	5	4	3	2	1
Easy credit	7	6	5	4	3	2	1
Competitive prices	7	6	5	4	3	2	1
Quality merchandise	7	6	5	4	3	2	1
Easy to find parking place	7	6	5	4	3	2	1

EXHIBIT 8-1 (continued)

High Numbers More Favorable—Low Numbers Less Favorable

	HIGHLY FAVORABLE					HIGHLY UNFAVORABLE	
Wide selection of merchandise	7	6	5	4	3	2	1
Carry well known brands	7	6	5	4	3	2	1
Well known to our friends	7	6	5	4	3	2	1
Quick delivery service	7	6	5	4	3	2	1
The type of customers patronizing the store	7	6	5	4	3	2	1
Convenient location	7	6	5	4	3	2	1
Well known generally	7	6	5	4	3	2	1

Would you please provide the following information about yourself:

1. Please check your AGE GROUP on the following:
   ___Under 20 years   ___30–39 years   ___50–60 years
   ___20–29 years   ___40–49 years   ___Over 60 years

2. Which of the following categories applies to your TOTAL FAMILY income:
   ___Under $5,000   ___$7,500–$9,999   ___$15,–20,000
   ___$5,000–$7,499   ___$10,000–14,999   ___Over $20,000

3. Person completing the questionnaire: ___Male ___Female

4. Occupation of the Head of the Household: _____

Questions

1. How do you evaluate MPS management's analysis of the problem? What alternative approach, if any, would you take in such a preliminary diagnosis of the problem?

2. Critically evaluate the agreed-upon research plan between the MPS management and the marketing consultant group.

3. Develop a set of guidelines for (a) constructing an effective questionnaire and (b) selecting a reliable sample.

Case 9

TIMPSON DEPARTMENT STORES

TIMPSON DEPARTMENT STORES owned and operated eleven retail department stores in the southeastern United States. In addition, in rural areas not large enough to support a department store, Timpson had set up 65 catalog stores on a franchise basis. The catalog stores generally did not stock merchandise other than a few major appliances and replacement parts and supplies. For over 30 years, the company had successfully marketed its private-label line of vacuum cleaners. Timson's vacuum cleaner line included three electric-broom models ($24.95 to $49.95 retail), four medium-priced upright models ($37.95 to $67.95), four higher-quality upright models ($164.95 to $237.95), and four cannister-type models ($47.95 to $77.95). Timpson's mail order catalog did not list horsepower ratings for electric motors except for cleaners with motors rated 1.0HP or more. The least expensive model with a 1.0HP motor sold for $97.95.

Timpson maintained an extensive testing and product development laboratory for vacuum cleaners and other electric appliances. While the actual manufacturing was performed by outside companies, every specification was set by Timpson engineers before the Timpson label was placed on the appliance. Whenever a competitor introduced a new vacuum cleaner model, Timpson's testing department would purchase several samples, and painstakingly disassemble and test every part to determine if there might be any way to improve the Timpson line.

Timpson management had made elaborate plans for a gala celebration sale featuring, among other best sellers, its well-known vacuum cleaners. Each of the 11 stores was to participate in the big sale. Several newspaper advertisements telling people to watch for the upcoming sale during February and March had run during the month of January. Since its vacuum cleaner

Source: Norman A.P. Govoni, Jean-Pierre Jeannet, and Terry F. Allen, *Marketing Problems: Cases for Analysis* (Columbus, Ohio: Grid, Inc., 1977), pp. 205–8. Reprinted by permission of Grid, Inc.

line was so well-known and could do so much to build store traffic, as had been demonstrated in the past, it was decided to feature a low-priced model in every pre-sale advertisement to help spark interest among consumers. Each advertisement contained, in addition to other copy, the following:

Spring Cleaning Special
Vacuum Cleaner

1.2HP electric motor
7-piece attachment set
Upright model
Our own brand

$58.00

A Fantastic Bargain

Since the $58.00 model was not listed in the catalog, it could not be purchased by direct mail or at the catalog store outlets. The customer had to actually visit a Timpson Department Store to inspect and order the "special" model. However, just a week before the sale was to begin, H & J Manufacturing Company, sole supplier of the Timpson brand vacuum cleaners, informed Timpson management that the promised delivery of the vacuum cleaners in time for the sale was impossible, due to severe labor problems at the plant. Up until several months previously, H & J had been extremely reliable, but then was plagued by a strike in its production plant. After an uneasy truce, vacuum cleaners again were manufactured. In planning for the February-March sale, Timpson management had consulted with H & J and was assured that delivery would take place about mid-January. Although this was too close to the sale date for Timpson, management agreed to go along with it for these reasons. H & J production to Timpson specifications was a known quantity, and management wanted to stick with its long-standing supplier of vacuum cleaners. But, another strike took place at H & J and production of the vacuum cleaners was at a standstill. And, it appeared unlikely that Timpson could get any vacuum cleaners before the end of the sale in March.

Because it was so close to the sale date and a one-month advertising campaign had been conducted to create and build interest in the sale, Timpson management felt there was no way it could turn back at this point and was forced to go through with the sale, even though it could not offer a single one of its advertised special vacuum cleaners for $58.00. As a result, out of desperation, a memorandum was dispatched to each of the unit store managers with a plan designed to weather the pending storm. The store managers were instructed to meet with the salesmen who were responsible for vacuum cleaner sales and to explain the situation in its entirety. The memo contained a blueprint that was to guide the salesmen during the sale.

Once the customer came into the store, the salesmen were instructed to make little or no effort to sell the advertised model (each store had a couple of the "special" cleaners, but only one was to be displayed). Instead, the salesmen were to try to sell higher-priced models through disparaging statements, including (1) the advertised model did not pick up half as much dirt as Timpson's more expensive models, (2) the 1.2HP rating was only under laboratory conditions (in home use, the effective horsepower rating was only about half that amount), (3) the advertised vacuum cleaner was excessively noisy, (4) it was guaranteed for only thirty days versus a full one-year guarantee on Timpson's more expensive models, (5) none of the advertised vacuum cleaners was available for off-the-floor sale and, if ordered, there would be a long delay in delivery, and (6) Timpson could not guarantee the availability of replacement bags and parts for the advertised special vacuum cleaners (such assurance could only be given for models listed in the catalog). After hearing these arguments, if a customer still insisted on the advertised special, the salesman was to make a gesture of exasperation and say something like, "I just couldn't face myself in the mirror if I let you buy this machine, Mr. Jones. Why don't you try our competitor down the street. As much as I would hate to see you go there, I would rather have you do that than buy one of these cut-rate cleaners." It was only after this, if the customer still insisted on the advertised model, that the salesman would sell it. Then and only then, the salesmen were instructed to tell the customer the machines were not available due to supplier problems and there would be about a four-month wait, for which a rain check would be issued, guaranteeing the customer the vacuum cleaner at the sale price when it became available.

During discussion of the plan to be used during the sale, a number of questions were raised by the salesmen concerning the ethics of the approach. Finally, all salesmen in each store agreed that, under these special circumstances, something had to be done to "save face" and this approach was as good as any.

Timpson salesmen received a salary plus 2 percent commission on all sales. However, there was no commission payable on the advertised special.

For several years, a nationally-known independent testing organization had consistently rated Timpson's higher-priced models as "Best Values" compared with most other major brands. (The independent testing organization would not allow its findings to be published by Timpson or anyone else, though.) Timpson management felt that it was best serving the interests of the public by making a strong effort to convince customers to buy the higher-priced, higher-quality merchandise. It was felt that immediate admission of the "mistake" would do more to incur the displeasure of customers and jeopardize the Timpson position than would adherence to the suggested plan. Timpson management felt that, at worst, its policy was of a "victimless crime" nature. It believed that a more appropriate appraisal of the policy would be that it was ultimately of great consumer benefit, because the customer ended up with a far better product value.

Questions

1. Is Timpson justified in running advertisements and then refusing to sell that product? Why or why not?

2. Do you feel the Timpson approach is legal? Moral? Ethical? Fair? Why or why not?

3. What would be the best course of action under these circumstances?

4. What are the ways for a department store to build traffic?

PART **5**

Retail Organization and Personnel Management

Case 10

AMWAY CORPORATION—DIRECT MARKETING SYSTEM

AMWAY CORPORATION is one of the fastest growing companies in North America. In only a few years it has grown from a small distributor of household products into a complete manufacturing and sales organization with a multi-million dollar annual sales volume. This growth includes all areas of operation. The company has completed several phases of a continuing program of increasing facilities for research, production, warehousing, and selling. Distributors have rapidly multiplied; today over 80,000 people are engaged in selling Amway products to homes and industry throughout the United States and Canada.

The corporation was founded by two men with broad experience in direct selling. Jay Van Andil and Richard DeVos each have over fifteen years of personal experience in developing direct sales distributorships. As President, Mr. DeVos is in charge of the sales division (including training, conventions, sales meetings, and recruiting and personnel). Mr. Van Andil, as board chairman, handles the finance, manufacturing, operations, marketing, and legal divisions.

Amway's U.S. home office and main manufacturing facilities are located on a 250-acre tract of land at Ada, Michigan, about nine miles east of Grand Rapids. In Amway's multi-million dollar complex is housed a modern, efficient manufacturing operation, including the most up-to-date equipment for formulating, packaging, bottling, and labeling dry and liquid products. Due to the importance of aerosol packages in the Amway line, the plant includes one of the most completely automatic aerosol-filling facilities in existence.

Laboratories at the Ada plant are staffed with specialized chemists, who carry out extensive testing programs on both raw materials and finished

Adapted from J. Taylor Sims, "Amway Corporation: Direct Marketing System," *Marketing Management: Strategies & Cases*, ed. M. Wayne DeLozier and Arch G. Woodside (Columbus, Ohio: Charles E. Merrill Publishing Company, 1978), pp. 376–88. In this case, the Amway distributor will be referred to as "he" or "she," alternating by sections.

products to assure rigid standards of quality control. In addition, these laboratories are used for research on new and improved products.

Other departments at the Ada plant include offices where the details and correspondence connected with millions of dollars worth of annual sales are handled; the creative and printing production department, which turns out hundreds of thousands of price lists, bulletins, brochures, and other printed pieces each month; and extensive storage facilities for inventories of raw materials and finished goods. Over twenty regional warehouses in strategically located cities in the United States and Canada serve distributors. Amway Home Products include such items as pesticides, room fresheners, and products to care for one's auto, clothing, floor, furniture, laundry, kitchen, and personal hygiene. Amway also manufacturers a line of commercial cleaning products. (See Exhibit 10–1.)

Amway Distribution System

Physical distribution

In the Amway system, products are produced and then sent to a central warehouse on location at the Ada plant facility. From this warehouse, Amway products are shipped to private warehouses all over the United States. In other words, the central warehouse handles orders from all of these individual warehouses. The central warehouse performs the transportation function of goods from the manufacturer to the private warehouses. Transportation of goods from the private warehouses are handled in two ways. The individual salesperson placing an order can furnish transportation or, if this is not feasible, the warehouse can handle the transportation in the most cost-efficient manner available.

Amway's Organizational Structure and Marketing Plan

The following points summarize Amway's organizational structure and marketing plan:

1. Each Amway distributor is either an independent business person or husband-wife partnership. Each distributorship is authorized to sell Amway products by Amway Corporation.
2. This independent business that an Amway distributor builds belongs to the distributor. In the event of the distributor's death, the business can be passed to legal heirs or estate as directed by applicable laws.
3. Amway distributors may sponsor new applicants for Amway distributorships. In exchange for motivating, training, and acting as wholesale supplier, the sponsor earns financial rewards through higher bonuses or "refunds" earned by combining the sponsor's purchase volume with that of the distributors sponsored.

Safety Care

Pesticides, Germicides, Herbicides

Auto Care

Clothing and Clothing Care

Floor and Furniture Care

Laundry Care

AMWAY HOME CARE PRODUCTS

Room Fresheners

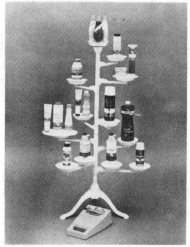

Personal Care

Kitchen Care

EXHIBIT 10-1

Amway home care products

4. Amway distributors can develop income through retail sales as a result of their own sales efforts or in the form of bonuses based on

total business volume, including wholesale sales to sponsored distributors.

5. Amway distributors have exclusive rights to the distributors and their customers. As long as they are properly serviced, customers cannot be switched from one Amway distributor to another without consent of both parties.
6. Amway distributors who sponsor other distributors have the right to continue that sponsorship without change as long as basic sponsorship requirements are met.
7. Because of the customer and distributor protection system, it is not necessary to restrict the general operations of Amway distributors to territories, and thus each Amway distributor has the entire nation as field for development.
8. The Amway Corporation distributes Amway products only through Amway distributors and does not solicit business except through distributors. All prospective customer leads coming to the Amway office are passed on to the nearest direct distributor; there are no "house accounts."

The Amway profit plan

Basic discount. The person selling Amway products can earn gross income two ways—the first of these is through "basic discount." The salesperson buys products from a sponsor at a wholesale price and sells them to customers at a retail price. The basic discount on most home-size products is 35 percent with a few at 25 percent. That percentage is the salesperson's gross profit—the basic discount received when the salesperson is paid by a customer. (The basic discount on larger size commercial products is usually 15 percent.) Most distributors average about 30 percent immediate profit. The sponsor sells the products to his sponsored distributors at the same price at which the products are bought, making no "basic discount" for the sponsor.

Refund. The second way the salesperson earns income is through monthly refund on all Amway products purchased for resale—home products, cookware, and commercial products (but not including literature or sales aids). In addition to the immediate "basic discount," the salesperson receives a refund each month based on the total combined purchase volume (PV) of all products sold for the month. The refund varies from 3 to 25 percent, depending upon a salesperson's PV as shown in Table 10-1.

Example of part-time group sponsorship profits

To see how the Amway salesperson earns part-time profits as a sponsor, take this example: The sponsor is selling on a part-time basis to personal customers, who purchase $320 worth of Amway products per month. She also sponsors five other part-time distributors, who add a total of $2,400 of monthly combined PV. Table 10-2 shows how each of the distributors she sponsors earns his full discount and refund, while the sponsor earns her full discount on her personal sales. She also earns a refund of 18 percent on her personal sales, plus the difference between 18 percent and the percentage refund earned by each of her distributors on his sales. If she were not a sponsor, her income would be $131.60—6 percent refund plus 35 percent discount. In this case, as a sponsor, she earns a total of $438.40 from part-time selling and sponsoring.

TABLE 10-1

Personal PV basic discount + refund = profit

Total Monthly PV*		Basic Discount on Personal PV	Refund	% of Profit on Personal PV
$ 1.00 to	$ 99.99	up to 35%	0	up to 35%
100.00 to	299.99	up to 35%	3%	up to 38%
300.00 to	599.99	up to 35%	6%	up to 41%
600.00 to	999.99	up to 35%	9%	up to 44%
1,000.00 to	1,499.99	up to 35%	12%	up to 47%
1,500.00 to	2,499.99	up to 35%	15%	up to 50%
2,500.00 to	3,999.99	up to 35%	18%	up to 53%
4,000.00 to	5,999.99	up to 35%	21%	up to 56%
6,000.00 to	7,499.99	up to 35%	23%	up to 58%
7,500.00 and	up	up to 35%	25%	up to 60%

*Total monthly PV includes both personal PV and PV of others you sponsor.

TABLE 10-2

Distribution of refund on $2,720 total group PV—18 percent refund equals $489.60

	Individual PV	Individual Refund %	Individual Refund $	% Refund Left for Sponsor	$ Refund Left for Sponsor
A	$ 640	9	57.60	9	57.60
B	560	6	33.60	12	67.20
C	480	6	28.80	12	57.60
D	400	6	24.00	12	48.00
E	320	6	19.20	12	38.40
Sponsor	320	—	—	18	57.60
TOTAL	$2,720		163.20		326.40

Total refund: $489.60

Paid out: $163.20

Sponsor maximum basic discount: $112.00

Sponsor maximum total earnings: $438.40

Note: A, B, C, D, and E also sponsor distributors under them.

Example of full-time group sponsorship profits

The following example shows how an Amway salesperson might earn even greater income as a full-time sponsor of a group of distributors. In this instance he is selling to a larger personal customer clientele, who make purchases from him totaling $500 of Amway products monthly. Also, the distributors he sponsors have increased their sales and have recruited some distributors of their own until they contribute an additional $5,000 to the sponsor's total PV. Now he is in the 21 percent refund bracket and gets the full basic discount on his personal sales; plus 21 percent refund on his personal sales; plus the difference between 21 percent and the percentage refund earned by each of his distributors on her sales. As a sponsor, he earns $736. In this example, as well as in the previous one, *note that he does not reduce the regular profits of the distributor he sponsors, and his sponsor does not reduce her regular profits.* Every distributor receives the full amount that he has earned on the discount and refund schedule, which will also include an override on the sales of those sponsored either directly or indirectly when his combined refund percentage is greater than theirs. (See Table 10–3.)

TABLE 10-3 ▬▬▬▬▬▬▬▬▬▬▬▬▬▬▬▬▬▬▬▬▬▬▬▬▬

Distribution of refund on $5,500 total group PV—21 percent refund equals $1,555

	Individual PV	Individual Refund %	Individual Refund $	% Refund Left for Sponsor	$ Refund Left for Sponsor
A	$1,000	12	120	9	90
B	900	9	81	12	108
C	1,200	12	144	9	108
D	1,500	15	225	6	90
E	400	6	24	15	60
Sponsor	500	—	—	21	105
TOTAL	$5,500		594		561

Sponsor's maximum basic discount: $175

Sponsor's maximum total earnings: $736

Note: A, B, C, D, and E also have distributors under them helping to make total. From here it is only a short step to direct distributor.

▬▬

The direct distributor

At the head of every distributor group in Amway's organizational structure is a direct distributor. This distributor has reached the maximum PV bracket and, thereby, the maximum refund bracket of 25 percent. There is no limit to the number of direct distributors; anyone can become one by reaching the qualifying PV of $7,500 monthly. Direct distributors buy directly from Amway Corporation; they can also become voting members of the ADA, and they may serve on the board. They enjoy other privileges as the sales leaders in the Amway sales system. Among these benefits are the added bonuses for which they qualify.

When a person sponsors a direct distributor, then both the sponsor of the direct distributor and the direct distributor are in the same refund percentage bracket. In order that the sponsor of a direct distributor may enjoy a profit also, Amway pays a special 3 percent bonus. To qualify for the 3 percent, the sponsor must either have at least $2,500 personal group PV, in addition to sponsoring the direct distributor below her, or sponsor two or more direct distributors. (See Table 10-4).

TABLE 10-4

Direct distributor profits

Distributor Group	Volume	% Earned	Total Refund Paid
A	$ 1,000	12%	$ 120
B	500	6	30
C	1,500	15	225
D	2,000	15	300
E	100	3	3
F	200	3	6
G	200	3	6
H	1,500	15	225
I	2,000	15	300
J	1,000	12	120
TOTAL	$10,000		$1,335

Refund received: $2,500

Refund paid out: $1,335

Profit from group: $1,165

Note: In this example, personal sales are not shown. If the sponsor had $500 in personal sales, his earnings would increase by $300 making a total of $1,465.

"Sub-direct" distributor. A "sub-direct" distributor in Amway's organizational structure is one who sponsors only one direct distributor (25 percent) group but does not have a minimum of $2,500 personal group PV. Such a person does get the 25 percent refund on whatever personal group PV he may have but does not qualify for the 3 percent bonus. Since it is the purpose of the Amway sales plan to compensate the distributor in proportion to the production resulting from the time and effort he has put forth, the direct distributor bonus is computed in such a way that it is more profitable to sponsor several direct distributors than just one. If a sponsor does happen to sponsor just one direct distributor, it is more profitable for the sponsor to have a sizeable personal group PV in addition to sponsoring that one direct distributor than it is to have little or no personal group PV or personal retail PV and sponsor only one direct distributor.

Sponsoring two or more direct distributors usually is the result of the direct distributor's sponsor having spent considerably more time and effort than his sponsoring of just one direct distributor, with little or no personal group PV maintained in addition. Therefore, the direct distributor bonus brings the most compensation to the direct distributor's sponsor who has put in the most time and effort and produced the best balanced groups.

The 3 percent bonus.   Although a direct distributor collects a 3 percent bonus on the personal group PV of the direct distributor she sponsors, she also must remember that her sponsor collects a 3 percent bonus on her personal group PV. Therefore, each direct distributor will collect a 3 percent direct distributor bonus on the personal group PV of the direct distributor she sponsors and will maintain sufficient personal group or personal retail PV herself to guarantee that her sponsor receives a 3 percent direct distributor bonus on her personal group PV of

1. At least equal to the amount of the bonus collected if she sponsors only one direct distributor, but not more than $225;
2. Equal to at least one half of the combined 3 percent bonus collected if she sponsors two direct distributors, but not more than $225;
3. Equal to at least one third of the combined 3 percent bonus collected if she sponsors three direct distributors, but not more than $225;

and so on, always guaranteeing to her sponsor a bonus equal to the total bonus received, divided by the total number of direct distributors sponsored but never more than $225 per month.

If a direct distributor sponsor's personal group PV is such that the sponsor would not receive a 3 percent bonus of at least the amount specified in the above paragraph, the difference between the amount that the 3 percent actually amounted to, and what it should amount to, is deducted from the direct distributor bonus of the *first* direct distributor sponsor and added to the direct distributor bonus of her sponsor. This same adjustment applies up a group sponsorship. The adjustment is limited to a maximum of $225, however. An example of how the 3 percent bonus system works is shown in Exhibit 10–2.

In the example, A sponsors B who in turn sponsors distributors C, D, E, and F. B receives a 3 percent bonus on the sales of each of her distributors. According to Amway's bonus guarantee structure, B must guarantee A the average of $217.50 ($870 divided by 4). Since B has no personal group PV, the $217.50 is deducted from her $870, leaving her a net profit of $652.50. Remember that each direct distributor deals directly with Amway so the $652.50 is paid to B even if she were sick, retired, or traveling around the world.

Sales-training bonus.   The sales-training bonus is designed to reward sponsors of multiple groups of direct distributors. Direct distributors who sponsor personally 3 or more groups of direct distributors share a fund consisting of one fourth of 1 percent of the national PV, which is distributed to them annually. This, in effect, gives them a percentage on all the volume in their total group, regardless of depth.

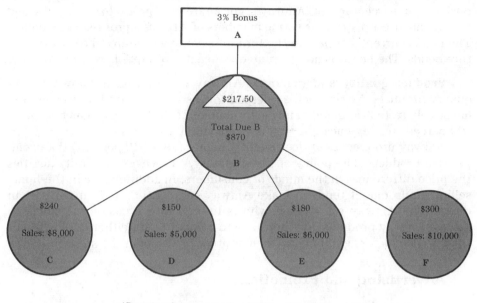

Direct Distributors

*B receives 3 percent on:
C— $8,000 × 3% = $240
D— $5,000 × 3% = $150
E— $6,000 × 3% = $180
F—$10,000 × 3% = $300
Total due B $870

EXHIBIT 10-2

Example of a 3 percent bonus (each circle represents a direct distributor)

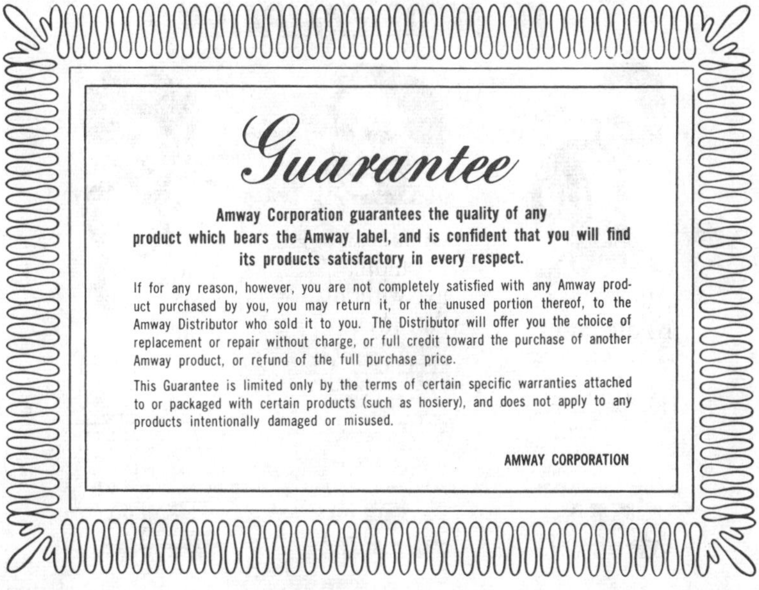

EXHIBIT 10-3

Amway guarantee

Profit-sharing bonus.   At the end of each year that Amway has been in business, a percentage of Amway's corporate net profit has been divided among the direct distributor voting members of ADA as a profit-sharing bonus. The bonus currently is paid in the form of seven-year interest-bearing debenture bonds. The bonus is not guaranteed since it is discretionary with Amway.

Product quality and pricing.   Amway Corporation is known for its quality products. No product is released for distribution until it has been exhaustively tested for quality and performance. Each Amway product carries a 100 percent money-back guarantee. See Exhibit 10–3.

Amway products are priced slightly higher (about 10 percent) than competitive products. The policy of "best quality," however, generally justifies the price differences in the minds of consumers. In addition, the in-the-home selling environment tends to make Amway competition more indirect than direct. The Amway salesperson who is invited into a customer's home to discuss Amway products does not have to compete with either the loyalty or the impulse factors exhibited by competitive products in the store.

Advertising and Promotion

National advertising

Amway Corporation supports its sales program on the national level through radio and magazine advertising. "Paul Harvey News," a staple of the ABC Radio network since 1951, was chosen by Amway in 1968 to present a nationwide radio program to bring the Amway home-care message to America's radio-listening public.

EXHIBIT 10-4

TV Guide campaign

AMWAY TRADEMARKS

Amway Trademarks Not To Be Used On Any Item:
Literature, Premium, Or Product Of Any Sort,
Without Advance Approval, In Writing, From Amway

EXHIBIT 10-5

Amway trademark

According to Jay Van Andel, chairman of the board, Amway's entrance into radio advertising is designed to support and strengthen the firm's national magazine advertising program initiated in the spring of 1965. One example of Amway's magazine-advertising program is its *TV Guide* campaign. (See Exhibit 10-4.) Featuring illustrations by Norman Rockwell, America's best-known artist, Amway's *TV Guide* ads are seen by over 12 million subscribers and newsstand buyers—an estimated 26 million readers! The entire *TV Guide* series is distributor oriented. The products are mentioned, but the distributor receives the major emphasis.

Regional and local promotion

In addition to national advertising, Amway has developed a great variety of promotional material, which the distributor may display to customers. Point-of-purchase advertising and aids have been more effective in retail sales. All sales literature and advertising material is printed by Amway for sale to their distributors. Direct distributors buy this material from Amway and resell it to the distributors in their groups at cost. The general types of advertising and promotional materials provided by Amway include

1. Outdoor billboards
2. Slide films, records, tapes
3. Catalogs and manuals
4. Annual international convention
5. Sales rallies
6. Home-care demonstration kit
7. Fund-raising brochure

8. Portable tape recorder
9. Personal shoppers' service catalog
10. Company trademark decals
11. Newsgrams
12. Personal sales award plaques
13. Point-of-purchase display kit
14. Meeting badges
15. Gift boxes for customers

Questions

1. Evaluate the organizational structure of Amway in terms of such organizational principles as (a) lines of authority and responsibility, (b) unity of command, and (c) span of control. Also consider in your evaluation the number of organizational levels and the job and task structure of the Amway organization.

2. The organizational structure of Amway's distribution system can best be described as "direct marketing," in that they market directly to the final consumer without using independently owned and operated wholesalers and retailers who are outside the Amway organization. Evaluate the direct distribution system used by Amway. Do you feel this is the most efficient type of distribution that could be used given the types of products Amway manufacturers? What other distribution systems might Amway consider? Why?

3. What are the sources of conflict in this type of distribution system? How important are such conflicts likely to be as a deterrent to Amway's sales and profit policies?

4. Evaluate the Amway sales and profit plan. How attractive are the plans from the point of view of the manufacturer? From the point of view of the resellers? From the point of view of the ultimate consumer?

5. Critically assess the advertising and promotional support supplied by Amway to its distributors. What changes would you make, if any?

Case 11 PARIS HOUSE

RONALD FRANK, a personnel manager in a large department store chain, was discussing a proposed change in the firm's branch organization with the president of the store.

The Paris House was a dominant department store in a large midwestern city. The sales volume of the main downtown store exceeded $75 million in each of the last five years. The largest sales growth of Paris House, however, came from its five branch stores located in the suburban areas surrounding the city. Each of these branch stores was under the direction of a store manager. Reporting to the store manager were as many as 25 department managers. These managers were responsible for the sales volume and total management of anywhere from 2 to 5 departments in the store. Although the department managers were directly responsible to the branch store manager, it was well-recognized that their jobs could not be performed efficiently without the full cooperation of the buyer for the organization and his assistant. Since the department manager was dependent on the downtown buyer for all of his merchandise, his relationship with this buyer was particularly important. In actuality, most department managers at the branch stores had to maintain good relationships with at least two or three buyers.

The management of the Paris House department store looked upon the branch department manager's position as a training ground for future merchandising positions that were becoming available as the firm grew.

Ronald Frank, however, was well aware of the fact that problems were developing in spite of management's view. It had been the policy of the firm to hire college graduates. After initial training, these graduates were offered assistant buyer positions within the main downtown store for a period not to exceed two years. At the end of this period the assistant buyers were assigned

Source: David J. Rachman and Houston G. Elam, *Retail Management Cases*, © 1969, pp. 42–44. Reprinted by permission of Prentice-Hall, Inc., Englewood Cliffs, N.J.

as department managers at the branch stores. It was at this stage, of course, that the firm hoped they would develop into top-level merchandising positions.

Within recent months, Mr. Frank's department made a tabulation of department managers in the branch stores and found that in a given year over one-third of the department managers left the firm. After carefully examining the personnel department's reports on exit interviews they had conducted with these department managers, he learned that:

1. Four of five department managers had taken similar positions in other competing retail stores in this same area.
2. Most of the department managers who were leaving gave as their reason the inability of the firm to recognize their worth. Many of the department managers complained that though they were responsible for increasing sales volume annually, they did not participate in the choice of merchandise selected for their store.
3. Many of these same department managers complained that during the time they were in the branch store they felt isolated from the firm's top management which ultimately made a decision concerning their future promotion.

In his discussion with the store president, Mr. Frank pointed out that the relationship of the store buyer and the department manager must be improved if the Paris House were to maintain its dominance in this metropolitan area. He recalled the president's comments a few months back when the firm launched an expensive recruiting program at the college level. In his remarks, the president pointed out that the future growth of the company meant that the firm must develop department managers who have attained a high level of merchandise sophistication since future branch stores would be located in areas considerably distant from the downtown branch store and hence their customers would probably demand very different merchandise from those who shop in the downtown area. Secondly, since the expansion of the branch stores places a greater burden on the downtown buyer, he must be in a position to receive more accurate merchandising information than ever before. Lastly, this expansion obviously would require the training of more buyers in the years ahead. The department manager would seem to be the major source for developing buyers.

Mr. Frank pointed out to the president that a merchandising committee that had been set up three months ago in cooperation with the personnel division developed a program aimed at correcting this problem. This program, tentatively titled MOP (Management by Objectives Program), has as its major function the attempt to gain a more active and meaningful participation in the merchandising decision making by the department branch manager. The program basically is very simple but takes into consideration a fact that came out in the discussions with the committee.

It was brought out that there actually exist two different types of department managers at the branch. The first type has been described earlier: the college graduate looking for a promotion within a short period after arriving at the store. However, the second type that exists within the branch store organization is the so-called "old timer" who is completely satisfied with a position as department manager and has little interest in taking on the responsibilities of a higher-level merchandising position. Thus, Mr. Frank pointed out that any program that is developed must take into consideration these two different types of department managers who operate within the confines of the branch store. He also added that the second type of manager was perfectly happy to allow the main store buyer to make all of the merchandising decisions for his departments.

The first step recommended in the MOP program was for each department manager to submit a detailed plan for the coming six-month merchandising period. This plan should include detailed sales breakdowns, stock turnover, and suggested improvements in the types of goods and assortments to be offered in each department. It was the feeling of the committee that the more ambitious department managers would submit detailed plans. On the other hand, the "old timers" would probably treat this work superficially as they had in the past. Once the plan was submitted, the buyers, the divisional merchandise manager, and the department manager would go over these plans in detail and make changes where necessary.

After the plan was approved, it became the distinct responsibility of the downtown buyer and the assistant buyer to buy the merchandise for the individual branch as outlined in the detailed plan. Concurrently, the computer department would supply exact information on all phases of the department operation, including markdowns and net profit. In the past, only departmental sales records had been kept for the branch stores.

At the end of the plan period the department manager would be evaluated on the basis of his ability to reach the goals as specified in his merchandising plan.

Questions

1. Evaluate the plan as submitted by Mr. Frank.
2. Are there any available alternatives to this plan?
3. What would be your recommendations?

Case 12

GALUP-HARRIS— PERSONNEL-HIRING COUNSELORS

MR. GALUP, the executive director of Galup-Harris, a nationally-known firm in the area of screening and selection of salesmen and executives, faced the task of reviewing the hiring practices of his client firms so that he could make specific recommendations as to which practices should be continued and which ones should be discarded. The task of screening applicants had increased in complexity due to new federal regulations, particularly those from the Equal Employment Opportunity Commission (EEOC). Galup's greatest concern was in the area of psychological testing. He was aware of a recent study of 2,500 companies, conducted by the American Personnel Administration which disclosed that a sizeable percentage of the firms queried had phased out testing, reduced it, or planned to stop.

Galup also was aware of a recent Supreme Court case in which the Court ruled that Albemarle Paper Company was discriminating in its hiring. Albemarle had validated its testing for some jobs but got in trouble when it didn't validate the same tests when applied to different jobs. Galup also knew that Flying Tiger Line, an air-freight firm, recently stopped giving its principal psychological test, the Wonderlic learning ability exam, because of all the uncertainties surrounding validation. Validation requirements also had scared off a big midwestern manufacturer from using psychological tests as a hiring tool at its many diverse plant and office locations. They decided to abandon their psychological examinations because the tests had not been validated by sex and race.

Due to his many years of successful experience with psychological testing, Galup was not ready to join the bandwagon of dissenters and to recommend that his clients drop tests as a hiring tool. His first move was to call the EEOC office where he talked with James Sharf, the commission's staff psychologist. This official was emphatic in stating that business was overreacting and misinterpreting the testing guidelines of EEOC. A common

---

This case was prepared by Steven J. Shaw, University of South Carolina.

misconception on the part of personnel managers was that the fastest way to get into trouble with the EEOC was to test. However, Sharf thought the best way for companies to stay out of trouble was to conduct good validation studies on the tests they gave. To support his assertions, Sharf pointed to several blue-chip companies which had extensive and sophisticated personnel systems. These firms still find testing so valuable that they have gone to the time and the expense to fully validate what they are doing. In particular, Sharf cited American Telephone and Telegraph Company and Exxon Corporation as companies doing an outstanding job in the area of test validation.

Attitude Testing by Exxon

To learn more about the validation procedures at one of the companies Sharf had cited, Galup called an Exxon personnel officer who was familiar with their testing procedures. Most of this firm's testing is the aptitude type for entry-level jobs in which candidates are trained in specialized skills. According to Paul Sparks, personnel/research coordinator for the oil giant, Exxon had begun their testing in 1948 to reduce a high rate of failure in training programs, and their testing had greatly reduced employee turnover. Moreover, Exxon strictly adhered to a policy of continuously validating its tests. They believed that although continuing validation studies cost money, the total expense was far less than the expense it would incur if they had to start from scratch to meet EEOC compliance with a massive crash-validation effort. The cost of test validation was low when compared to the alternative of a large number of "bust-outs" in training programs. Sparks estimated that it cost Exxon at least $8,000 to train one refinery worker, for example.

Sparks explained that the EEOC had received very few discrimination complaints about Exxon's testing procedures. He cited one case, as an example, in which a Black claimed discrimination. However, Exxon was quickly exonerated when the EEOC learned that the job he or she wanted had been given to another Black.

Reference Checks

After his talks with the EEOC and Exxon officials, Galup was convinced that proven tests, properly administered, were still the most effective selection tools available to personnel managers. Galup had little faith in reference checks. From his experience, Galup believed that references could not be trusted because previous employers may have had unfounded personal biases against the applicant. Also, former bosses, Galup knew, were often unwilling to divulge the true reasons why employees were discharged, even though it might have been entirely justified. Conversely, applicants who truly did a rotten job might wind up with glowing recommendations simply because the previous employer either wanted to get rid of them or because he or she feared a lawsuit in the event the bad recommendation fell into the employee's hands. Several such suits had been won in court.

Personal Interviews

While personal interviews can be used to explain job specifications and screen out misfits, Galup did not want his clients to rely heavily on them since numerous studies have shown that flagrant biases exist among interviewers. For instance, Galup read that tall men did markedly better in sales interviews because subconsciously interviewers generally equate height with potential sales success. Galup had also learned from another famous experiment that in a traditional face-to-face meeting, a group of businessmen could not judge consistently job applicants. The interviewers were twenty-three experienced men, mostly sales managers who hired salespersons all the time. Each of them individually talked to and rated the same twenty-four applicants. The results were almost as helter-skelter as if the names had been written on sheets of paper and churned up by an electric fan. No single applicant was ranked first by more than three of the twenty-three interviewers. As an example, one man was ranked first by one interviewer but sixteenth, nineteenth, and twenty-second by others.

Galup also learned that sociologists had conducted several studies which proved that flagrant biases exist among interviewers. One study assigned twelve people to interview 2,000 homeless men to find out what had put them on the skids. Among the interviewers were an ardent prohibitionist and a confirmed socialist. The prohibitionist found that the chief cause of the men's downfall was drink. The socialist determined that the chief cause was capitalism. The experiment proved that no interviewer can really see beyond the end of his or her own prejudices.

What Types of Tests to Recommend

There were hundreds of tests in use and Galup's next task was to make recommendations on specific types his clients should use. In a letter he was drafting, Galup decided to recommend five types of tests.

1. Intelligence tests. These tests present, in varying combinations, tasks involving word meanings, verbal relationships, arithmetic reasoning, form classifications, spatial relationships, and other abstract symbolic material. Galup was leaning toward a test like the Wechsler Adult Intelligence Scale which was designed to measure capacity to learn as opposed to past actual achievement.
2. Personality inventory. These tests frequently are referred to as social intelligence examinations. They are designed to measure an applicant's method of handling himself or herself in various social situations. Various socially sensitive situations might be described and the applicant is asked to check which method he would use from a checklist of alternatives. Some of the tests try to measure the examinee's degree of extroversion or introversion by asking the person to check favorite hobbies and interests from a list that might include

playing bridge, solitaire, attending social functions, and hunting or fishing alone.

3. Proficiency tests. These are examinations which are designed to test a job applicant's present skill or ability. Thus, an individual applying for a secretarial position can be given a typing speed test and a test designed to measure accuracy in transcribing from shorthand notes. Likewise, a person applying for a sales position could be given a word-meaning and an oral test to determine both understanding of words and command of spoken English. Also, he or she could be asked to stage a mock sales presentation.

4. Aptitude tests. In these tests, the aim is to measure an applicant's potential. That is, does the applicant have the qualities and traits that successful job performers have. Most successful aptitude tests are those that have been custom-built specifically for the company by a psychologist hired by that company. For instance, an insurance company might retain a psychologist to develop a test to measure applicant ability to sell its form of insurance. The first step for the psychologist would be to study the personnel files of the company and to isolate a group of characteristics that might be labeled as success traits. Once it is decided what characteristics seem to make up the profile of a good insurance salesperson for that company, a test then has to be designed to measure either the presence or absence of these traits among applicants. Finally, the test has to be administered to both good and bad company salespersons to see if the test actually separates the successes from the failures. The psychologist and his staff might have to work several years before a valid examination is developed.

5. Attitude scales. An attitude scale contains a series of questions or statements which are designed to measure a job applicant's strength of feeling toward or against an idea, person, or object. For example, through an attitude scale of the Likert type, it would be possible to measure a job applicant's attitude toward Blacks and other minority groups. Obviously, a salesperson for a company that had many black customers should not have negative feelings against this race. Likewise, a person being considered for the personnel department of a firm should not be negatively disposed toward women as executives. A question similar to the following could determine the degree of open-mindedness of an applicant. "In your opinion which one or ones of the following roles can women play effectively?" Check one or more from the following list: ( ) homemaker, ( ) secretary, ( ) clerk, ( ) supervisor, ( ) executive." If two applicants for a position in the personnel department had equal abilities but one of them checked just the first three categories while the other checked all five, the firm would be wise to give the job to the second applicant. The EEOC is pressing hard to get companies to hire and promote women to executive positions, and the first applicant might sabotage company efforts in this direction.

For Discussion

1. If you were in Galup's position, which one or ones of the five types of tests would you recommend to your retailer clients the most? Why?

2. Which one or ones of the tests would you be reluctant to recommend strongly? Why?

3. What role should personal interviews play in selecting retail employees? Mention as many situations as you can where personal interviews might be very important in the hiring process.

4. What should be the place of reference checks in the selection process?

5. Can you suggest any other techniques that Galup might consider? For instance, could the polygraph or lie detector test be a useful screening device in situations where employees handle money?

PART 6

Retail Facilities Management

Corporate Background: Big Mac Gets Bigger

MCDONALD'S CORPORATION is one of the best-known companies in America and is increasingly becoming one of the best-known in the world. It even qualifies as a legend in the history of modern marketing success stories. In 1955, McDonald's opened its first fast-food outlet in Des Plaines, Illinois, not too far from its current headquarters on McDonald's Plaza, Oak Brook, Illinois. The current chain of 4,000 restaurants is in all fifty states and twenty-one countries. Seventy percent of these outlets are licensed to independent firms, called "franchisees," and thirty percent of the outlets are directly owned by McDonald's. Hardly any of these restaurants has failed.

The 1975 sales volume was $2.5 billion, making it the largest food service in the world. By September 1976, the sign posted near the Golden Arches outside each McDonald's outlet boasted 20 billion hamburgers sold. While it took eight years for the company to sell its first billion burgers, it now takes only four months for the sign to be revised another billion. In 1975, McDonald's spent $60 million on advertising. Profit has been on a steady increase with an average annual rise of forty percent.

Growth has clearly been the driving force of McDonald's two-decade history. Coinciding with an increasing population and the great expansion of the suburbs, McDonald's has added more restaurants and significantly raised the sales volume per restaurant. The modern building, Golden Arches, and parking lot have become familiar fixtures on the American suburban landscape.

In pursuing its growth objectives in the mid-1970's, McDonald has vigorously placed outlets within cities—including downtown areas and shopping avenues adjacent to residential neighborhoods. These restaurants have no

Adapted from Larry J. Rosenberg, "McDonald's Corporation," *Marketing Management: Strategies & Cases,* ed. M. Wayne DeLozier and Arch G. Woodside (Columbus, Ohio: Charles E. Merrill Publishing Company, 1978), pp. 66–72.

parking lots and the architecture is adapted to the tighter space requirements of city properties.

McDonald's management has been surprised by the increasing eruption of community groups protesting the building of local McDonald's restaurants. These reactions have occurred mainly in urban neighborhoods, but also in some suburban communities as well.

What shall we do about West 86th Street?*

The place is the McDonald's Eastern Regional Office, in Bloomfield, N.J. The date is March 15, 1975. A meeting of three executives is about to begin in preparation for tomorrow's confrontation with a neighborhood group opposing the location of a McDonald's restaurant in its community at 168 West 86th Street, Manhattan, a major borough of New York City. The protest leaders claim to have a petition with 3,000 signatures against the proposed outlet at a major intersection of the Upper West Side. This area is populated by diverse ethnic groups, artists, professionals, and the elderly, and most are living in fairly old, once elegant, high-rise apartment buildings and three-story townhouses.

Today's meeting is chaired by Henry Pace, Assistant Regional Manager—a hardliner regarding expansion in Manhattan. In the last two years he supervised the opening of thirteen restaurants (there is a total of forty in New York City). Also at the meeting is Mary Lambert, Director of Public Information, who advocates image building and careful compromise. The third participant is Kenneth Roman, Senior Market Analyst, who has considered the community point of view to which he has recently been personally exposed and about which he feels some merit may exist.

Growth is great

Henry Pace, at forty-five years of age, is an Assistant Regional Manager with responsibility for directing the expansion of the McDonald's chain in New York City. Although he did not graduate from college, he has advanced as the McDonald's organization grew. Next month he will be considered for promotion to Vice President, which would give him prestige and a host of excellent fringe benefits. He has worked hard to attain this goal, and he dreams of little else.

Success at McDonald's has meant expansion in number of outlets and sales. His record in Manhattan has been excellent; however, top management has expressed displeasure at his cancellation of plans for two previous Manhattan outlets in the face of community protests.

Pace feels McDonald's has been a national, indeed an American cultural, success. Virtually every new outlet does well, demonstrating that McDonald's is meeting consumer demand for, as he puts it, "good, cheap

*The meeting and characters described in this case are fictional. But the account of the McDonald's general situation in Manhattan and the West 86th Street protest in 1975 are based largely on facts.

food." Location decisions are based on solid marketing research. First, the company studies demographic data (which neighborhoods have the population to support a new McDonald's and how intense the competition is). Second, it pursues the goal of providing convenient locations in already commercially-zoned areas. Pace knows that McDonald's has an economic right to try to satisfy existing consumer demand and a legal right to own property to do it. On the other hand, he regards a neighborhood group of twenty members or so, springing up to claim that *their* rights are being violated, as elitist, radical, and illegitimate. He suspects that this group is comprised mainly of local food store and restaurant owners who fear competition from a new McDonald's. He can't quite understand why some businesspeople—such as clothing, antique, and other non-food store owners—are among the protest supporters. He feels that they all will benefit from the added flow of people who will end up around West 86th Street to eat at the new McDonald's. He is unimpressed with the 3,000-signature petition, even assuming all the names are of real people. With all "those liberals" in Manhattan on a sunny February day, it would be relatively easy to get that many passers-by to sign practically anything. This would hold true especially if the protest is against an "establishment" corporation like McDonald's.

As a future strategy, Pace is thinking about a plan to avoid, or at least minimize, protests against a new McDonald's by some fringe community members and outside radicals. After the former building is demolished, no announcement should be made nor sign erected (stating "on this site will be built...") regarding the coming McDonald's restaurant. Not until the new McDonald's building is nearly completed should the Golden Arches and name sign be installed. If the protestors don't know what is coming, he reasons, then how can they either object to it or seek support against it?

Another side of the story

Mary Lambert, now thirty-five years old, came to McDonald's after a brilliant career with J. Walter Thompson, the New York advertising agency. There she did public relations for the L&M cigarette account, advising them on responding to anti-smoking attacks in the 1960's. As Director of Public Information, she believes that image building for McDonald's is its best long-term defense.

Lambert has skillfully created a case based upon the facts and assumptions, as she sees them, regarding the McDonald's story. This case states that a new McDonald's would upgrade the neighborhood; store personnel would keep the premises clean and well policed; the store would serve a family clientele; added street lighting and pedestrian traffic would reduce crime; the franchisee would be a new small business person who would be "Mr. or Ms. McDonald" in the neighborhood; the franchisee would hire local people to work in the restaurant, especially teenagers who have difficulty finding decent part-time jobs. She is encouraged by reinforcement of the notion that McDonald's contributes to the social and economic life of a community in the form of two recent "average citizens'" letters in the *New York Times* (see Exhibits 13-1 and 13-2).

5,347,890,386,903,274,711,310 Sold

By David S. Sampson

The old woman crossed herself, pushed aside her tattered coat and knelt down by the table to pray. Her lips moved, her head nodded up and down. Nobody paid much attention, even though she was nowhere near a church.

This happened at a restaurant. Not just any restaurant, because, even though this is New York, the old woman would probably have been tossed out, along with the rest of the somewhat ragged crew that shared the same eating quarters.

The restaurant was McDonald's. I like McDonald's.

The McDonald's restaurants are, of course, an eyesore to behold. The little golden arches seem to pop up in the least likely and most unpopular spots; property values are lowered; "undesirables" flock in.

But the "undesirables" are all around us anyway. McDonald's simply gives them a place to go. Anyone with a little change in the pocket can come up with a pretty full meal. Instead of shuddering on an outside corner, there is warmth. There are other people. There is the assurance that no one will come up and ask you to leave because you happen to be a little crazy.

Gourmets shudder at the mere mention of McDonald's. Property owners and nearby residents cringe; hungry people don't.

McDonald's, on the West Side, at least, are perhaps the only restaurants around that come equipped with full-time security men, all decked out in policeman-blue and a billy club.

They are places filled with lonely people who have no place else to go. Residents of the welfare hotels don't exactly hit your finest restaurants. But they can go to McDonald's and, for a brief time maybe, not feel like they're on welfare.

And the chain seems to encourage it. Little tickets are passed out offering free meals for $5 in pennies.

Stop and think about that for a while and it's actually a pretty nice thing to do. Stop and think a little longer and realize that no one else is doing it. Unemployment is up, prices are up. McDonald's still says come on in and have a cheap meal, we don't care who you are.

I like McDonald's. I don't like the food. I don't like to eat there. I feel uncomfortable when I go in. But I like McDonald's because they seem to care a little. Maybe it's all business and they really don't. But they seem to, and even that's rare enough these days.

David S. Sampson, a lawyer who is studying natural resources for the Commission on Critical Choices for Americans says he has "absolutely no connection" with McDonald's.

EXHIBIT 13-1

To defuse the West 86th Street protestors' demands at tomorrow's meeting, Lambert wants to suggest a "compromise." She personally would admit that it is more real in appearance than in substance. She will propose that McDonald's try to sell the West 86th Street property with the so-far unbuilt restaurant. Should it not be possible to find a customer, however, McDonald's then would be able to go ahead and build the restaurant. Given the slow real estate market on the Upper West Side, she estimates that there is less than a fifty percent chance that a buyer will be found.

IN DEFENSE OF McDONALD'S

To the Editor:

I am appalled at the concerted action that is being taken against McDonald's. I fail to see anything reprehensible about the operation of an inexpensive, wholesome establishment like McDonalds—at least nothing more reprehensible than could be said against Burger King, Kentucky Fried Chicken, Papaya, Orange Julius or any of many other fast-food places that have been allowed to flourish without a voice being raised.

The argument of undesirables gathering at McDonald's is ridiculously unfair. All my children and their friends go to McDonald's and I'd rather have them eat there than consort with the motley crew that is to be found in, for example, the Blimpie Base at 86th Street and Broadway.

As for cars double-parking, could that be any more extreme than what I've seen outside Zabar's and Murray's Sturgeon Shop—rows of Rolls-Royces and Cadillacs and assorted other metal monsters, exuding fumes while their engines idle?

Are intelligent New Yorkers going to listen to remarks such as that of Dr. Gabriel Roz—a "social psychiatrist"—that "the hamburger stand" (at 86th and Amsterdam) "would lower the quality of mental health in the area"? Please, something's gone awry when neighborhoods with real problems choose to waste their energies fighting against an innocuous fast-food chain.

Miranda Knickerbocker
New York, Feb. 4, 1975

EXHIBIT 13-2

Letters to the Editor, *New York Times*, February 22, 1975, p. 26, © 1975 by the New York Times Company. Reprinted by permission.

Time for a change?

Ken Roman, at the age of fifty-five, has long been a specialist in restaurant site selection before joining McDonald's as a senior research analyst five years ago. He was transferred last month from McDonald's Oak Brook headquarters to help with further expansion in the New York metropolitan area. He found an apartment in Manhattan at 125 W. 86th Street because he wanted one of those grand old, roomy, high-ceiling Upper West Side apartments he had seen in movies. At the time he signed the lease, he was unaware his apartment was near an intended location for a McDonald's outlet. He recently discussed the neighborhood protest with some of its leaders, not identifying himself as a McDonald's employee in order to hear their full story.

Roman learned the community group's feelings about the new outlet harming the tenuous balance in the present character of community, resulting from its blend of population and distinctive store types and dwelling units. The negative consequences of the McDonald's is believed to seriously accelerate the decline of this community's uniqueness. The quality of life in the community would be subverted without its being consulted. Specific fears centered on the McDonald's producing more street noise, litter, auto traffic, congestion and pollution; teenagers hanging out and drug-dealing types being attracted; and additional fast-food chains opening and pushing up rents to the detriment of the long-time small independent stores in the area. He visited other Manhattan sites and found that each neighborhood is struggling in one way or another to maintain its quality of life. It was surprising for him to see two major newspaper editorials, in the *New York Times* and *Wall Street Journal,* discuss this issue in such strong terms (see Exhibits 13–3 and 13–4).

Battle of the Burger

The battle of the burger continues in New York, generating heat and litter. Community protest increases as the number of fast-food places grows. "Protest is a fact of life which we accept," says one McDonald's spokesman. "We must be doing something right," says another, referring to an apparently insatiable demand for Big Macs.

Undimmed opposition from almost every neighborhood threatened with the blessings of Burger King and its brothers suggests more clearly that they must be doing something wrong. The message just doesn't seem to be getting through their demographic data.

City neighborhoods are more than population figures indicating potential markets. The impact of fast-food chains in an urban setting is completely unlike the effect on suburbia or the open road, because the environmental patterns are different. It has taken planners decades to find out what makes a successful city neighborhood tick. It works because it is a strongly individualized collection of close-knit, small-scaled, personalized, related living,

service and amenity facilities stacked together in tight pedestrian proximity. The balance shifts constantly and precariously, but these are the stable constants. It can be ruptured easily, and physical damage can lead to social dislocation.

Therefore it is not a question of esthetics or decorum, or the good will of the franchisee. The promise of voluntary policing, or clean-up, or changes in design to make fast-food outlets more acceptable neighbors are beside the point. What is fatal to city residential neighborhood character is the mass market formula itself, with its high volume turn-over and mass-produced plastic image that sabotages individuality and a sense of place.

Fast-food places are neighborhood-busters before one burger is bitten or one redundant wrapper dropped. It is a matter of scale, style and standards that are destructively incompatible with the urban fabric and functions. They simply do not cut the mustard in New York.

EXHIBIT 13-3 ══════════════════════════════════════

Roman is reasonably certain about the ignore-the-protestors position Pace will take. He also senses that someone like Lambert will advocate a public relations offensive. However, Roman is not as sure about either strategy's success given this new kind of community issue. He begins to question what McDonald's has learned from the three community protests so far, and he believes that others will occur unless the company does something. He seriously doubts that McDonald's can win on this issue. He is leaning toward a new location policy that focuses on community criteria developed in a dialogue with community representatives. But he is quick to ponder What are these criteria? Who should these representatives be? The question troubling him most is Should his corporation somehow give a community a "veto" over whether a McDonald's can be built there? In his thirty-year career in marketing research and site selection, he has never had to deal with questions like these.

Trouble in River City

Those New Yorkers who are ever alert to signs that their city is threatened from within are now up in arms, waving petitions and promising lawsuits, because McDonald Hamburger, Burger King and their like are making inroads in New York City. The watchdogs of public taste are alarmed at the "apparently insatiable demand for Big Macs," in the words of The New York Times.

According to the Times, "The impact of fast-food chains in an urban setting is completely unlike the effect on suburbia or the open road, because the environmental patterns are different. It has taken planners decades to find out what makes a successful city neighborhood tick.... What is fatal to city residential neighborhood character is the mass market formula itself, with its high volume turnover and mass-produced plastic image that sabotages individuality and a sense of place."

Besides, it is simply not necessary that the style, the grace, the ambience of lovely New York be spoiled just because the great unwashed mob has a craving for double cheesers and whoppers. If a New Yorker wants to take his wife and kiddies out for hamburgers and fries, he can always hail a cab and hop down to P.J. Clarke's. Or, if he's a poor person, an outing via subway to Coney and Nathan's Famous is always a lot of fun. As for the watchdogs of public taste, they can pile the family in the old bus and take to the open road for a visit to suburbia. This activity is only recommended for those New Yorkers whose will is strong enough to resist the plastic and dehumanizing influence of those golden arches.

EXHIBIT 13-4

Discussion Questions

1. Are there any social responsibility aspects to this marketing situation? What are they?

2. Given the nature of Manhattan neighborhoods like West 86th Street, can McDonald's growth policy be justified today?

3. What good can a public relations response do? What harm? In the short run? In the long run?

4. What are the rights of a community? Who should determine them?

5. Do you feel there should be any new marketing strategy similar to what Ken Roman is suggesting? What kind?

6. What recommendations would you make to McDonald's?

Case 14

LEFTY'S LTD.

LEFTY'S LTD. is a men's clothing store located in a mid-western college town. In twenty years Lefty's has grown from little more than a storefront operation to a 3,200-square-foot men's specialty shop and college student boutique. Amost since entering town, Lefty's assumed the leadership position in retailing for men in the under-forty age group and for the college student. While Lefty's has been profitable over the years, the last two years have shown a decline in sales and profit. (See Table 14-1.) Norman Mathews, the owner, feels the problem is that Lefty's does not project the same image to the market that was so carefully cultivated over the years. In an effort to ascertain what the community thinks of Lefty's, Mathews hired Kingman and Associates, a small advertising agency, to find out how consumers perceive his store.

TABLE 14-1

Sales and profits of Lefty's (1972-1975)

	1972	1973	1974	1975
Net sales	$251,255	$302,717	$299,247	$282,134
Net profit	75,950	81,128	29,147	74,927

Background

Lefty's Ltd. was opened in 1956 by Norman Mathews after he had spent five years learning the business in his brother's men's wear shop. Lefty's began with a store layout of little more than 1,000 square feet and used display fix-

Adapted from Carter L. Grocott, "Lefty's Ltd.," *Consumer Behavior Dynamics: A Casebook,* ed. M. Wayne DeLozier (Columbus, O.: Charles E. Merrill Publishing Company, 1977), p. 29–36.

tures. In the next ten years, Mathews modestly expanded his store area and upgraded its facilities by always buying used items. Such frugality provided Lefty's with a pleasing if unexciting decor, at a fraction of normal cost.

In 1965 Lefty's was able to acquire second floor storage space above the store. This allowed for an expansion of the sales area to almost 1500 square feet. While new carpeting was added throughout the store, again only used cabinets and fixtures were purchased.

Although Mathews desired more space, Lefty's expansion was blocked at the current location by existing leaseholders on both sides of the store. Because the location was ideal for his customers, Mathews looked to other alternatives to satisfy his space requirements. In 1969 Mathews opened the forerunner of his student boutique in the basement of a nearby building. The new 288-square-foot store had very simple appointments and operated under the name of ''The Downstairs Shop.'' The store carried jeans, shirts, belts, sandals, and other items of interest to the male and female college student.

The Downstairs Shop operated successfully until early 1973 when Lefty's was able to obtain additional floor space next door. The acquisition of the new space allowed for a doubling of sales space and a vast increase in much needed storage areas. With the expansion of the store, Mathews completely redecorated the facilities. With new carpets, display and lighting fixtures, cabinets and wall and ceiling treatments, the store was a changed operation from top to bottom. The exterior also was refurbished with brick veneer and new signing. About 800 square feet of the new area was allocated to the student boutique. The student boutique is rustic in nature and carries many of the same items offered in the former Downstairs Shop. Although often a hardship, Lefty's operated throughout the redecoration process. The store had its ''Grand Opening'' in October 1973.

Merchandising Practices

Until recently, Lefty's carried a wide range of nationally advertised brands. This broad selection of merchandise seemed to enable Lefty's to meet the needs of all their customers. Over the last several years, Mathews, who does all the buying, has been able to obtain some excellent buys on unbranded merchandise. As a result, the Lefty's brand name now appears more frequently on suits, sport coats, shirts, and other items. During this process, the number of national brands carried was sharply reduced. Mathews suggested that the unbranded was the same quality level as the national brands, but privately some of his salesmen did not agree with his assessment.

Along with the increased use of the Lefty's brand there was a shift in the type of national brands offered. The store now is stocked with unfamiliar national brands. Mathews again claims no change in quality, but rather just good buying on his part. Within the past year Mathews has begun to purchase some irregulars and extras to offer as specials in the college boutique. While this policy has not been extended to the rest of the store, Mathews indicated it might be possible in the future.

When compared with stores in other communities, Lefty's has always tended to be rather conservative in its offering of styles. But, this policy matches the character of both the student market as well as the community as a whole and Mathews feels it has made Lefty's successful.

The Mathews pricing philosophy has changed in the last several years from one with moderate prices with few price lines to that of high prices with few price lines. In a practical sense, the prices are fictional, for Lefty's runs what amounts to a continuous sale on at least some of the store's merchandise. It has become almost a standing joke in the community that no one would buy an item from Lefty's unless it were on sale, and that seems to be all the time. Mathews feels that the sales add excitement to the store and that people like them.

The only advertising Lefty's does is through the local newspapers, morning and evening, and the student paper. All of Lefty's advertisements stress the same thing—a sale. Mathews accepts no cooperative advertising. He feels that sales items are what bring the customer into the store, not any fancy copy with its pseudo-sophisticated pictures.

Competition

The competitors have come and gone over the twenty years Lefty's has been in operation, but only one full-line men's store, Gordon's, is providing serious competition. Gordon's caters to the same market as Lefty's but its student-oriented clothing is included within the rest of the store's merchandise. Gordon's is located only one block away. Gordon's management suggests that the only reason Mathews remodeled Lefty's is because Gordon's redecorated the year before. Competition between the two stores has become quite intense in the last several years. In an effort to counter Lefty's pricing policies, Gordon's has run advertisements in the local papers stressing their normally low prices. Copy in other ads has suggested that customers need not wait for a sale to obtain a good buy. Both advertisements have been directed toward Lefty's customers.

Additional local competition comes from two "jean shops" and two men's wear shops in a nearby mall. While the "jeans shops" do offer strong competition in their specialty, their merchandise lines are very limited. The two men's shops appear to be having a good deal of difficulty generating any type of business. The two mall shops offer merchandise at the same price and quality level as Lefty's and Gordon's, but have generated little interest in the community. Most people seem to feel that the two men's stores provide a much higher quality and style level than the rest of the mall stores and as a result are of little interest to the typical "value-conscious" mall customer. Rumors have spread that the owners of these two men's shops have realized their mistake, and plan to relocate next year within the downtown area. Mathews has some concern over this possibility.

Consumers

The consumers in this community have been and continue to be very mobile. Even with the recent recession, the community had a much higher population turnover than the national average. The city has a population of 40,000 with an additional 30,000 suburban residents. There also are 16,000 student consumers who play an important role in the clothing market. (Although Mathews is unsure how important the student is to Lefty's business, it would be safe to assume that 50 percent of sales emanate from the student population.) Both the community and student populations have increased about 33 percent over the last twenty years.

As one would expect of a college town, the population is well educated with the college degree being the rule rather than the exception. It should be noted that the high educational level is the result not only of the university, but also the existence of several federal agencies which operate facilities in the area. These operations require highly educated personnel.

For some unexplained reason, members of the community tend to be very localized in their shopping behavior. Little shopping is done outside of town, even though there are many shopping areas in a twenty-five- to seventy-five-mile range of town reachable by an excellent new highway system. The majority of television viewing in the community comes from this twenty-five- to seventy-five-mile range via cable television. Although the community is exposed to advertising from large retailers in neighboring areas, it seems to make little difference in their shopping patterns.

Regarding the tendency to shop locally, the student population operates in much the same fashion as the townspeople. However, the majority of students make only 50 percent of their clothing purchases in town. The remainder of their clothing is usually obtained in their home towns. While the student population is not very affluent, its size alone makes it an attractive market.

Image Study

Because Mathews felt uncomfortable about the image his store might be projecting to the community, he decided to hire Kingman and Associates to conduct an image survey for him. Jim Kingman suggested the following:

1. Compare Lefty's advertised image with the customers' image of the store.
2. Compare Lefty's store image with Gordon's store image.
3. Compare the image of Lefty's customers who used a charge account with those who did not use one.

To conduct the survey, Kingman decided to test three kinds of consumers: those who preferred to shop at Lefty's, those who preferred to shop at Gordon's, and a group of consumers from another community who were unfamiliar with Lefty's.

Over a two-week period, subjects for the first two groups were selected randomly from individuals shopping in the downtown area. Shoppers were assigned to one of two groups on the basis of their answer to the following question: "When considering a clothing purchase, at what store in town do you prefer to shop?" The subjects were then asked to complete a seventeen-item, six-point semantic differential questionnaire. In the case of those who preferred to shop at Lefty's, they were asked if they generally used a Lefty's charge account in making purchases there. Demographic data was obtained at the end of the interview.

Lefty's advertised image was generated by interviewing subjects drawn from a nearby city. The subjects had no knowledge of the store. They were shown a series of Lefty's advertisements and were asked to form a mental picture of the store which did the advertising. With this picture in mind, the subjects were asked to complete the same seventeen-item semantic differential scale.

Survey Results

The data generated from the three subject groups were analyzed and arithmetic means for scale values were calculated. A summary of the results is provided in Exhibits 14–1 through 14–3. These exhibits provide image profiles for Lefty's, Gordon's, and Lefty's advertising.

Mr. Kingman's report to Mr. Mathews was basically a descriptive report on his research procedures and the data. Very little interpretation of results were included. Mathews had the report, but was uncertain of just what it meant or what to do. He felt something was wrong and that he must decide what changes to make in his marketing effort if he were to reverse the sales and profit decline. A quick decision was especially important since he believed that the possible relocation of the two mall stores to the downtown area would further erode his business.

Discussion Questions

1. What do you see as the problems, if any, with Lefty's image?

2. What action should Mr. Mathews take to make a turnabout in Lefty's sales and profits?

3. How would you evaluate the research that Mr. Kingman performed?

4. What additional image data would you have collected? For what purpose?

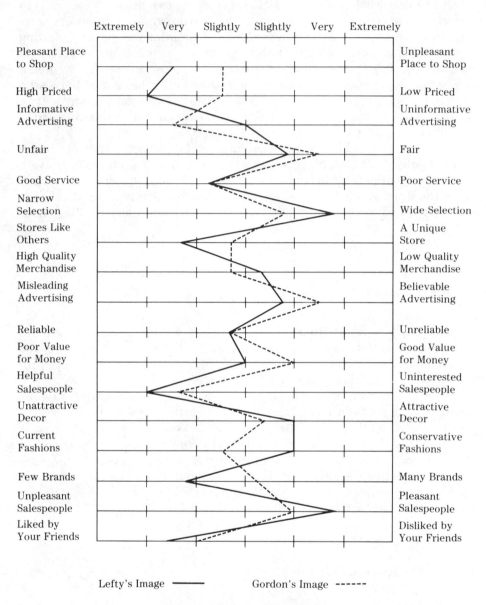

EXHIBIT 14-1

Lefty's image versus Gordon's image (mean values)

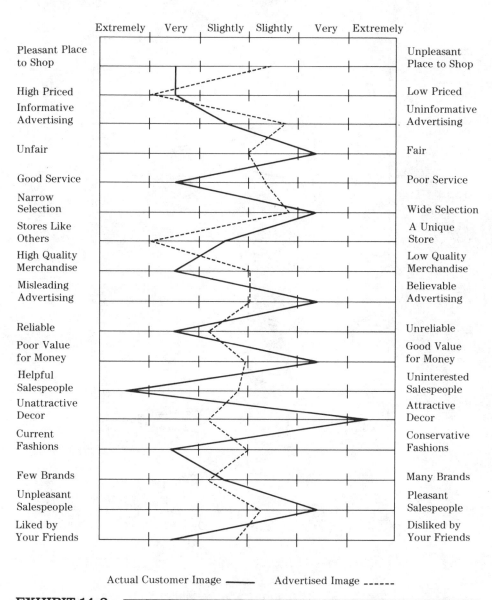

Actual Customer Image ——— Advertised Image ------

EXHIBIT 14-2

Lefty's advertised image versus actual customer image (mean values)

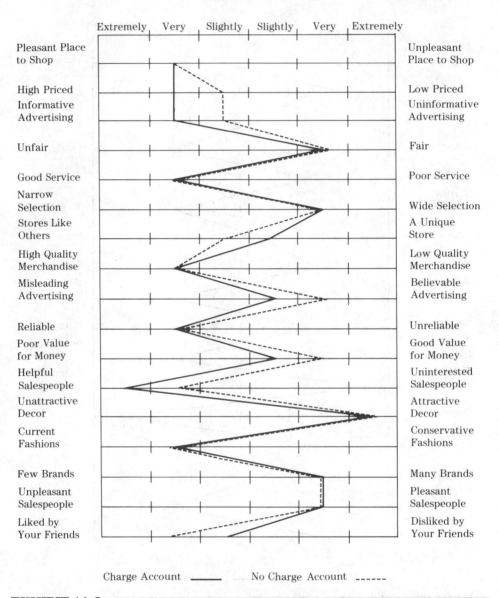

Charge Account ——————　　No Charge Account ------

EXHIBIT 14-3

Lefty's customers' image: charge account versus no charge account (mean value)

Case 15

DUPONT

THE CONCEPT OF INTEGRATING inner and outerwear merchandise is still considered provocative and radical by many retailers. It is certainly not the way things have always been done.

Resistance, however, may be more a political problem than a marketing one for many control garment retailers. The idea has long been accepted in other areas of retailing. In furniture departments, for example, sterile rows of similar furniture pieces have been replaced in many stores by integrated arrangements whose area is completely decorated with accessories from many departments to create a total room look. The stimulus to sales of all items by such integration no longer needs proving in the departments where it has been tried.

The need for this clear visualization of the concept is even greater in fashion than in furniture. Women who already know that rooms must have a coordinated look must be taught how the concept works in apparel. The "lost market" for women's control undergarments may be recapturable. It is possible that given the right garments and incentives, women may become customers again.

The Retailing Strategy

The strategy—here called "Outerwear Enhancers"—is based on the concept of coordinating apparel from the skin out, a total system for buying clothes. It is designed to reposition control undergarments in the customer's mind, showing what they can do for the body as well as what they can do for

---

Source: *Contemporary Cases in Marketing*, 2nd ed., pp. 222–26, by W. Wayne Talarzwk. Copyright © 1979 by The Dryden Press, a division of Holt, Rinehart and Winston, Inc. This case is an edited version of "A Strategy for Selling 'Control' Garments," a report prepared by DuPont for retailing organizations. Reprinted by permission of Holt, Rinehart and Winston and of DuPont.

the finished fashion look. Such a different philosophy naturally requires substantial changes in a retail store's department design, marketing, and personnel training.

Selling a look, not a garment is the overall philosophy of "Outerwear Enhancers." The control garment should relate to a woman's clothes, not to her body. Dressing should be a system, with all outerwear coordinated with compatible underwear to make the finished look work.

Integrated Department Layout

The traditional intimate apparel department set-up will no longer work, since it has been shown that women in the target market avoid this department. If they happen in, usually looking for robes or sleepwear, they find the displays dull and the merchandise outdated. They tend to ignore altogether the section for "bottom" garments.

The traditional separate intimate apparel department must be abandoned. Instead, related merchandise must be sold together, in integrated departments. To buy a total look, a woman must be able to try and buy all the pieces at the same time. To one degree or another, innerwear must be integrated with outerwear in departmental organization. This is the most wrenching change suggested by the new strategy, for it requires close cooperation among all involved departments and management personnel, but it is essential for success. Some possible ways to achieve the desired integration are described below.

The optimum plan

Optimally, every outerwear department would contain an appropriate undergarment section and system selling would prevail, with sales people oriented to sell innerwear-outerwear outfits.

The mini-boutique

A modification of the optimum plan is a mini-boutique of undergarments in every major ready-to-wear department, with a sample inventory of related, popular garments available for trying on and powerful displays to illustrate the concept.

The "hub" department

Received with great enthusiasm in the suburban store it was designed for, this idea places one undergarment department at the hub of encircling ready-to-wear departments. All departments are contiguous, but each retains its historic identity. Exhibits 15–1 and 15–2 illustrate some possible layouts for this type of department.

Cross-department displays

Instead of actual undergarments available in ready-to-wear departments, reciprocal displays in both departments would carry the message. This method depends on displays of great persuasiveness and prominence—such as side-by-side manikins or paired photographs—to illustrate the concept.

A walk-through "fashion magazine"

An exciting version of the cross-department display mounts three-dimensional, full-sized photographic blow-ups on department walls or room dividers. These displays, changed frequently to show new styles, would be traffic-pullers in themselves.

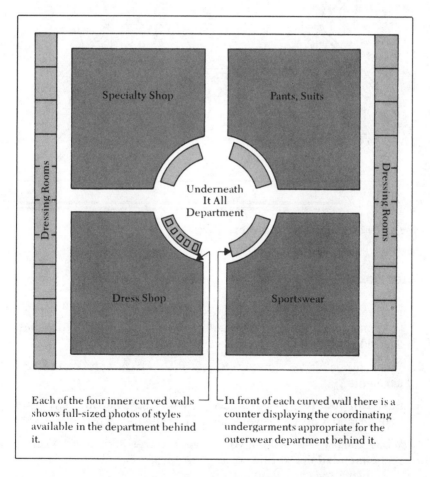

EXHIBIT 15-1

Possible layout for the hub department

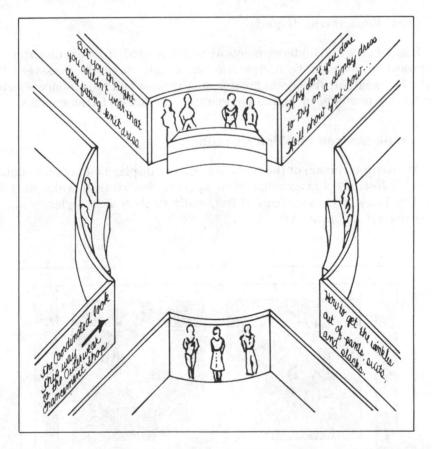

EXHIBIT 15-2

Another view of the hub department layout

Questions

1. Evaluate the relative advantages and disadvantages, as perceived by the consumer and the retailer, of the five possible ways to achieve the desired integration of innerwear and outerwear.

2. What other ways can you suggest to effectively market control garments?

3. Based on your responses to 1 and 2, which strategy for marketing control garments do you recommend most highly? Why?

4. What suggestions would you have for the implementation of our recommended marketing strategy in terms of
    a. display of merchandise
    b. advertising strategy
    c. type of sales personnel and their training

PART **7**

Retail Location
Management

Case 16

PRIME CUT STEAKHOUSES, INC.

PRIME CUT STEAKHOUSES is a regional chain of steak house restaurants in what is often described as the family-priced steak house field. The Great Plains region of the United States serves as the primary market for the firm's 84 company-operated restaurants and its 120 franchised outlets. By using a marketing-mix strategy consisting of standardized product offerings, quick service, uniform quality, convenient locations, and "family" prices, the firm has attracted a large segment of the Great Plains population.

Management Policies and Marketing Mix

The firm's product mix consists of a standard menu of prepared foods. The menu is restricted to a limited number of steak cuts, specials, and sandwiches. In addition, there is a limited support menu of beverages, salads, side orders, and desserts. Product depth is limited to approximately four items per product line. The limited product mix is part of the firm's operational policy of maintaining strict centralized management control. This policy provides for operational efficiency in the following ways:

1. High-volume, low-cost procurement of foods, beverages, and restaurant items
2. Fewer product procurement costs and requirements because of the limited menu
3. Consistent product quality throughout the company-owned and franchised restaurants
4. Fewer preparation problems because of the limited menu

Adapted from Dale M. Lewison, "Prime Cut Steakhouses, Inc.," *Consumer Behavior Dynamics: A Casebook*, ed. M. Wayne DeLozier (Columbus, Ohio: Charles E. Merrill Publishing Company, 1977), pp. 165–77.

5. Lower advertising expense per restaurant, since all outlets benefit from the same campaign within the media's market area

The firm's pricing structure is designed to attract middle income ($15,000 to $30,000) families. Product-item pricing is based on a single price for a basic meal. The basic meal includes the meat (usually a steak), potato (french fries or baked), and toast. Additional product items are priced separately. The base price plus the individual product-item pricing system is believed to be the most attractive to the widest range of potential consumers. The wide appeal is due to the consumer's desire to select only those items he wants. Essentially, it is the firm's policy to offer a quality product at a reasonable price. This policy has worked for Prime Cut, because they have been willing to accept a low unit-profit margin, believing that they could generate high sales volume while keeping overhead to a consumer-accepted minimum.

Management feels that their high sales volume is due to their fast-food, self-service policy. The basis of this approach is management's belief that a large segment of its customers must operate within a limited time schedule, which is particularly true of the luncheon trade. Reasonable profits result from greater customer turnover in a limited space during limited trade hours and through lower operating overhead by eliminating table service personnel.

The firm's communication mix consists primarily of newspaper, radio, and television advertisements; however, personal selling and public relations are also employed informally and to a limited extent. The firm invests about 3 percent of its gross sales in promotional activities. General regional promotion costs for Prime Cut Steakhouse are 2 percent of gross sales while individual store promotions account for 1 percent. Part of the firm's promotion costs is invested in special promotional programs. They include: (1) a free ice cream cone with each meal purchased, (2) discount coupons, (3) price specials, (4) newcomer programs, such as welcome wagon, and (5) gifts for new babies in the family. Management considers these "special promo" campaigns essential in creating new restaurant patronage as well as revitalizing former patronage. It also is important for promoting its family image.

The firms's distribution mix consists primarily of a central distribution center which supplies all outlets (company and franchised) with most of the necessary operating inventory. Some perishable items (such as meats, vegetables, and dairy products) are obtained directly from a prescribed list of vendors.

Management believes that one advantage Prime Cut has over conventional restaurants is the standard architecture of its outlets. By using a standardized architectural style, sign, and interior layout, the firm has been able to create wide consumer recognition of its outlets. Each restaurant is of a standard size (ninety by sixty feet) with a seating capacity of 180 people. The interior layout is designed to maximize customer turnover during peak demand periods, while providing the consumer with a clean, uncluttered dining atmosphere.

The atmosphere of each of the firm's outlets can be described as a "western" or an "authentic ranch-house style." This style, management feels, is consistent with the people's life style in this region of the country.

The Firm's Operating Environment

On the national level, Prime Cut has several major chain competitors in the family-priced steak house field which are Bonanza, Pondarosa, and Sizzler. While Bonanza and Pondarosa are primarily concentrated in the eastern sections of the country and Sizzler is basically a far-western operation, there are several market areas in which there is direct competition between Prime Cut and the three national chains. In addition, there are numerous smaller regional chains as well as single, independent operations which are in direct competition with Prime Cut. In addition, Prime Cut restaurants are located within trading areas which contain a variety of other well-known, nationally franchised restaurants. The competitive impact of Kentucky Fried Chicken, McDonald's, Roy Rogers Roast Beef, Pizza Hut, Sambo's, and other chain, fast-food operations is uncertain since the cumulative attraction versus competitive effects of these restaurants on the sales performances of Prime Cut outlets has not been determined.

Two peak demand periods (the noon and dinner hours) characterize the Prime Cut operation. Prime Cut must maximize sales during peak demand periods to maximize total daily sales. However, daily sales maximization is complicated by the differences in consumers for each of the two peak demand periods. Typically, the noon-hour customers (11:00 A.M. to 2:00 P.M.) tend to come from different source areas than dinner-hour customers (5:00 P.M. to 9:00 P.M.). Furthermore, there are substantial differences in demographic characteristics and patronage motives for each of the peak-period customers. Prime Cut management believes that these differences must be taken into account in developing the firm's marketing program.

Prime Cut Steakhouses: An Expansion Program

E.V. Smith, newly appointed Vice President of Real Estate and Development for Prime Cut, is faced with his first major company decision. Smith must recommend to the firm's review board one of four site alternatives for immediate development. The decision is required by the end of the week in order to meet the firm's present expansion schedule of opening two additional outlets per month. Smith's long association with the fast-food industry and the commercial real estate business has given him considerable knowledge and experience in the problems of retail site evaluation and selection.

The four available site alternatives were selected from an original list of twelve alternatives by Mr. Smith's predecessor and the staff of the Real Estate and Development Department. The list was narrowed down by an on-site inspection of the twelve alternatives. Reports indicate that land development and real estate costs were the principal criteria in selecting the four alternatives.

The northeastern area of Killian, Texas (Standard Metropolitan Statistical Area population 1.1 million) is the general trade area location of all four site alternatives. Killian also is the original market area for Prime Cut as well as the firms's corporate headquarters. The northwestern section of Killian has experienced tremendous growth in recent years. With the development of several low-, medium-, and high-income residential areas and a corresponding commercial development, a market has been created that is not being served by one of the firm's eight existing Killian locations.

In an earlier discussion with the firm's president, Mr. Smith got the distinct impression that filling the void in the Killian market was an objective which needed immediate attention. The general location and expansion strategy to which Prime Cut management adheres is market saturation. The policy involves "freezing out" the competition in a local market area by using a distributional pattern of outlets which creates a spatial monopoly. Because the Killian market is the corporate headquarters for Prime Cut, this strategy takes on even greater importance.

Contemplating the importance and the rush nature of the decision, Mr. Smith decides first to clarify in his own mind the nature of the problem. As viewed by Mr. Smith, the major objective is to select the site alternative that offers the greatest sales potential. The current average monthly sales for the firm's existing outlets vary from $40,000 to $80,000. Reasoning that sales potential is primarily a function of locational attributes (all other marketing mix variables are standardized from one store to another), Mr. Smith believes the problem is to determine the site alternative which best serves the type of consumer which patronizes Prime Cut outlets. Realizing that the firm's outlets tend to draw different consumer groups at different peak hours, Mr. Smith decides to start the evaluation by considering a list of locational factors which have served him well in similar past decisions. Locational factors such as accessibility, cumulative attraction, compatibility, interception, store association, competition/saturation, and trade area demographics are, in Mr. Smith's experience, all spatial expressions of consumer preference in determining consumer store choice behavior.

TABLE 16-1 ▬▬▬▬▬▬▬▬▬▬▬▬▬▬▬▬▬▬▬▬▬▬▬▬▬▬▬▬▬▬▬▬

Customer type based on frequency of patronage

Customer Type	Patronage Frequency	Average Percentage*	Percent Range*
Passer-by, drop-in-trade	At least one time	21.6%	15–25
In-vicinity, drop-in-trade	At least once a year	12.1	10–20
Occasional return trade	At least once a month	23.6	15–30
Steady return trade	At least once a week	42.7	35–50

*Percentage of all customers for all existing outlets

Because of the time limitation, Mr. Smith feels that he must base his decision primarily upon the information in the two reports prepared by the staff of his predecessor. (See Tables 16–1 through 16–7.) While the reports appear to have been prepared in a reasonably scientific manner, there are certain obvious omissions in the available information such as the lack of demographic data. Mr. Smith feels that he must fill in the demographic and other missing data (at least subjectively) if he is to arrive at the best possible decision within the next week.

Questions

1. What are the relative advantages and disadvantages of each of the four site alternatives?

2. Are there significant differences in the locational requirements and store choice behavior among the four consumer types? If so, what?

3. Which of the four site alternatives should Mr. Smith recommend to the firm's review board? Why?

4. What are the strengths and weaknesses of Prime Cut's retailing mix relative to consumer store choice behavior?

5. In terms of consumer store choice behavior, how appropriate is the firm's locational strategy of market saturation?

TABLE 16-2

Customer reasons for patronage (percentages)

Patronage Reason / Customer Type	Good Quality Food			Fast Service			Convenient Location			Menu Selection			Reasonable Prices			Store Atmosphere			Other		
	1*	2**	3***	1	2	3	1	2	3	1	2	3	1	2	3	1	2	3	1	2	3
Passer-by, drop-in-trade	9	12	17	16	17	22	40	29	12	21	23	26	12	18	22	1	1	0	1	0	1
In-vicinity, drop-in-trade	16	15	12	16	18	23	30	26	17	20	20	16	15	20	28	2	1	2	1	0	2
Occasional return trade	20	22	20	18	15	20	18	19	20	18	20	15	21	21	25	4	3	0	1	0	0
Steady return trade	25	26	10	15	14	22	15	10	37	23	20	10	20	23	18	2	6	3	0	1	0

*1 = First choice
**2 = Second choice
***3 = Third choice

TABLE 16-3

Noon hour origin characteristics (percentages)

Customer Type	Home			Work			Shop[1]			Visit[2]			R and E[3]			Misc.			Total		
Origin Type	P[4]	S[5]	T[6]	P	S	T	P	S	T	P	S	T	P	S	T	P	S	T	P	S	T
Passer-by, drop-in-trade	0	2	11	1	7	23	0	18	12	1	1	2	1	2	4	0	7	8	3	37	60
In-vicinity, drop-in-trade	0	8	4	14	10	1	30	10	0	6	0	0	8	1	0	8	0	0	66	29	5
Occasional return trade	5	12	1	20	12	0	21	8	1	4	1	0	5	0	0	9	1	0	64	34	2
Steady return trade	11	2	0	40	16	1	14	3	1	2	1	0	3	2	0	4	0	0	74	24	2

1. Individuals on commercial shopping trips (goods or services)
2. Individuals on personal visits
3. Recreation and entertainment
4. P = Primary trading area (0 to 0.99 miles)
5. S = Secondary trading area (1 to 2.99 miles)
6. T = Tertiary trading area (3 miles or more)

TABLE 16-4

Noon hour destination characteristics (percentages)

Customer Type \ Destination Type	Home			Work			Shop[1]			Visit[2]			R and E[3]			Misc.			Total		
	P[4]	S[5]	T[6]	P	S	T	P	S	T	P	S	T	P	S	T	P	S	T	P	S	T
Passer-by, drop-in-trade	0	1	12	1	10	25	0	8	18	0	2	3	1	3	6	1	3	6	3	27	70
In-vicinity, drop-in-trade	0	2	7	1	3	8	31	17	3	7	2	1	6	0	0	12	0	0	57	24	19
Occasional return trade	3	14	0	16	20	1	22	5	0	4	1	1	5	2	0	6	0	0	56	42	2
Steady return trade	12	2	1	40	13	2	15	3	0	2	0	0	6	0	0	4	0	0	79	18	3

1. Individuals on commercial shopping trips (goods or services)
2. Individuals on personal visits
3. Recreation and entertainment
4. P = Primary trading area (0 to 0.99 miles)
5. S = Secondary trading area (1 to 2.99 miles)
6. T = Tertiary trading area (3 miles or more)

126

TABLE 16-5

Dinner hour origin characteristics (percentages)

Customer Type	Home P[4]	Home S[5]	Home T[6]	Work P	Work S	Work T	Shop[1] P	Shop S	Shop T	Visit[2] P	Visit S	Visit T	R and E[3] P	R and E S	R and E T	Misc. P	Misc. S	Misc. T	Total P	Total S	Total T
Passer-by, drop-in-trade	0	6	20	1	7	19	1	7	17	0	2	4	1	4	6	1	2	2	4	28	68
In-vicinity, drop-in-trade	0	14	12	1	5	9	15	16	0	3	6	1	4	4	0	5	5	0	28	50	22
Occasional return trade	30	13	1	15	15	0	8	7	1	3	1	0	2	2	0	2	0	0	60	38	2
Steady return trade	34	8	0	27	10	3	10	2	0	2	0	0	1	1	0	2	0	0	76	21	3

1. Individuals on commercial shopping trips (goods or services)
2. Individuals on personal visits
3. Recreation and entertainment
4. P = Primary trading area (0 to 0.99 miles)
5. S = Secondary trading area (1 to 2.99 miles)
6. T = Tertiary trading area (3 miles or more)

TABLE 16-6

Dinner hour destination characteristics (percentages)

Customer Type	Home			Work			Shop[1]			Visit[2]			R and E[3]			Misc.			Total		
Destination Type	P[4]	S[5]	T[6]	P	S	T	P	S	T	P	S	T	P	S	T	P	S	T	P	S	T
Passer-by, drop-in-trade	0	8	43	0	3	6	1	2	12	1	3	3	0	7	6	0	3	2	2	26	72
In-vicinity, drop-in-trade	2	4	29	5	3	4	10	4	7	1	4	6	1	7	8	1	3	1	20	25	55
Occasional return trade	24	18	4	7	4	1	12	6	0	3	1	0	9	2	0	8	1	0	63	32	5
Steady return trade	48	6	1	8	1	1	12	0	0	6	0	0	10	2	1	4	0	0	88	9	3

1. Individuals on commercial shopping trips (goods or services)
2. Individuals on personal visits
3. Recreation and entertainment
4. P=Primary trading area (0 to 0.99 miles)
5. S=Secondary trading area (1 to 2.99 miles)
6. T=Tertiary trading area (3 miles or more)

TABLE 16-7

Locational survey report

Location characteristics[1] / Site alternative	1	2	3	4
A. Residential characteristics				
1. Number of single dwelling units	1,714	2,341	905	3,172
2. Number of multiple dwelling units	670	64	1,248	102
3. Number of transient dwelling units	20	0	50	0
4. Owner-occupied units (%)	42	58	24	67
B. Nonresidential characteristics				
1. Total number of retailing units	94	100	81	57
a. Convenience goods retailers (%)	64	48	61	71
b. Shopping goods retailers (%)	30	42	31	29
c. Specialty goods retailers (%)	6	10	2	0
2. Total number of service units	128	134	311	54
a. Personal service units	24	26	19	35
b. Business service units	6	8	24	0
c. Automotive service units (%)	10	9	4	11
d. Recreation/entertainment units (%)	18	10	15	15
e. Legal, financial, medical service units (%)	16	18	24	7
f. Governmental service units (%)	17	10	10	5
g. Educational service units (%)	5	9	1	10
h. Religious service units (%)	5	8	1	16
i. Miscellaneous service units (%)	3	2	2	1
3. Total number of wholesale units	7	7	21	0
4. Total number of manufacturing units	1	0	2	0
C. Population characteristics				
1. Total population	13,000	15,000	14,000	10,900
2. Mean family income	11,200	12,800	14,100	13,200
3. Low-income population: 7,000 (%)	24	8	10	28
4. High-income population: 20,000 (%)	2	12	24	32
5. Nonwhite population (%)	31	8	8	0
6. Elderly population: over 62 (%)	18	6	4	8

TABLE 16-7 (continued)

Location characteristics[1] \ Site alternative	1	2	3	4
7. Teenage population: under 18 (%)	20	35	6	44
D. Site characteristics				
1. Site size: Front footage	80	140	110	100
2. Site size: Total square footage	16,000	19,600	22,000	15,000
3. Site block position	corner	interior	interior	interior
4. Type of location	free standing	free standing	free standing	free standing
5. Number of entrances/exits	4	2	2	4
6. Footage of entrances/exits	100	140	100	120
7. Facing street: Number of traffic lanes	4	4	6	4
8. Facing street: Turn on-off lanes	no	yes	yes	no
9. Facing street: Medians	crossable	crossable	uncrossable	crossable
10. Facing street: Speed limit	35	40	45	35
11. Facing street: Average daily traffic volume	19,791	20,213	28,428	14,005
12. Side street: Number of traffic lanes	2	N/A[2]	N/A	4
13. Side street: Turn on-off lane	no	N/A	N/A	no
14. Side street: medians	crossable	N/A	N/A	crossable
15. Side street: Speed limit	35	N/A	N/A	35
16. Side street: Average daily traffic volume	4,952	N/A	N/A	6,200
E. Real estate characteristics				
1. Percent of gross sales	5.25	5.75	5.75	4.75
F. Competitive characteristics				
1. Number of "like" establishments	2	1	2	0
2. Number of specialty sandwich units	6	7	8	2
3. Number of specialty nonsandwich units	7	9	10	2
4. Number of variety sandwich units	6	6	4	1
5 Number of variety nonsandwich units	9	10	12	2

[1]Location characteristics are for the primary trading area only.
[2]Not applicable

Case 17 READY-MARKET, INC.

READY-MARKET, INC. is a small regional chain of grocery supermarkets operating in a midwestern state. The first unit was opened in 1913 in a city of 10,000 population. The success that followed led to the opening of a second store in a neighboring community three years later. At various times during the next fifty years, the firm operated as many as five stores in as many small to moderately sized communities.

Beginning in 1950, Ready-Market began to close its small stores and replace them with larger units. In most of these conversions, the larger stores were opened in the same community where a smaller unit had previously existed. However, by 1980, the firm began to place larger units in a number of cities where the company previously had not had stores.

Plain City: A New Store

One of the new locations considered was Plain City, a town of 30,000. Plain City is a blue collar, lower-middle socioeconomic-class community. Many of its residents are employed in light industries and service industries in the city, while many others work at industrial jobs in several surrounding communities.

Ready-Market's executive staff carefully studied the competitive scene in Plain City before deciding to locate a major unit there. The lack of strong major chain competitors helped influence their choice of Plain City. Other factors included proximity of Plain City to distribution facilities used by Ready-Market and access to a location relatively near two growing middle class residential neighborhoods on the east side of town. This location—with a

Adapted from Gordon L. Wise, "Ready-Market, Inc.," *Consumer Behavior Dynamics: A Casebook*, ed. M. Wayne DeLozier (Columbus, Ohio: Charles E. Merrill Publishing Company, 1977), pp. 178–86.

large drug store and a moderate-size variety store on the same site—featured more than ample space for parking. Because the location site was further from the center of Plain City than any of its competitors, Ready-Market would be able to offer the most spacious and easily accessible parking in town.

Before the Ready-Market store was opened, cost analyses and projections of sales volumes led company officials to believe that the store could break even on a weekly sales volume of $105,000. In an effort to offer as many inducements to customers as possible, Ready-Market's Plain City unit would be lavishly decorated, and carpeting would be used in many areas of the store.

The Competition

As Ready-Market prepared to move into Plain City, a gigantic fire struck the downtown business district. Included among the victims of the fire was Jones Food Center, a major independent grocery supermarket which had long held a fairly strong market position in Plain City. Another strong anticipated competitor also was destroyed by the fire, and its central headquarters announced that the store would not be rebuilt and would cease all operation in Plain City. Jones Food Center later reopened in Plain City, but located in a rather small building with very inadequate parking facilities.

Other major competitors in Plain city include Most-Rite Supermarkets and Konstant Brothers. Both of these are large independent supermarkets which have long-held, strong positions in Plain City. Each has grown over the years in spite of their mediocre physical facilities. Both are in cramped locations with tight accommodations for display and storage, narrow aisles, and barely adequate parking facilities.

The "Super-Store" Concept

By late 1976, Ready-Market opened its new store in Plain City. This store was patterned after the "super-store" concept with a bakery, delicatessen, a full-service restaurant in the store, a flower shop, and a spacious seafood section.

Aisles were unusually wide. Only the most modern and beautiful fixtures were installed, and lighting was emphasized throughout the store. Each of the special departments (delicatessen, bakery, restaurant, produce, etc.) were given spacious prime locations in the store and many of the floor areas were carpeted. It was announced that the store would operate twenty-four hours a day and seven days a week.

The store was opened with the customary promotion and fanfare. Door prizes, free gifts, and numerous specials were featured. Response from Plain City residents was instant and gratifying. Average weekly sales immediately passed $130,000 and climbed steadily to nearly $145,000. At that point sales appeared to peak and then began to fluctuate between $120,000 and $140,000.

Accounting statements soon showed that the estimated break-even weekly sales figure was too low. Over the period of the first six months of operation, the profit from the Plain City unit was barely existent.

To counter the situation, Ready-Market began to offer more price specials. After some considerable internal debate, the company decided to cease its heavy use of newspaper advertising and concentrate more on promotional pieces mailed directly to the homes of residents of the Plain City area.

A Study of the Market

In an effort to determine whether further steps could be taken to expand market penetration in the Plain City area, Ready-Market conducted a market research study designed to identify and measure such factors as What features and services are most desired by Plain City consumers from the grocery supermarkets which would serve them? What image does Ready-Market have for the major patronage-inducing factors (price, location, promotion, etc.)? What images do its major competitors have? Where are the competitive strengths and weaknesses possessed by Ready-Market?

A personal interview was conducted in more than 300 homes in the Plain City area. The selected sample was patterned in such a way that an approximately equal number of respondents were drawn from the geographical areas in the "natural" market of each of the four major Plain City supermarkets. Respondents were given approximately twenty-five possible features/services available through a supermarket and asked to indicate for each whether they believed the dimensions were "very important," "somewhat important," or "not at all important" to them in choosing a grocery supermarket. Responses to these features/services are shown in Table 17-1. The responses are shown in three categories: all respondents in the samples, respondents who do at least some shopping at Ready-Market, and respondents who do most of their shopping at Ready-Market.

Respondents then were asked to choose from among all of the features/services those which they considered the single most important and the second most important in selecting a supermarket. Responses to these questions are shown in Table 17-2.

A series of direct questions was asked of all respondents. These questions dealt with such matters as Which store in Plain City does the most advertising? Has the lowest prices? Responses to these questions are shown in Tables 17-3 through 17-8.

Respondents then were asked to use several patronage factors to evaluate each of the Plain City supermarkets in which they shopped. Table 17-9 provides a summary of responses to these questions.

After all of the data were gathered and the results were presented, the management of Ready-Market turned its attention to analysis of the results in light of a less-than-acceptable profit performance.

Some members of the management staff wondered whether they were expecting too much from the Plain City unit. After all, the store had captured approximately 24 percent of the Plain City grocery dollar. Konstant Brothers had a 23 percent market share and the Jones Food Center had 12 percent. Only Most-Rite with 41 percent enjoyed a larger market share than Ready-Market. However, Ready-Market management was generally unhappy with the profit figures and all agreed that some action must be taken.

TABLE 17-1

Responses to supermarket features and services

Feature	Total Response Sample			Shop "Some" at Ready-Market			Shop "Most" at Ready-Market		
	Very Important	Somewhat Important	Not Important	Very Important	Somewhat Important	Not Important	Very Important	Somewhat Important	Not Important
Store is located close to my home	59.3%	26.8%	13.9%	58.8%	27.2%	14.0%	61.2%	26.5%	12.2%*
Very wide aisles	54.1	32.5	13.4	50.9	34.2	14.9	63.3	26.5	10.0
Lots of parking	84.7	12.4	2.9	82.5	15.8	1.8	89.8	8.2	2.0
Employees easy to find if I need help	69.9	21.5	8.6	67.5	21.1	11.4	65.3	22.4	12.2
Low prices	90.4	7.2	2.4	91.2	7.0	1.8	91.8	4.1	4.1*
High quality food products	90.0	8.6	1.4	89.5	9.6	.9	85.7	12.2	2.0
Friendly, courteous employees	82.3	15.3	2.4	83.3	14.0	2.6	83.7	14.3	2.0
Offers many well-known national brands	64.1	25.4	10.5	59.6	29.8	10.5	59.2	32.7	8.2
Locally-owned; not part of a big chain	17.7	25.4	56.9	11.4	28.9	59.6	2.0	30.6	67.3*
Stays open 24 hours	20.6	18.7	60.8	25.4	24.6	50.0	36.7	26.5	36.7*
Has a delicatessan	14.4	21.5	64.1	14.9	21.9	63.2	26.5	20.4	53.1
Wide selection of food products	85.2	12.0	2.9	83.3	23.3	4.4	89.8	6.1	4.1
Has a bakery	19.6	29.2	51.2	21.9	29.8	48.2	26.5	28.6	44.9
Offers a wide variety of produce	85.6	12.1	2.1	87.1	11.8	1.1	88.9	8.3	2.8

TABLE 17-1 (continued)

Feature	Total Response Sample			Shop "Some" at Ready-Market			Shop "Most" at Ready-Market		
	Very Important	Somewhat Important	Not Important	Very Important	Somewhat Important	Not Important	Very Important	Somewhat Important	Not Important
Small store, with everything close together	5.3%	10.1%	84.6%	4.4%	8.8%	86.7%	4.2%	8.3%	87.5%
New store with modern equipment and fixtures	25.0	31.3	43.7	23.9	27.4	48.7	29.2	16.7	54.2
Puts coupons good for reduced prices in mailers or in the newspaper	55.0	22.0	23.0	56.1	21.1	22.8	51.0	16.2	32.7
Offers many non-food items	28.2	25.8	45.9	30.7	27.2	42.1	36.7	12.1	51.0
Has an express check-out lane	72.3	16.5	11.2	79.6	12.9	7.5	72.2	16.7	11.1
Offers weekly specials	71.8	19.6	8.6	67.5	21.9	10.5	63.3	24.5	12.2
Offers cash to nonprofit organizations for collecting cash register tapes	17.8	28.8	53.4	19.5	26.5	54.0	14.6	29.2	56.2
Has a restaurant	8.6	8.6	82.8	12.2	10.5	77.2	20.4	6.1	73.5*
Offers free carry-out service	57.4	22.5	20.1	58.8	21.1	20.2	71.4	14.2	14.3
Neat and clean	97.1	2.4	.5	96.5	2.6	.9	95.9	2.0	2.0
Offers a wide variety of meat and fish	84.1	11.1	4.8	83.3	8.8	7.9	89.8	6.1	4.1

*Significant at .05

136

TABLE 17-2

"Forced choice" responses to supermarket features and services

Feature or Service	Most Important	Second Most Important	Total First and Second
Low prices	41.%	20.6%	61.7%
Neat and clean	8.6	14.4	23.0
High quality food products	10.0	12.4	22.4
Wide selection of food products	9.1	8.1	17.2
Friendly, courteous service	7.2	7.2	14.4
Store is located close to my home	6.2	7.2	13.4
Offers a wide variety of meat and fish	5.3	3.8	9.1
Offers a wide variety of produce	1.4	5.7	7.1
Offers many well-known national brands	2.4	4.3	6.7
Lots of parking	1.0	2.9	3.9
Offers free carry-out service	1.4	2.4	3.8
Very wide aisles	—	3.3	3.3
Has an express check-out lane	1.9	1.4	3.3
Employees easy to find if I need help	1.4	1.4	2.8
Put coupons good for reduced prices in mailers or in newspaper	.5	1.4	1.9
Locally-owned; not part of a big chain	.5	.5	1.0
Stays open 24 hours	1.0	—	1.0
Has a delicatessan	—	.5	.5
Offers weekly specials	.5	—	.5
Has a restaurant	—	—	—
Offers cash to nonprofit organizations for collecting cash register tapes	—	—	—
Has a bakery	—	—	—
Offers many nonfood items	—	—	—
New store with modern equipment	—	—	—
Small store; everything close together	—	—	—

TABLE 17-3

"Which Plain City grocery store does the most advertising?" (controlling for the store shopped most frequently)

Response	Overall Sample	Ready-Market	Most-Rite	Konstant Brothers	Jones
Ready-Market	10.5%	26.5%	4.8%	6.7%	—
Most-Rite	41.1	24.5	59.0	17.8	59.1%
Konstant Brothers	21.1	10.2	14.5	53.5	4.5
Jones	1.4	—	1.2	—	9.1
Don't know	25.8	38.8	20.5	22.2	27.3

Note: Differences observed in the data presented in this table were found to be statistically significant at the .05 level.

TABLE 17-4

"Which Plain City grocery store do you think has the lowest prices?" (controlling for the store shopped most frequently)

Response	Overall Sample	Ready-Market	Most-Rite	Konstant Brothers	Jones
Ready-Market	9.1%	24.5%	4.8%	2.2%	4.5%
Most-Rite	56.5	36.7	86.7	26.7	50.0
Konstant Brothers	8.1	2.0	1.2	31.1	—
Jones	3.3	4.1	—	2.2	18.2
Don't know	23.0	32.7	7.2	37.8	27.3

Note: Differences observed in the data presented in this table were found to be statistically significant at the .05 level.

TABLE 17-5

"Which Plain City grocery store do you think has the highest prices?" (controlling for the store shopped most frequently)

Response	Overall Sample	Ready-Market	Most-Rite	Konstant Brothers	Jones
Ready-Market	41.1%	10.2%	63.9%	42.2%	40.9%
Most-Rite	2.9	2.0'	—	6.7	4.5
Konstant Brothers	19.1	22.4	21.7	13.3	9.1
Jones	11.5	20.4	9.6	8.9	—
Don't know	24.4	44.9	4.8	28.9	45.5

Note: Differences observed in the data presented in this table were found to be statistically significant at the .05 level.

TABLE 17-6

"Which Plain City grocery store would you most likely recommend to a friend who had just moved into town?" (controlling for the store shopped most frequently)

Response	Overall Sample	Ready-Market	Most-Rite	Konstant Brothers	Jones
Ready-Market	18.7%	65.3%	1.2%	8.9%	—
Most-Rite	44.5	16.3	92.8	6.7	4.5%
Konstant Brothers	19.1	6.1	2.4	73.1	9.1
Jones	7.7	2.0	1.2	—	63.6
Don't know	10.1	10.2	2.4	11.3	22.7

Note: Differences observed in the data presented in this table were found to be statistically significant at the .05 level.

TABLE 17-7

"Which of the following Plain City stores has (in your opinion) the best produce department?" (controlling for the store shopped most frequently)

Response	Overall Sample	Ready-Market	Most-Rite	Konstant Brothers	Jones
Ready-Market	43.5%	72.2%	34.6%	42.5%	38.1%
Most-Rite	19.6	8.3	38.5	—	4.8
Konstant Brothers	21.2	2.8	19.2	52.5	4.8
Jones	6.5	5.6	1.3	2.5	33.3
Don't know	9.2	11.1	6.4	2.5	19.0

Note: Differences observed in the data presented in this table were found to be statistically significant at the .05 level.

TABLE 17-8

"Which of the following Plain City stores has (in your opinion) the best meat department?" (controlling for the store shopped most frequently)

Response	Overall Sample	Ready-Market	Most-Rite	Konstant Brothers	Jones
Ready-Market	34.2%	63.9%	29.5%	27.5%	23.8%
Most-Rite	23.9	5.6	43.6	10.0	9.5
Konstant Brothers	16.3	—	12.8	47.5	—
Jones	9.8	8.3	3.8	5.0	42.9
Don't know	15.8	22.2	10.3	10.0	23.8

Note: Differences observed in the data presented in this table were found to be statistically significant at the .05 level.

TABLE 17-9 ═══

Consumers' competitive image of Plain City supermarkets (1-5 scale)

(1)	Ready-Market	Most-Rite	Konstant Brothers	Jones Food Center	(5)
Very low prices	3.11	2.30	3.12	3.02	Very high prices
Friendly, courteous employees	1.96	1.78	1.67	1.71	Unfriendly, discourteous employees
Very clean	1.47	1.74	1.80	1.89	Very dirty
Highest quality products	1.71	1.87	1.93	2.18	Low quality products
Very good advertising	2.33	1.65	2.00	2.05	Very poor advertising
Has good specials	2.50	1.69	2.22	2.29	Does not have good specials
Has a good selection of food products	1.51	1.73	1.73	2.18	Has a poor selection of food products
Plenty of parking	1.35	1.84	1.79	2.44	Not enough parking
I like this store very much.	1.96	1.69	2.07	2.00	I don't like this store.

Questions

1. From the data presented in the case, how would you characterize the criteria used by Plain City grocery shoppers in choosing a store at which to shop? Are there other important choice criteria overlooked in the study? If so, what?

2. How well do the store characteristics of Ready-Market match the choice criteria used by Plain City grocery shoppers?

3. Ready-Market has 24 percent of the Plain City market. Based on the consumers' choice criteria and the store's perceived characteristics, should Ready-Market expect a larger market share, about what they have, or a smaller market share? Explain.

4. Develop what you feel Ready-Market's strategy should be in the Plain City market. Based on the data, describe the promotional approach you would use, i.e., advertising, sales promotion, etc.

Case 18

SHORTSTOP RESTAURANTS— EVALUATING RETAIL SITE ACCESSIBILITY

SHORTSTOP RESTAURANTS enjoyed considerable success in the fast-food business during the decade of the 70's. In fact, during the last ten years the firm's expansion program has taken the firm from a local chain of four restaurants to a successful regional operation of sixty-four fast-food outlets. While expanding operations into five southeastern states, the firm has yet to expérience a single failure. Being able to say that the firm has "never had a failure" is a matter of personal pride to Gary Bauer, the founder and president of Shortstop Restaurants, Inc. The lack of a failure is also an excellent selling point in the firm's attempts to attract potential investors—an important consideration if the firm's growth objective of opening ten new restaurants each year for the next five years is to be achieved.

The Firm and Its Marketing Mix

Shortstop's success has been predicated on offering the fast-food customer the best in both time and place convenience. For Shortstop Restaurants, the key marketing mix ingredients are offering a variety of well-prepared food items at very convenient locations supported by quick service. By targeting its marketing efforts toward the mobile, outdoor lifestyles of the southern consumer and by appealing to the working-wife family, the firm hopes to continue expanding on its past successes and to meet its future growth objectives.

The product mix

The firm's product mix consists of a specialized menu of prepared foods featuring a limited selection of sandwiches and related complementary items.

This case was prepared by Dale M. Lewison, The University of Akron, and Bill C. Tadlock, University of Arkansas at Little Rock.

The menu is restricted to those food items that can be prepared (1) in a quick and efficient manner, (2) with uniform product quality, (3) for carry-out service, and (4) in a variety of ways for the largest product selection possible.

The breakfast menu (served from 6 A.M. to 10 A.M.) offers a selection of two sandwiches: (1) the "Yankee"—a poached egg with Canadian bacon and Wisconsin cheese served on an English muffin and (2) the "Rebel"—a poached egg with southern pork sausage served on a homemade biscuit. Breakfast complements include hot apple or cheese danish, hash browned potato pattie, juices (orange, tomato, and grape), milk, and coffee. The breakfast menu has been quite successful and accounts for 26 percent of total sales for the typical Shortstop Restaurant.

The lunch and dinner menu (served from 10 A.M. to 11 P.M.) consists of a selection of three different size hamburgers, a chicken sandwich, a ham sandwich, a fish sandwich, and a Coney hot dog. Each sandwich is made to order from a selection of standard condiments (e.g., pickles, onions, tomatoes). Lunch and dinner complements include french fries, onion rings, cole slaw, green salad bowl, deep fried pies, soft-serve sundaes or cones, and a wide assortment of beverages (soft drinks, tea, coffee, milk, and shakes). In addition, each of the above sandwiches can be ordered as a platter that includes a choice of french fries or onion rings and cole slaw or salad bowl.

The service mix

Shortstop Restaurants offers its customers the choice of self-service in-store seating or drive-up window service. Originally, the drive-up service was added to the service mix to attempt to distinguish the firm's operations from those of its competitors. However, the drive-up window service has clearly become the single most important factor in explaining Shortstop's success. While the exact percentage varies from one restaurant to another, drive-up window sales account for approximately 47 percent of the total sales volume for the typical Shortstop Restaurant. A recent survey of the firm's regular customers identified the convenience of the drive-up window service as being the most important patronage reason for 36 percent of the survey's respondents. The importance of drive-up window sales in the fast food business if further evidenced by the large number of McDonald's and Burger King restaurants that have been remodeled to include this service.

The pricing mix

Competitive parity is the primary pricing tactic employed by Shortstop Restaurants. With the exeption of a daily price special, the firm strives to maintain prices that are comparable with the local prices of such nationally franchised prepared food retailers as McDonald's, Wendy's, and Burger King. For the price-conscious consumer, the sandwich platters represent a notable savings over the sum of the individual prices for each item—a 10 to 15 percent savings.

The promotion mix

Supported by a 4 percent of gross sales budget, the firm's promotional mix involves the use of a variety of advertising media and sales promotion devices. First, Shortstop uses heavy radio advertising during the morning and evening rush-hour traffic periods. Management believes these audiences are most susceptible to the convenience appeals and messages featured in the firm's advertisements. Second, to build awareness of the firm and its operations, a local television advertising blitz is employed in selected markets on a periodic basis. Shortstop also makes extensive use of local newspaper advertising which is often tied to various sales promotions such as discount coupons and premiums (e.g., free glasses with a purchase of a large soft drink). To reinforce the promotional mix and to promote customer recognition, Shortstop's facilities (store and signs) are highly standardized.

The Firm's Location Strategy

From the beginning, it has been the opinion of Shortstop's management that the crucial element in explaining the success they have enjoyed is the attention they have given to the careful selection of locations. While a considerable amount of money and effort is devoted to identifying and evaluating potentially viable trading areas, the key feature in Shortstop's location strategy is site accessibility. In the words of the firm's founder, "the single most important physical site attribute is direct site accessibility; an inaccessible site is of little value to us in the fast-food business, even if it is located within a potentially high sales volume trading area." As viewed by the firm, the site accessibility factor encompasses the four basic accessing activities of (1) approaching a site, (2) entering a site, (3) traversing a site, and (4) exiting a site. Any evaluation of the accessibility of a site must take into account the ease with which the consumer can accomplish each of these four tasks. If the potential consumer encounters any major difficulty in any one of the four tasks, the site's accessibility is notably affected in a negative manner. To ensure close attention to the site accessibility problem and to guide the firm's site accessibility evaluation process, a site accessibility checklist was developed for use in the evaluation of all site alternatives. The site accessibility checklist is presented in Exhibit 18-1. This check list identifies the principal factors Shortstop management wants to consider when evaluating the accessibility of a site.

EXHIBIT 18-1 ═══════════════════════════════════

Site accessibility checklist

I. Traffic Factors

    A. Traffic Arteries
        1. Number of traffic arteries adjacent to site
        2. Number of traffic lanes associated with each of the site's traffic arteries

EXHIBIT 18-1 (continued)

    3. Designated directional flow of each traffic artery
    4. Number, location and configuration of intersections
    5. Type and configuration of mediums
    6. Presences or absences of protected traffic lanes

  B. Traffic Flow
    1. Total volume of traffic on each of the adjacent traffic arteries
    2. Directional variations in the volume of traffic flow (northbound, southbound, eastbound and westbound flows)
    3. Temporal variations in the volume of traffic flow (seasonal, monthly, weekly and daily variations)
    4. Spatial variations in the volume of traffic flow in terms of traffic lanes (inside, middle, and outside lanes)
    5. Composition of the traffic flow in terms of its trip behavior (work trips, shopping trips, pleasure or recreation trips and through trips)

  C. Traffic Controls
    1. Speed limit of each of the adjacent traffic arteries
    2. Number, type, and location of traffic lights
    3. Number, type, and location of stop signs
    4. Number, type and location of traffic rule signs (U-turn, left-turn and no parking signs)
    5. Number, type and location of traffic guidance lines (lane dividers, turning-arrows and thru-arrows)

II. Site Factors

  A. Site Layout
    1. Size of site (square footage)
    2. Shape of site (square, rectangular, triangular and odd)
    3. Elevation of site (at, above or below street level)
    4. Boundaries of site (front footage, number and character of entrances and exits)

  B. Site Location
    1. Side of street (left or right-hand side)
    2. Part of block (corner or interior location)

  C. Site Position
    1. Interceptor qualities—the ability of the site to intercept customers as they travel between identifiable origins and destinations
    2. Intervening opportunities—the ability of the site to serve as an intervening shopping opportunity between the location of competitors

The Firm's Expansion Program

For the last three years Steve Smith, Store Operations Manager for Short-stop Restaurants, Inc., has had the responsibility for conducting the firm's expansion program. Part of that responsibility includes the identification and evaluation of new locations. Based on the sales performance records of existing restaurants, Steve has become a firm believer in the necessity of good site accessibility. Sales records show a direct correlation between high levels of site accessibility and above-average sales performances. Having become a student of the art and science of selecting profitable locations, Steve recognized long ago that site accessibility has both physical and psychological dimensions. Physical site accessibility is viewed in terms of the tangible attributes of a site and its surrounding area, and how those tangible factors interact either to enhance or hinder potential customers as they approach, enter, traverse, and exit a site. The psychological dimensions of accessibility are ones related to how the potential customer perceives the ease of accessing a site. From past experience, Steve has learned that the customer's perception of a site's accessibility is as important as the site's actual physical accessibility. If a consumer believes that a site is difficult, dangerous, or inconvenient to access, then a psychological barrier has been created equal to any physical barrier.

For the 1980's expansion program to be as successful as the one the company experienced in the 1970's, Steve will have to ensure that the time and place convenience needs of the firm's targeted consumers are satisfied. To meet the convenience needs of the typical Shortstop consumer, Steve realizes that he must find new locations that are both physically and psychologically accessible.

The Waynesville Site

Currently under consideration for a new Shortshop Restaurant is a site in Waynesville, Mississippi (population 186,000). The site is located at the intersection of Ross Boulevard and Green Avenue. The results of the trading area analysis for the Waynesville site are very favorable. There appears to be no question that the site's trading area contains both the number and type of consumers necessary to support a Shortstop Restaurant. What remains to be completed before making a recommendation on the site is the analysis of the site accessibility information collected by the firm's field survey team. The field survey team's report contains the following information: (a) a general land use and major traffic arteries map of Waynesville (Exhibit 18-2), (b) a traffic control map of the proposed trading area (Exhibit 18-3), (c) a twenty-four-hour traffic count by direction and traffic lane (Table 18-1), (d) a twenty-four-hour traffic count by time period (Table 18-2), (e) a competitor-location map of the proposed trading area (Exhibit 18-4), and (f) a site layout map of the Ross/Green site (Exhibit 18-5).

The Problem

Assume the role of Steve Smith and prepare a written analysis of the accessibility of the Ross/Green site using the information provided in the field survey team's report. Make a specific recommendation as to whether the Ross/Green site should be selected as a future location for the Shortstop Restaurant.

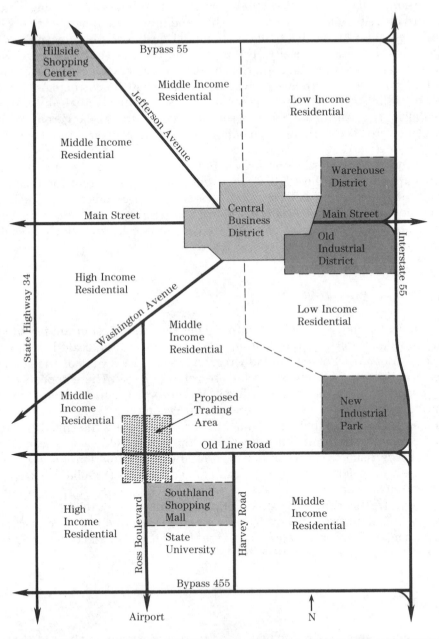

EXHIBIT 18-2

**General land use and major traffic arteries map
Waynesville, Mississippi**

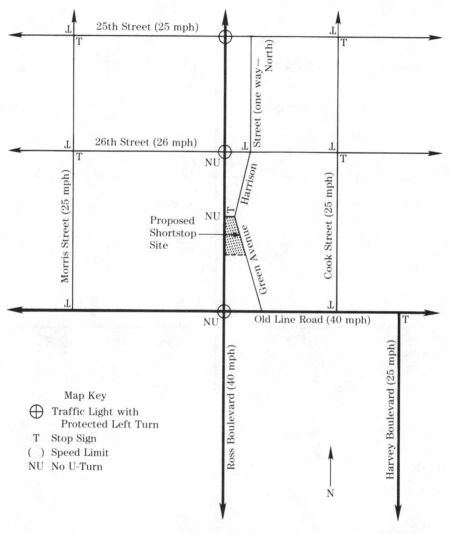

EXHIBIT 18-3

Traffic control map of proposed trading area

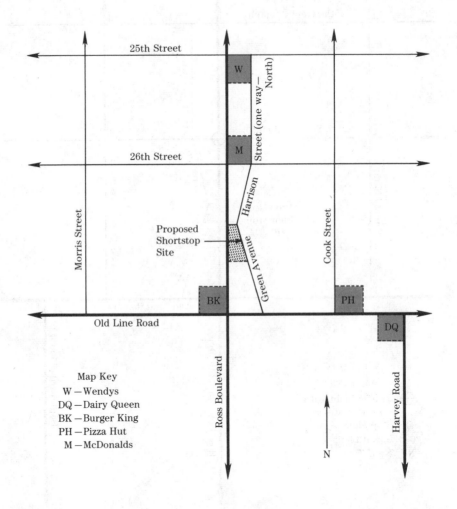

EXHIBIT 18-4

Competitor location map of proposed trading area

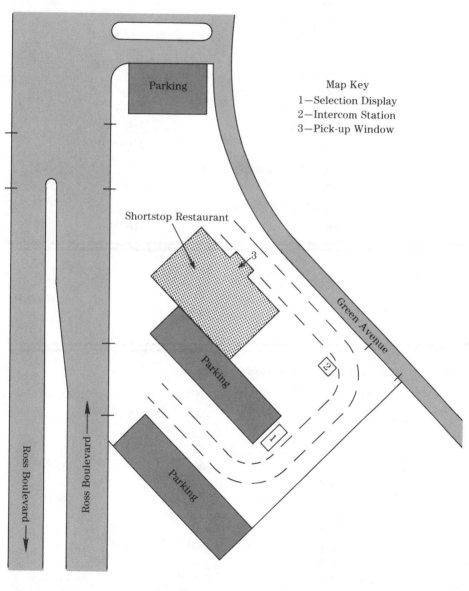

Map Key
1—Selection Display
2—Intercom Station
3—Pick-up Window

EXHIBIT 18-5

Layout of the Ross/Green site

TABLE 18-1 ═══════════════════════════════════════

24-hour traffic count by direction and traffic lane

Southbound on Ross Boulevard	
Left Lane	3,370
Middle Lane	4,120
Right Lane	3,710
Total	11,200
Northbound on Ross Boulevard	
Left Lane	3,490
Middle Lane	4,470
Right Lane	4,440
Total	12,400
Southbound on Green Avenue	
Total	80
Northbound on Green Avenue	
Total	1,190

TABLE 18-2 ═══════════════════════════════════════

24-hour traffic count by time period (weekdays)

Time Period	Ross Boulevard	Green Avenue
1 A.M. to 3 A.M.	300	30
3 A.M. to 5 A.M.	300	40
5 A.M. to 7 A.M.	1,100	110
7 A.M. to 9 A.M.	3,800	200
9 A.M. to 11 A.M.	2,200	120
11 A.M. to 1 P.M.	3,600	220
1 P.M. to 3 P.M.	2,400	115
3 P.M. to 5 P.M.	2,100	75
5 P.M. to 7 P.M.	8,400	210
7 P.M. to 9 P.M.	2,000	70
9 P.M. to 11 P.M.	800	55
11 P.M. to 1 A.M.	600	25
TOTAL	27,600	1,270

PART 8

Retail Merchandise Management

SHAW'S DEPARTMENT STORES—THE NEED FOR ADAPTIVE MERCHANDISING

RETAIL MANAGEMENT constantly is faced with decisions regarding adjustments to its dynamic operating environment. Changing consumer and retail structure patterns create a continuing need for reevaluation of market positions and merchandising strategies. The director of stores for Shaw's Department Store and his staff are faced with a series of product-mix decisions as a result of the planned introduction of a large regional shopping mall into the firm's local retail market and the opening of an additional Shaw's outlet within the new mall. A recently-completed impact study conducted at the University of South Carolina intensifies the need for decisions.

The City: Columbia, South Carolina

Centrally located within the state, Columbia reaps the economic and political benefits associated with that position. The pleasant physical environment (climate, terrain, and vegetation) of the uplands area of South Carolina provides highly desirable "quality of life" factors that contribute greatly to the population and economic growth of the area. As the capital of South Carolina, Columbia has evolved into the cultural, political, and economic hub of the state.

The Columbia SMSA's current population of 313,200 is expected to continue its steady growth rate of the last decade. This continuing growth rate is predicated on a strong and balanced economy. The city's economic base is reasonably well balanced between primary and secondary production, distribution, and service sectors of the economy. As the seat of state government, Columbia enjoys the benefits of a stable state and federal employment sector. In addition, this governmental employment sector is enhanced by the

---

This case was prepared by Dale M. Lewison, The University of Akron, and Wilke English, University of Arkansas at Little Rock.

presence of the University of South Carolina and a major federal military base, Fort Jackson.

The diversity of the production sector is illustrated by the presence of such industries as (1) chemicals, (2) electronics, (3) textiles, (4) wood and paper products, (5) machine tools, (6) food processing, (7) component parts, (8) subassemblies, and (9) apparels and accessories. The national trend of southern migration of industry is having its positive impacts on the Columbia area.

The centrality of Columbia makes it ideal for local and statewide distribution activities. In recent years, the percent of labor force employed in the distributive trades has shown a sharp increase. In addition, a few distributors have found Columbia ideally suited for interstate distribution. The area has experienced a slow but steady increase in district and regional distribution facilities.

The growth rate of both Columbia and South Carolina has produced a great need for services. Columbia has become the state's hub for medical, social, cultural, legal, and educational services. The natural beauty of the area and the state also has increased the need for recreation and entertainment services; these services are becoming a major mainstay of the economy.

The population structure of Columbia

The demographic characteristics of Columbia's population is shown in Tables 19–1, 19–2, and 19–3. The six demographic variables presented are (1) total population, (2) racial composition, (3) median family income, (4) age composition, (5) occupation status, and (6) employment status. Exhibit 1 is a map of census tracts.

TABLE 19-1

Population characteristics: total population and racial composition

| Census Tract | Total Population | | Racial Composition | | | |
| | | | % White | | % Black | |
	1970	1980	1970	1980	1970	1980
1	1,050	900	26	18	74	82
2	2,800	2,100	18	18	82	82
3	5,400	4,300	32	30	68	70
4	6,100	6,200	34	14	66	86
5	4,900	4,950	38	36	62	64
6*	—	—	—	—	—	—
7	6,400	6,950	64	68	36	32
8	5,700	5,700	72	72	28	28
9	5,350	5,400	70	70	30	30
10	4,750	4,700	72	71	28	29
11	6,200	6,300	35	34	65	66
12	5,750	5,700	81	80	19	20
13	4,900	4,900	77	77	23	23
14	5,100	5,000	83	81	17	19
15	6,450	6,350	74	70	26	30
16	6,100	6,700	52	46	48	54

TABLE 19-1 (continued)

Census Tract	Total Population 1970	Total Population 1980	Racial Composition % White 1970	% White 1980	% Black 1970	% Black 1980
17	5,200	5,300	50	39	50	61
18	7,400	7,300	21	7	79	93
19	6,700	6,900	58	58	42	42
20	4,100	4,100	64	62	36	38
21	5,350	5,250	94	94	6	6
22	6,100	6,050	63	62	37	38
23	5,100	5,250	97	97	3	3
24	3,000	3,400	69	68	31	32
25	3,100	3,300	70	70	30	30
26	2,200	2,900	74	73	26	27
27	3,900	4,700	84	84	26	26
28	1,900	3,400	83	82	17	18
29	1,200	5,100	84	90	16	10
30	1,700	3,900	87	89	13	11
31	2,100	6,300	95	98	5	2
32	2,600	4,900	92	96	8	4
33	3,700	5,650	94	94	6	6
34	3,650	5,100	88	88	12	12
35	1,200	2,900	74	75	26	25
36	800	7,000	50	95	50	5
37	200	800	100	100	0	0
38	1,700	3,700	98	99	2	1
39	2,300	5,250	99	99	1	1
40	1,800	6,100	100	100	0	0
41	1,250	2,700	98	99	2	1
42	1,600	8,200	96	99	4	1
43	1,000	4,800	90	96	10	4
44	1,200	6,400	94	99	6	1
45	800	5,100	98	99	2	1
46	1,400	5,400	92	99	8	1
47	1,300	4,900	94	99	6	1
48	1,300	3,900	81	87	19	13
49	1,200	4,100	87	97	13	3
50	1,700	3,700	96	98	4	2
51	1,100	4,400	96	99	4	1
52	1,400	7,100	99	99	1	1
53	1,100	6,100	100	100	0	0
54	300	4,100	100	100	0	0
55	1,300	8,000	96	99	4	1
56	2,100	7,000	97	99	3	1
57	800	6,000	99	99	1	1
58	1,100	4,000	100	100	0	0
59	1,600	8,700	100	100	0	0
60	900	6,900	99	100	1	0
61	1,700	4,700	96	100	4	0
62	1,900	6,300	99	100	1	0
TOTAL	181,900	313,200				

*Census tract 6 is the University of South Carolina consisting of 16,000 full-time students. Approximately one third of the student body resides in campus housing in census tract 6.

TABLE 19-2 ━━━

Population characteristics: median family income and age composition

Census Tract	Median Family Income		Age Composition			
			% under 18		% over 65	
	1970	1980	1970	1980	1970	1980
1	$4,500	$4,900	22	16	12	28
2	4,750	5,150	26	21	10	29
3	5,100	5,450	20	20	8	12
4	5,700	6,100	21	16	7	10
5	5,500	6,350	16	12	9	14
6	—	—	—	—	—	—
7	6,900	6,300	28	16	12	8
8	5,500	6,000	26	21	15	15
9	6,600	8,100	21	20	14	16
10	8,100	7,400	19	10	12	26
11	7,300	8,100	18	13	10	18
12	7,400	9,300	23	23	11	13
13	7,000	9,100	21	21	9	9
14	7,100	10,700	22	26	7	7
15	7,700	9,600	20	23	6	10
16	7,000	7,900	18	20	6	14
17	6,700	7,400	16	17	7	19
18	5,100	6,100	17	22	6	10
19	5,900	6,700	14	14	7	14
20	5,700	6,900	17	16	8	17
21	6,200	8,300	19	19	10	10
22	6,500	7,900	16	18	7	8
23	6,800	9,100	24	24	4	3
24	5,900	8,300	23	22	3	5
25	6,100	8,100	21	22	3	4
26	6,300	8,200	20	21	5	5
27	7,100	9,600	18	19	3	3
28	7,200	9,400	19	20	4	5
29	7,000	10,200	18	19	4	3
30	6,800	9,600	17	17	5	5
31	7,300	10,300	16	16	4	4
32	7,000	10,400	14	18	6	5
33	7,400	10,500	16	19	2	2
34	7,000	9,300	19	21	2	4
35	6,800	8,900	21	21	1	4
36	5,800	8,900	20	21	4	3
37	6,100	8,800	20	24	6	1
38	6,400	9,300	19	21	1	1
39	6,300	9,400	18	22	2	1
40	6,400	9,700	18	23	3	1
41	6,500	10,000	14	20	2	2
42	6,900	11,200	13	20	2	0
43	7,000	10,100	14	18	3	2
44	6,800	11,300	15	18	3	1
45	7,500	12,900	14	19	2	0
46	7,000	11,900	15	18	1	1
47	8,100	14,500	10	16	0	0
48	8,300	15,200	14	18	1	1
49	6,200	9,900	20	20	2	2

TABLE 19-2 (continued)

| Census Tract | Median Family Income | | Age Composition | | | |
| | 1970 | 1980 | % under 18 | | % over 65 | |
			1970	1980	1970	1980
50	$6,800	$9,700	21	20	2	3
51	7,100	10,000	20	20	3	3
52	6,900	10,800	21	21	2	1
53	6,400	11,700	16	23	2	0
54	6,800	14,300	10	21	4	1
55	6,000	16,800	11	19	3	0
56	6,400	16,200	12	18	4	1
57	7,100	15,900	13	18	5	2
58	7,100	16,000	11	17	5	3
59	7,800	18,200	14	19	5	1
60	7,700	21,000	14	16	4	0
61	6,900	19,100	12	20	8	2
62	7,700	20,300	11	17	6	1

*Census tract 6 is the University of South Carolina consisting of 16,000 full-time students. Approximately one third of the student body resides in campus housing in census tract 6.

TABLE 19-3

Population characteristics: occupation and employment status

| Census Tract | Occupation (Head of Household) | | | | Employment Status (Head of Household) | |
| | % Blue Collar | | % White Collar | | % Unemployed | |
	1970	1980	1970	1980	1970	1980
1	64	88	36	12	18	21
2	66	90	34	10	12	14
3	70	88	30	12	10	10
4	50	74	50	26	8	12
5	58	70	42	30	10	10
6*	—	—	—	—	—	—
7	34	58	66	42	7	6
8	52	56	48	44	6	4
9	53	63	47	37	5	5
10	49	59	51	41	3	3
11	46	63	54	37	3	4
12	70	70	30	30	4	2
13	60	65	40	35	4	3
14	34	40	66	60	4	3
15	33	48	67	52	1	1
16	74	80	26	20	2	5
17	90	91	10	9	4	5
18	83	92	17	8	4	8
19	75	79	25	21	5	4
20	68	70	32	30	4	4

TABLE 19-3 (continued)

Census Tract	Occupation (Head of Household)				Employment Status (Head of Household)	
	% Blue Collar		% White Collar		% Unemployed	
	1970	1980	1970	1980	1970	1980
21	75	78	25	23	4	3
22	70	70	30	30	4	4
23	68	72	32	28	2	2
24	58	52	42	48	3	2
25	50	52	50	48	3	3
26	40	36	60	64	3	4
27	38	32	62	68	2	1
28	42	42	58	58	2	1
29	22	20	78	80	2	1
30	30	26	70	74	2	2
31	12	10	88	90	1	0
32	20	20	80	80	1	1
33	18	17	82	83	0	0
34	34	36	66	64	2	1
35	48	50	52	50	2	2
36	37	35	63	65	4	1
37	55	60	45	40	1	1
38	70	75	30	25	0	0
39	80	78	20	22	0	1
40	78	82	22	18	0	0
41	60	61	40	39	1	0
42	60	32	40	68	0	1
43	24	22	76	78	3	1
44	30	30	70	70	1	1
45	35	30	70	65	0	0
46	30	25	70	75	2	1
47	22	21	78	79	1	1
48	39	37	61	63	3	1
49	42	43	58	57	2	1
50	58	57	42	43	1	1
51	59	67	41	33	1	0
52	70	70	30	30	3	4
53	80	82	20	18	3	3
54	74	70	26	30	3	5
55	52	24	48	76	2	0
56	27	27	73	73	2	2
57	25	27	75	73	2	3
58	27	16	73	84	2	1
59	21	10	79	90	0	0
60	18	17	82	83	0	0
61	23	20	77	80	0	0
62	14	12	86	88	0	0

*Census tract 6 is the University of South Carolina consisting of 16,000 full-time students. Approximately one third of the student body resides in campus housing in census tract 6.

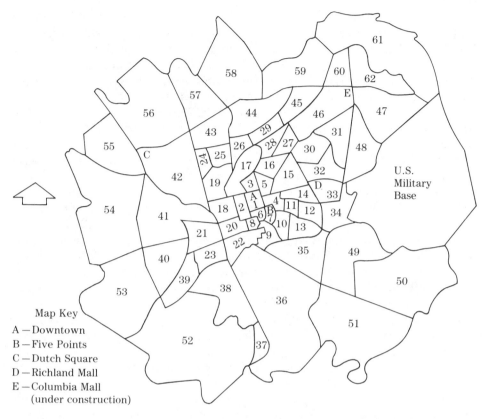

EXHIBIT 19-1

Census tract map

The Retail Structure of Columbia

The retailing structure of Columbia consists of the following clusterings: (1) regional shopping clusters, (2) community and neighborhood shopping centers, and (3) free-standing string developments along major traffic arteries. Due to the limited sales potential of the localized trading areas of the latter two clusterings, Shaw's Department Store has limited its store locations to those clusterings having regional attraction. Four regional shopping clusters exist in the Columbia area. They are (1) Downtown, (2) Dutch Square, (3) Richland Mall, and (4) Five Points Shopping Center. Currently, Shaw's operates a store in each of the four clusters. While the size (square footage of selling space) of each store varies, the percentage of the selling space devoted to a given product line remains constant. The location of each major cluster is shown in Exhibit 19–1.

Downtown cluster

Currently, the largest shopping cluster is the downtown area with 102 retailing establishments. Three "full-line" department stores, including J.C.

Penney, Belk, and Davidson's, provide the principal retail attraction for the downtown area. Several quality softgoods retailers with local and regional reputations also serve as an important attraction force for the area; they include Tapp's Department Store, Berry's on Main, Britton's, Lourie's, and Shaw's Department Stores. In addition, the downtown area has the largest concentration of furniture and appliance stores, as well as specialty stores. The willingness of consumers to spend considerable time, money, and effort in making price and quality comparisons relative to these hard and specialty goods should provide the downtown with additional attraction power. In general, the tenant mix of retailers in the downtown area is quite conducive to consumer trip generation and comparison shopping.

The downtown has several positional strengths from a retailing perspective; they are (1) centrality to the entire city's population, (2) close proximity to the federal, state, and local governmental office complex, (3) close proximity to the city's major complex of business offices, and (4) close proximity to the University. Additional positional qualities include the adjacent location of the city's sports and convention complex and its associated hotel complex. With the completion of the new Main Street pedestrian mall, the shopping atmosphere of the downtown area should be greatly enhanced.

The downtown area is not without its retailing weaknesses. External and internal accessibility to and within the area is extremely limited. The accessibility problem is further complicated by a lack of sufficient parking in the immediate area. While the new pedestrian mall should improve the shopping atmosphere, it could well represent a further deterioration in the accessibility and parking problems. Shopper security, especially during the evening and weekends, creates additional problems. Muggings, robberies, and auto vandalism have had a serious adverse effect on consumers' willingness to shop in the downtown area. This security has resulted in a 6:00 P.M. closing for most stores except during the annual holiday seasons and special events. With the slow but steady increase in the number of low-status retailers in and around the downtown area, the consumer security problem easily could get worse.

The general shopping atmosphere of the downtown area also places certain limitations on consumer attraction. Even with the new pedestrian mall, many of the buildings are old and in need of extensive repair. The numerous vacant buildings take their psychological toll on consumer purchase motivation. For the white, middle-class suburban shopper, the minorities-majority makeup of the downtown shopper is psychologically discomforting and results in a poor shopping "frame of mind." Rumor has it that some of the major department stores plan to adjust downward their pricing points and carry a lower quality of goods in order to appeal to the lower income minorities consumer.

Finally, the "cost of doing business" in the downtown area currently is the highest in the city. High rent, extra security, and high storage rates all add to this cost. In addition, with very defined daily peak shopping periods (noon hour, coffee hours, and post-workday), labor costs are necessarily higher to meet these peak demand periods.

Dutch Square

The Dutch Square Mall and its adjacent area is the second largest retailing cluster in the Columbia SMSA. When completed in 1973, the Mall consisted of forty-eight retailing establishments. In four years, the cluster has grown to its present size of eighty-nine retailing establishments. The tenant mix of the cluster consists of (1) one full-line department store, J.B. White; (2) three discount department stores, Woolco, K-Mart, and Richway; (3) two catalog showrooms, Sam Solomon's and Key Wholesalers; and (4) five major softgoods retailers, Tapp's Department Store, Berry's on Main, Britton's, Lourie's, and Shaw's Department Store. In addition, there is the usual mix of specialty, shopping, and convenience goods retailers.

Located in South Carolina's fastest growing upper-middle class suburban areas, Dutch Square has been extremely successful. Sales per square foot are among the highest in the Columbia area. Lack of competition is the reason most often cited for the success of the cluster. With good external accessibility, the Mall area attracts from the entire metro area, as well as numerous surrounding communities. The recent addition of several office complexes should also enhance the cluster's drawing power.

Retailing weaknesses are relatively few, but two are noteworthy. First, with the rapid expansion of the last four years, the internal accessibility within the shopping cluster has been severely retarded. Long-term effects are certain to be felt as consumers seek more convenient and accessible shopping opportunities. The second weakness concerns the tenant mix. With only one major full-line department store, the Mall lacks sufficient "store name" drawing power that comes with major full-line retailers such as J.C. Penney, Sears, Montgomery Ward, Belk, and Davidson's. This lack of major "shopping-center anchors" creates competitive vulnerability with respect to other malls which have such "full-line anchors."

Richland Mall

Columbia's third largest shopping cluster with regional drawing power is Richland Mall. Located within a well-established, middle-class section of Columbia, the Mall obtains the bulk of its customers from local eastside neighborhoods. Forty-eight retail establishments are located within the Mall and the surrounding area. J.B. White, Berry's on Main, Britton's, and Shaw's Department Store provide the nucleus of the regional drawing power. A limited number of specialty shops also aid in drawing consumers from outside the local markets. Excluding surrounding neighborhoods, Richland Mall usually ranks as either the third or fourth shopping cluster choice for most Columbians.

The principal limitations on inter-regional consumer drawing power are (1) extremely poor external and internal accessibility, (2) poor tenant mix (many of the establishments are convenience retailers which conflict with the shopping and specialty retailers in terms of traffic and parking congestion and the type of consumer attracted), and (3) insufficient number of full-line department stores, other establishments, and activities that are capable of drawing consumers from considerable distances. There are rumors that J.B. White is considering relocating.

Five Points Shopping Center

Next to the downtown area, the Five Points Shopping Center is the oldest shopping cluster in Columbia. Consisting of approximately three dozen shopping, specialty, and convenience goods retailers, the Center's ability to attract regional consumers is based on two factors. First, Columbia's only Sears store is located adjacent to the cluster. In Columbia, Sears by itself is capable of drawing consumers from considerable distances. Second, historically, all of Columbia's old-line specialty and shopping goods retailers (Berry's on Main, Britton's, Tapp's, Lourie's, and Shaw's Department Store) have branch locations within the Center.

Located adjacent to what was Columbia's most exclusive residential area (University Heights), Five Points was once the exclusive shopping district of the upper-income Columbia consumer. With the migration to the suburbs in the 1950's and 1960's, University Heights subsequently evolved into a low-income multi-dwelling residential area populated with University students and minority groups. The conversion of many of the single-family dwellings into multiple-family dwellings hastened the physical deterioration of the area. Recently, however, restoration of the area and its dwellings has become a passion for many young, middle-class professionals. Its adjacency to the University makes it a highly desirable place of residence for the University administration, faculty, and staff.

The advantages associated with the cluster's adjacency to the University and the downtown area are far outweighed by the disadvantages of the reduced external and internal accessibility and increased competition. In terms of the Columbia metro area, Five Points is by far the least accessible. Internal traffic conjestion and the lack of parking facilities is an extreme limitation, but conjestion will probably be reduced with the closing of Sears soon. In addition, there has been some talk about refurbishing the Center's many older buildings.

Columbia Mall

The opening of the new Columbia Mall, scheduled for the fall, will signal a new era in retailing for the greater Columbia area. Located in the northeastern section of Columbia (see Exhibit 19–1), the two-story, 1.5 million square-foot development will contain 145 retailing establishments. Success of the venture is almost certain, given the consumer drawing power associated with such noted shopping center "anchors" as Belk, J.C. Penny, Sears, and Rich's. What is certain are some of the profound changes in the retailing structure of the Columbia metropolitan area. Speculation abounds as to the effects of the new mall. To the Columbia area consumer, it will offer new and exciting shopping opportunities. To the existing and would-be Columbia area retailer, it will represent a business opportunity and/or a source of potential competition.

A recent study completed by the Marketing Research Division of the University examined the potential impact of the Columbia Mall on existing major shopping clusters. Four shopping clusters (Downtown, Dutch Square, Richland Mall, and Five Points) and seven product categories (clothing, footwear, apparel accessories, furniture and appliances, household accessories, recreational and entertainment, and personal) were included in the study. Using a probability model, the study estimated the probability of a consumer in a given census tract traveling to a particular shopping cluster for a given product category. To ascertain the impact of the new mall, a "before" and "after" research design was employed. The conclusions of the study are as follows:

> Of the seven product categories considered, the new mall should assume the dominant market share position in the five areas of clothing, footwear, household accessories, recreation and entertainment, and personal products. In addition, Columbia Mall's market share in apparel accessories should be second only to the Downtown area. Only in the furniture and appliance product category is the Columbia Mall's market share expected to be of a limited scope. . . . If the market share positions projected here are assumed to be valid, then it would be appropriate to expect the Columbia Mall to become the dominant force in the retailing activities of the Columbia area. . . . Further, these projections would indicate that the impact of the Columbia Mall would not be evenly distributed. Substantial differences, given these conditions, would occur between product categories and shopping clusters. For most of the four existing clusters, substantial decreases in market share would be expected for most product categories. Overall, most of the existing clusters would experience their largest market share decreases in clothing and footwear product categories. . . . The entrance of the mall into the retailing structure of the Columbia area poses several difficult problems for existing and potential retailers. Initially, decisions regarding locational strategies will need to be made. Later, as the effects of the new mall become apparent, marketing strategies relative to product, promotion, and price will require adjustment.

The impact of the Columbia Mall already is being felt. In the area surrounding the mall, several firms have announced that they have purchased land and plan to build within the next year. Among these are two major discount-department stores, a major catalog showroom, a developer who specializes in small (ten to fifteen stores) specialty shopping clusters, and a firm that specializes in four-screen theaters. In addition, there are rumors that two major department stores have purchased adjacent properties.

The new Columbia mall will be two levels completely enclosed and, therefore, climatically controlled. Sunken gardens and a lower level walkway have been designed to provide customers with an excellent shopping atmosphere. The planned activities for the garden and walkways include concerts, exhibits, shows, and displays.

Tenants of the mall include most of the major local retailers, as well as many nationally-known retailers. The developers are attempting to control the tenant mix in terms of product, price, and promotional mix. Hopefully, the tenant mix will be such that it will attract consumers from many income categories ranging from upper-lower to upper-upper income groups.

The Firm: Shaw's Department Store

Shaw's Department Store, a leading softgoods merchandiser in the Columbia area for over eighty years, was first established by William L. Shaw in 1889. Over the years, the name Shaw's has become synonymous with quality and style in the Columbia area. Appealing to the upper 40 percent of the market, Shaw's product, pricing, and promotional strategy is directed toward those consumers whose principal purchase motives are high quality, high style, and excellent service. For the last two decades, Shaw's merchandising strategy has been to offer high quality merchandise in a limited number of product lines at various pricing points. Sales departments, product lines, sales areas, pricing ranges, and annual sales are shown for each store in Tables 19-4, 19-5, 19-6, and 19-7. This standardized mix has proven to be quite successful for the last twenty years. However, ultraurban population shifts have created considerable sales variation from one store to another. These variations become more pronounced when reviewed in terms of sales per square foot. Perhaps some changes in the standardized mix are needed. Gross margin characteristics and operating expenses by department for each store also are shown in Tables 19-5 through 19-7.

The management of Shaw's Department Stores has secured a highly desirable corner location on the first level of the new mall. It consists of approximately 35,000 square feet of space; the firm's management believes that it has obtained one of the most desirable locations within the mall. The question now becomes one of how to use the location and the space in the most productive manner possible.

The Problem

Mary Hoy, Director of Marketing Research for Shaw's Department Stores, has been assigned the task of analyzing the impact of the new mall and store on Shaw's existing Columbia operations. She also has been asked to make recommendations regarding any changes that are needed in Shaw's merchandising strategies (product and price mixes) as a result of the new mall and store. In preparation, Mary has itemized the following questions to guide her investigation.

1. What are the potential positive and negative impact factors of the new mall and the new store on Shaw's downtown, Dutch Square, Richland Mall, and Five Points locations?

2. Should any of Shaw's existing locations (downtown, Dutch Square, Richland Mall, or Five Points) be abandoned? Why or why not?

3. What, if any, adjustments are required in Shaw's merchandising strategy (product and price mixes)? Will these adjustments vary by store location? How?

4. What merchandising adjustments are required in Shaw's merchandising strategy for the new store in the Columbia Mall?

Assume the role of Mary Hoy and develop a research report that will completely cover the basic concerns outlined in the above questions.

TABLE 19-4

Sales operations by department: downtown store

Sales Department	Price Range ($)	Sales Area (sq. ft.)	1980 Sales ($)	1979 Sales ($)	1978 Sales ($)	1980 Gross Margin (% of sales)	1980 Operating Expenses (% of sales)
Men's Department							
Suits	100–400	1,500	321,000	220,000	191,750		
Sportswear	15–100	3,800	345,000	222,750	188,500		
Accessories	10–100	1,500	243,000	178,750	136,500		
Total	*10–400*	*6,800*	*909,000*	*621,500*	*516,750*	44.1	40.3
Women's Department							
Moderate Dresses	25–100	6,350	417,000	371,250	347,750		
Moderate Sportswear	15–100	3,050	252,000	222,750	227,500		
Better Dresses	50–800	5,750	75,000	178,750	315,250		
Better Sportswear	30–900	2,250	33,000	167,750	312,000		
Lingerie	10–90	3,350	90,000	88,000	123,500		
Cosmetics	1–50	3,000	333,000	327,250	357,500		
Accessories	1–100	3,500	285,000	231,000	256,750		
Total	*1–900*	*27,250*	*1,485,000*	*1,586,750*	*1,940,250*	46.2	41.5
Junior's Department							
Sportswear	15–100	2,250	183,000	173,250	217,750		
Dresses	20–100	2,250	69,000	74,250	94,250		
Coats	20–200	500	33,000	27,500	32,500		
Total	*15–200*	*5,000*	*285,000*	*275,000*	*344,500*	45.8	41.7
Children's Department							
Boys	10–100	2,250	24,000	35,750	100,750		
Girls	10–100	2,250	12,000	30,250	94,250		
Infants	3–40	1,100	18,000	49,500	123,500		
Total	*3–100*	*5,600*	*54,000*	*115,500*	*318,500*	46.5	41.8
Gifts-Linen Department							
Total	*5–500*	*5,350*	*267,000*	*151,250*	*130,000*	47.4	42.0
TOTAL	1–900	50,000	3,000,000	2,750,000	3,250,000		

TABLE 19-5

Sales operations by department: Dutch Square

Sales Department	Price Range ($)	Sales Area (sq. ft.)	1980 Sales ($)	1979 Sales ($)	1978 Sales ($)	1980 Gross Margin (% of sales)	1980 Operating Expenses (% of sales)
Men's Department							
Suits	100–400	1,000	125,100	130,000	133,000		
Sportswear	15–100	2,500	213,800	190,000	127,000		
Accessories	10–100	1,000	150,100	155,000	126,000		
Total	*10–400*	*4,500*	*489,000*	*475,000*	*386,000*	*47.1*	*38.1*
Women's Department							
Moderate Dresses	25–100	4,200	377,100	380,000	401,000		
Moderate Sportswear	15–100	2,000	210,100	185,000	129,000		
Better Dresses	50–800	3,800	299,800	315,000	377,000		
Better Sportswear	30–900	1,500	171,100	165,000	119,000		
Lingerie	10–90	2,200	116,900	120,000	90,000		
Cosmetics	1–50	2,000	379,500	367,000	316,000		
Accessories	1–100	2,300	281,500	289,000	230,000		
Total	*1–900*	*18,000*	*1,836,000*	*1,821,000*	*1,662,000*	*48.2*	*38.6*
Junior's Department							
Sportswear	15–100	1,500	414,300	374,000	301,000		
Dresses	20–100	1,500	134,900	153,000	167,000		
Coats	20–200	300	45,000	46,000	36,000		
Total	*15–200*	*3,300*	*594,200*	*573,000*	*504,000*	*47.8*	*39.7*
Children's Department							
Boys	10–100	1,500	87,900	60,000	52,000		
Girls	10–100	1,500	104,000	77,000	66,000		
Infants	3–40	700	84,900	82,000	53,000		
Total	*3–100*	*3,700*	*276,800*	*219,000*	*171,000*	*48.5*	*38.8*
Gifts-Linen Department							
Total	*5–500*	*3,500*	*209,600*	*208,000*	*180,000*	*49.4*	*40.3*
TOTAL	1–900	33,000	3,405,600	3,295,000	2,903,000		

TABLE 19-6

Sales operations by department: Richland Mall

Sales Department	Price Range ($)	Sales Area (sq. ft.)	1980 Sales ($)	1979 Sales ($)	1978 Sales ($)	1980 Gross Margin (% of sales)	1980 Operating Expenses (% of sales)
Men's Department							
Suits	100–400	1,000	69,000	78,750	82,080		
Sportswear	15–100	2,500	94,300	114,750	118,560		
Accessories	10–100	1,000	94,300	114,750	118,560		
Total	*10–400*	*4,500*	*257,600*	*308,250*	*319,200*	*45.1*	*38.0*
Women's Department							
Moderate Dresses	25–100	4,200	282,900	297,000	321,480		
Moderate Sportswear	15–100	2,000	200,100	155,250	114,000		
Better Dresses	50–800	3,800	115,000	137,250	143,640		
Better Sportswear	30–900	1,500	135,700	114,750	70,680		
Lingerie	10–90	2,200	73,600	69,750	57,000		
Cosmetics	1–50	2,000	232,300	229,500	280,440		
Accessories	1–100	2,300	186,300	186,750	214,320		
Total	*1–900*	*18,000*	*1,225,900*	*1,190,250*	*1,201,560*	*47.2*	*38.4*
Junior's Department							
Sportswear	15–100	1,500	257,600	234,000	228,000		
Dresses	20–100	1,500	94,300	92,250	91,200		
Coats	20–200	300	29,900	22,500	22,800		
Total	*15–200*	*3,300*	*381,800*	*348,750*	*342,000*	*46.8*	*39.2*
Children's Department							
Boys	10–100	1,500	71,300	63,000	61,560		
Girls	10–100	1,500	73,600	67,500	63,840		
Infants	3–40	700	69,000	45,000	41,040		
Total	*3–100*	*3,700*	*213,900*	*175,500*	*166,440*	*47.5*	*38.8*
Gifts-Linen Department							
Total	*5–500*	*3,500*	*220,800*	*227,250*	*250,800*	*48.4*	*39.9*
TOTAL	1–900	33,000	2,300,000	2,250,000	2,280,000		

TABLE 19-7

Sales operations by department: Five Points

Sales Department	Price Range ($)	Sales Area (sq. ft.)	1980 Sales ($)	1979 Sales ($)	1978 Sales ($)	1980 Gross Margin (% of sales)	1980 Operating Expenses (% of sales)
Men's Department							
Suits	100–400	1,200	53,200	58,500	66,600		
Sportswear	15–100	3,040	109,200	105,000	86,400		
Accessories	10–100	1,200	72,800	70,500	66,600		
Total	*10–400*	*5,440*	*235,200*	*234,000*	*219,600*	*41.1*	*37.5*
Women's Department							
Moderate Dresses	25–100	5,080	114,800	160,500	219,600		
Moderate Sportswear	15–100	2,440	114,800	120,000	95,400		
Better Dresses	50–800	4,600	29,400	55,500	95,400		
Better Sportswear	30–900	1,800	75,600	61,500	66,600		
Lingerie	10–90	2,680	35,000	39,000	48,600		
Cosmetics	1–50	2,400	123,200	120,000	198,000		
Accessories	1–100	2,800	95,200	90,000	118,800		
Total	*1–900*	*21,800*	*588,000*	*646,500*	*842,400*	*45.2*	*38.0*
Junior's Department							
Sportswear	15–100	1,800	260,400	255,000	253,800		
Dresses	20–100	1,800	128,800	120,000	104,400		
Coats	20–200	400	43,400	48,000	46,800		
Total	*15–200*	*4,000*	*432,600*	*423,000*	*405,000*	*42.8*	*38.8*
Children's Department							
Boys	10–100	1,800	14,000	30,000	86,400		
Girls	10–100	1,800	22,400	43,500	95,400		
Infants	3–40	880	11,200	33,000	66,600		
Total	*3–100*	*4,480*	*47,600*	*106,500*	*248,400*	*42.5*	*38.1*
Gifts-Linen Department							
Total	*5–500*	*4,280*	*96,600*	*90,000*	*86,600*	*44.4*	*38.9*
TOTAL	1–900	40,000	1,400,000	1,500,000	1,800,000		

Case 20

ARCOT DAIRY PRODUCTS

ARCOT DAIRY PRODUCTS produces a wide variety of dairy products for distribution in supermarkets in the Middle and South Atlantic states from Pennsylvania to Georgia. Originally a processor of fluid milk and a manufacturer of ice cream, Arcot has diversified its product lines over the past 15 years to include cottage cheese, cheese dips, biscuits, and a variety of wedge and sliced cheeses. In fact, fluid milk and ice cream account for less than 25 percent of Arcot's total product sales.

All of the Arcot family of products are normally sold in the dairy case, although occasionally biscuits or cheese dips are displayed in the meat case or an outside cooler at the end of a store aisle.

Arcot seeks to elicit consumer preference by having a reputation for freshness and quality at a fair price. The firm believes that the appeal of its packaging must convince the consumer to buy and that the quality of the products must bring the consumer back for repeat business. Arcot also tries to elicit preference and loyalty through a program of extensive advertising keeping the Arcot name in the eyes and the minds of consumers. The objective has been to let people know that when they buy the Arcot name, as opposed to buying private brands, that they will be getting the same uniformity and quality wherever they buy the product. This is in contrast to private brand (packer's label) merchandise that may offer the retailer a lower price but inconsistent quality and limited continuity of labels. Arcot's salespersons stress to their retail customers the following advantages of marketing Arcot products as compared with marketing private brands:

1. They are known by the customer.
2. They need only where-to-buy advertising by the retailer.

Source: "Arcot Dairy Products" (pp. 141–55) from *Cases in Marketing Channel Strategy* by Foster, Woodside and Sims. Copyright © 1977 by Harper & Row, Publishers, Inc. Reprinted by permission of the publisher.

3. They add prestige to the store.
4. They can be used as traffic builders.
5. They are price-protected.
6. The services provided by Arcot representatives include technical advice on product promotion, displays and promotional material, and services for store openings.

In addition, Arcot sends out millions of recipes each year and encourages the use of Arcot and related store items through television and other advertising. Arcot helps its dealers by supplying displays at no cost to the dealer, promotional allowances, and other services that build up a healthy dealer-producer relationship. Arcot provides operating aids and services to the retailer on the premise that increasing total store sales will increase food product sales, which will, in turn, increase Arcot sales.

Arcot tries to adjust the type of products displayed in dealer stores, depending on the area income level and the location of the store (see Table 20-1). In a low-income area, for example, the higher-priced cheese products might not be displayed, while the more popular and average-priced cheeses would tend to have good sales. In this case the dealer would be discouraged from purchasing a slow-moving high-profit item in favor of a fast-moving average-profit item.

TABLE 20-1

Dairy department sales in a high- and low-income area store

Product group	Low-income area (store A) (%)	High-income area (store B) (%)
Milk	38.0	30.8
Milk beverages	1.6	1.5
Cream and cream substitutes	1.4	1.5
Butter	2.8	3.9
Margarine	9.0	4.6
Eggs	21.2	12.7
Cottage cheese	3.3	3.3
Processed cheese loafs	1.5	1.1
Sliced processed cheese	4.3	15.7
Store packaged cheese	—	—
Prepackaged natural cheese	4.3	12.6
Graded and special cheese	1.2	0.9
Cream cheese	0.7	0.7
Cheese spreads and foods	0.5	1.4
Sour cream and dips	0.9	1.9
Biscuits and dinner rolls	5.8	1.7
Cookies and pastries	1.0	2.5
Miscellaneous	2.5	3.2
Total department	100.0	100.0

Promotional Techniques

In selecting the combination of sales promotion devices that will be used, Arcot uses the following techniques to induce retail customers to buy its products:

1. Arcot distributes its product directly to larger retail and store chains and to the small customers through wholesalers to get their product displayed on as wide a basis as possible. Arcot has chosen direct sales for the following reasons:
   a. More aggressive selling through control of its own sales force.
   b. A chance to get closer to the ultimate consumer and hence a means of learning more about his reaction to the manufacturer's product.
   c. Rapid movement of products to market.
   d. An opportunity to work directly with the retailer in training him in selling methods, advertising, and display programs.
   e. A method of combating the promotion of private brands.
   f. A chance to reduce marketing costs.
2. Arcot salespeople perform the following services in promoting successful supplier-retailer relationships:
   a. They assist retailers in noting and controlling out-of-stock conditions. Adequate stocks of merchandise on the shelves are essential for maintaining maximum sales. Various research studies indicate that sales increase by 25 percent when full-stock conditions exist. Also consumers are not forced to shop competitors for out-of-stock items. Arcot salespeople point out to the retailer specific periods of the year when demand for an item will peak, so that inventories can be increased to limit out-of-stock conditions. They help the retailer to forecast his future needs and seasonal needs of Arcot products.
   b. They assist the retailer in laying out various departments to gain maximum sales. They calculate facings for Arcot products in new stores, help set up displays and promotions during grand openings, and talk to the consumers, encouraging them to buy Arcot products.
   c. They assist retail store personnel in checking the control dates on products and in rotating the product.
   d. They pick up unsalable Arcot products and compensate the dealer for them. This helps the dealer to avoid a loss and to use the money he has tied up in the product in purchasing another more profitable product.
   e. They take time out to talk to dealers about resale problems, knowing that the best way to increase Arcot sales is by helping retail customers sell more of the product. More sales volume and greater efficiency are achieved through a retailer-producer cooperation. The firm believes that a good retailer-producer relationship develops reliable feedback resources that will give valuable marketing information.

3. Arcot attempts to motivate retail sales excitement through an extensive advertising program featuring the use of television, regional editions of magazines, and local newspapers spot advertising. On the local level sales excitement is built through dealer's displays of the product which are designed to promote the Arcot product and related items for higher retailer sales and profits. One Arcot executive described this as painting a profit picture for the store manager through advertising and promotion support.

4. Arcot maintains continued retailer patronage through producing quality products with a money-back guarantee:

   a. Arcot will cut the price of a product up to one-third until the product is sold.

   b. After the control date has expired, Arcot will replace the product, giving the retailer credit. (Cream cheese, for example, would be replaced after 60 days.)

5. The use of promotional allowances is needed to encourage the retailer to be a strong member of the Arcot channel of distribution. Promotional allowances are not to be considered as a discount or reduction in price and are offered only for advertising and/or promotional support. Arcot offers the following promotional allowances to its customers:

   a. Off-invoice allowance. The retailer is not required to advertise to receive the promotional allowance but is asked to promote the product to generate additional sales during the cooperative merchandising period.

   b. Advertising allowance. The retailer must advertise the product to receive the allowance. The usual practice is for newspapers to run an advertisement, on a selected Arcot product, at least once during each four weeks of the performance period. If newspapers are not used as a regular means of advertising, the product must be featured through whatever other medium of direct consumer advertising is normally used (handbills, radio, direct mail). In the event all stores operated or serviced by the retailer are not included in the advertising coverage, deliveries to stores outside the advertising coverage are to be deducted from dealers' purchases to determine which purchases qualify for payment.

   c. Display allowance. The retailer must display the product in special displays, referred to as "shopper-stoppers," use acceptable Arcot point-of-sale material provided at no cost to the dealer, with credit issued to his account if he meets the requirements featuring the floor or table displays in all stores for the specified time period.

   d. Special options. These are various options for promotional money such as other off-invoice allowances, advertising allowances for items featured twice, and allowances for items sold at a reduced price.

The company assists the retailer in seasonal promotions (Thanksgiving, Christmas) and other special promotions to increase retailers' sales and profits.

Counseling and promotional assistance are intended to produce a more efficient retailer who in turn will become a better customer of the company.

These promotional offers are available on the same terms to all dealer-customers competing in the sale of the product in the same area. For a large food chain, for example, these allowances are credited to the chain's account, whereas for the members of a voluntary retail chain handled by wholesalers the allowances are paid by check to the individual retailer or by credit memo to the wholesaler for the individual retail member of the cooperative account.

Cooperation with Retail Accounts

Arcot account representatives meet once every month with the merchandising executives of each major food chain served by Arcot to develop and set up advertising and merchandising techniques and displays to be used during the month in all of the chain's stores. At this time, a promotion planning book is shown to the merchandiser and buyer, illustrating the various display materials that can be used to tie in with the accompanying schedules of television spots, magazine advertising, and local newspaper advertising. The objective is to coordinate the advertising and promotional effort of local retail chains with Arcot's effort to promote products when the demand is highest. The Arcot representative gives the suggested dates for store advertising and promotion of specific Arcot products. This information is included in the promotion planning book which contains presentation information and a number of merchandising ideas for each promoted product. There is a description of the product and information on regular case cost, the allowance available to dealer and its effective date, net cost, the accompanying magazine ad and television ad schedules, and other promotions available.

The section on merchandise ideas contains illustrations of how the particular product item might be effectively promoted in a dairy case, outside cooler, or meat case. The illustrations served to point up the use of the display cards, product dividers, and cents off promotions that are available. The promotion planning book also gives examples of the profit and sales experience of retailers who have had successful promotions. Suggestions are also made concerning appropriate order quantities and for other promotional tie-ins.

On the basis of the facts and ideas gleaned from the promotion planning book, the account executive then consults with the merchandiser and buyer and develops a coordinated plan for the marketing of specific Arcot products for a one-month period in the particular food chain. The account executive also helps the buyer control his inventory by maintaining data on previous years' sales to the account of specific products. This also includes help in predicting seasonal purchases, such as cheese purchases at Christmas, from previous years' figures. Through the use of punch cards and computers these trends and seasonal predictions can be handled for each account with relative ease.

In the case of new products, major retailers rely on a buying committee to make buying decisions. Arcot sought acceptance for its new products with samples distributed personally by the account executive to members of the buying committee and their families two to three weeks in advance of the meeting of the buying committee. Then the product is presented to the committee by the account executive and its advantages and disadvantages are discussed, for the purpose of determining whether to accept the new Arcot product for distribution.

The Arcot account executive helps the buyer schedule incoming and outgoing products through the chain or wholesaler warehouse. The biggest problem in the typical chain warehouse is the shortage of space for the thousands of different products handled. Through proper coordination, products spend minimal time in the warehouse before being shipped to local stores. Thus a product might enter the warehouse from an Arcot plant on Monday and be on the dealer's case by Wednesday, and by that afternoon a different Arcot product would be occupying the same warehouse space. This coordination is essential for the efficient operation of the warehouse and the supply channel. Companies are able to effect stronger patronage by offering more in the way of service than competitors or by cutting prices through successfully reducing physical-distribution costs.

Arcot sales representatives have tried many strategies from the use of programmed display to unplanned operations. In a typical promotion program involving a 39-store chain in September 1979, a promotion featuring Arcot biscuits and chicken sales was planned at the chain warehouse level with the district managers, buyers, and merchandisers. The promotion was based on the idea of selling chicken and biscuits together. Attractive display cards were provided to be fitted on the dairy or meat case, which featured an illustration of fried chicken served with hot biscuits. Attached to the display card was a cents-off offer involving a refund of 40 cents on the purchase of four cans of Arcot biscuits and a fryer. In addition to the display of biscuits in the dairy case, a combination display of chicken and Arcot biscuits in the meat case was planned for all stores. Product dividers featuring the promotion theme were to be installed in the meat case to call attention to the special offer. In addition, recipe pads featuring chicken and biscuits were made available to each store. Weekend newspaper advertising was planned to feature fryers at 29 cents per pound as well as the 40-cents refund offer on Arcot biscuits. Arcot account representatives supplied the merchandising pieces—local ads and display materials. After the basic planning, district dinners were held with the individual store managers and merchandisers. Suggested ways of merchandising and best ways of merchandising the products and the program were presented to the store-level personnel. After this, product orders were taken on the spot to the individual stores. Pressure was exerted on the store managers by the district managers to make a full effort for the program in their individual stores. As a result of this promotion, sales more than doubled one month's normal business. Some 1,440 cases of biscuits were moved.

In September 1980 another equally successful promotion theme involving biscuits and chicken was accepted by the same chain, with Arcot supplying the ads and displays in consultation with the buyers and merchandisers at the warehouse level. This time a letter was sent to the district managers and store managers explaining the promotion and specific items to be promoted. The display materials were sent to the stores with instructions on use. The promotion was not pushed by the chain's district managers, nor were the merchandising techniques to be used explained to the store managers. The promotion raised sales by approximately 10 percent. Average storewide sales for September through October 1979 were ten times as great as sales for the same period in 1980.

In-store Research Effort

In addition to the various promotional efforts, Arcot's marketing research personnel cooperated with the various retail organizations in undertaking in-store research to help retailers increase dairy-case sales by determining the most advantageous ways of displaying dairy products.

For example, Arcot marketing research people selected a particular store (store 101) from the previously-mentioned 39-store chain. In doing the study the researchers selected 40 weekend shoppers at random and followed their movements throughout the test store. The result was a mapping of the number of shoppers entering each aisle or store area. (See Exhibits 20-1 and 20-2.) They found, for example, that 95 percent of the 40 shoppers (or 38) shopped the dairy case, while as few as 45 percent of the shoppers visited one side of the frozen food gondola. Shoppers were also observed concerning their average shopping time, average check-out time, average number of items purchased, and dollar amount of order purchased. Customers were also observed with respect to whether they used a shopping list, asked for assistance, carried the store advertisement, or bought special items. Finally, the observer recorded the sex, race, estimated age of each shopper, and whether he or she shopped alone or with other family members. (See Table 20-2.)

The Arcot research team also recorded the incidence of purchases for 100 shoppers who visited the dairy case during a weekend day. The purpose of this aspect of the study was to observe to what extent consumers shopped the entire dairy case. Only 3.8 percent of the items (or 10 items) were selected from the very top level of the dairy case by the 100 shoppers. Appreciably more items were selected at lower levels in the case, with 114 selections, or 43 percent, being made from the lowest level which permanently features fluid milk, random-weight cheese, margarine, and biscuits.

Further analysis revealed that the pattern of shopping for the dairy case results in the distribution of sales and gross profit in proportion to the amount of cubic space each dairy product occupies in the dairy case, as illustrated in Exhibit 20-3. A further comparison was made among the departmental sales in the test store, the published departmental sales of a 50-store study, and the results of a study of a southern food chain. (See Table 20-3.)

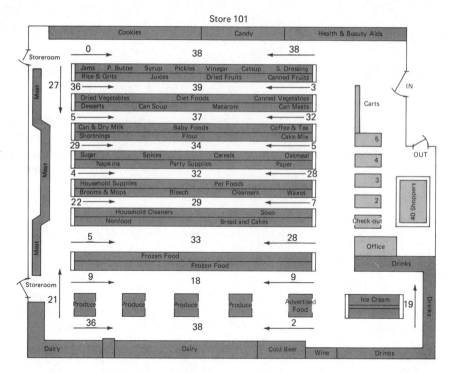

EXHIBIT 20-1

Store directory and layout

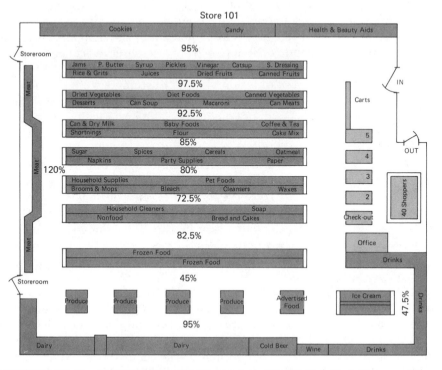

EXHIBIT 20-2

Mapping of the number of shoppers entering each aisle or store area

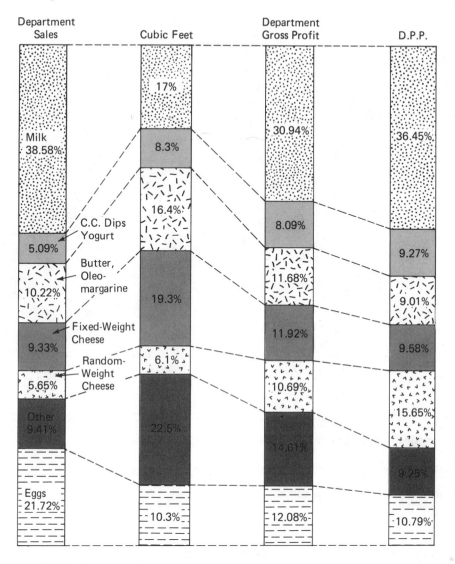

EXHIBIT 20-3

Store 101: a matter of profitability relationships and balance

As a consequence of the comparison studies, an adjustment was made in the arrangement of products in the store 101's dairy case, at the suggestion of the Arcot account representative. The new arrangement emphasized a greater vertical alignment of some products, like fluid milk, while lowering some of the special dairy items to the middle of the case. A follow-up research study involving 200 shoppers was employed to investigate the incidence of purchase. (See Exhibit 20-4.) The study revealed that the incidence of purchase on the top shelf was 15 percent under the new arrangement and that a more uniform distribution of purchases existed throughout the entire dairy case.

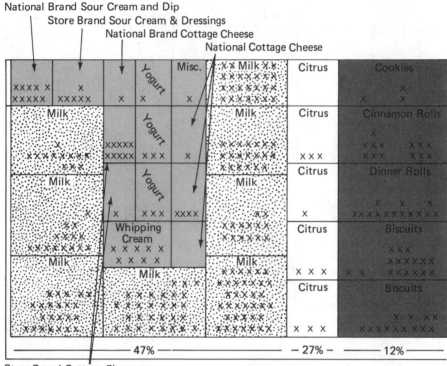

National Brand Sour Cream and Dip
Store Brand Sour Cream & Dressings
National Brand Cottage Cheese
National Cottage Cheese

Store Brand Cottage Cheese

EXHIBIT 20-4

Incidence of purchase: new arrangement plan for store 101

TABLE 20-2

Customer flow analysis (40 shoppers) for store 101

Average shopping time	27.8 minutes
Average time to check-out	5.5 minutes
Customers using shopping lists	17
Cost of average order purchased	$22.87
Average number of items purchased	35.4
Sex	
Female	36
Male	4
Race	
White	38
Nonwhite	2
Average customer age	41.6 years
Customer	
Men only	10
Women only	16
Woman and children	15
Man and woman	4
Man, woman, and children	5
Customers redeeming coupons	2
Customers carrying store ad	3
Customers asking store personnel for help	8
Customers buying special sale items	30

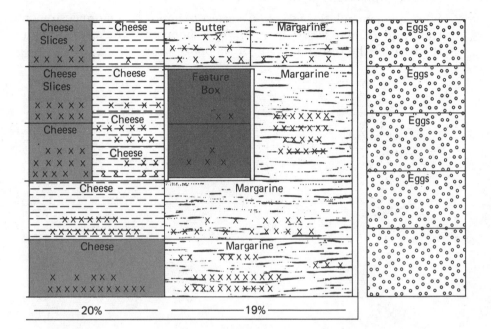

TABLE 20-3

Percentage of department sales: contribution analysis

Product category	Store 101 (%)	50-store study (%)	Chain X (southern) (%)
Fluid milk	38.58	36.3	35.94
Cheese, dip, yogurt, etc.	5.09	8.8	5.24
Butter, oleomargarine	10.22	15.4	13.65
Fixed-weight cheese	9.33	8.7	7.79
Random-weight cheese	5.65	6.6	6.75
Eggs	21.72	17.9	20.32
All other	9.41	6.3	10.31

Questions

1. Evaluate the Arcot merchandising program in light of how well you believe the program fulfills the firm's channel requirements and satisfies the retailers' expectations.

2. What recommendations would you make to improve the future sales efficiency of special promotion events, such as the biscuit-and-chicken promotions in 1979 and 1980?

3. What recommendations can you suggest to improve in-store customer traffic flow and to assure more uniform shopping of the dairy case on the basis of the research study of shopping patterns?

Case 21

THE HINDMAN STORES—THE ADDITION OF A CUSTOMER SERVICE

HINDMAN'S is a four-store chain of women's ready-to-wear establishments located in shopping centers in widely scattered areas of suburban Denver. The major management functions and the bookkeeping for the four stores are conducted in a central location. The parent store is incorporated while the other three are operated as a sole proprietorship.

The owner of the stores has an extensive retail background in the Denver area beginning with a single downtown store in the late 1950's. By the early 1960's, though the downtown location was successful, the owner recognized a trend away from the core city and toward the suburbs, so the original store was relocated in a shopping center. In the next four years the owner opened two additional stores, and in 1973 added a fourth operation, all in shopping centers.

The stores are designated 1, 2, 3, and 4 by the owner according to the order in which they were opened. The owner is concerned about store 4's declining sales.

Store 4 is a family-held corporation that began in operation in January 1973. The store carries a full line of women's ready-to-wear clothes with sales in the store divided among product lines as follows: 50 percent dresses and suits, 30 percent sportswear (slacks, blouses, swimwear, etc.), 10 percent coats, and 10 percent lingerie and sleepwear. The dresses in the store range from casual to cocktail styles and are priced from $15 to $75 with the most sales in the $20 to $40 category. Coats range in price from $20 to $60 with $40 being the median sale.

Adapted from Michael J. Etzel, "The Hindman Stores: The Addition of a Customer Service," *Marketing Management: Strategies & Cases*, ed. M. Wayne DeLozier and Arch G. Woodside (Columbus, Ohio: Charles E. Merrill Publishing Company, 1978), pp. 365–75. This case is taken from an actual situation. The names have been changed to protect confidentiality.

The sales staff of the store consists of the equivalent of five full-time people (four full-time and two part-time). One of the employees acts as store manager responsible for supervising store personnel, interviewing prospective employees, opening and closing the store, handling general housekeeping, and completing daily report sheets. The store also has the part-time services of a stockboy and a bookkeeper.

The store is located in a shopping center which has a total floor area in excess of 400,000 square feet and a parking area for 3,000 cars. There are forty-six merchants in the center, including three additional women's ready-to-wear outlets. Two of these are larger than store 4 and one is smaller. There also are two major department stores in the center with women's ready-to-wear departments larger than store 4. The center is approximately four miles from the downtown area. Three small (less than 100,000 square feet) shopping centers, which provide two additional competitors, are located within three miles. Store 4, situated on the edge of the shopping center without exposure to the main shopping mall, has 1,800 square feet of selling space with additional area for storage and dressing rooms.

TABLE 21-1

Store 4—total sales by month, 1973-1976

Month	1973	1974	1975	1976
January	$ 4,387	$ 4,611	$ 3,396	$ 3,800
February	4,412	5,501	5,171	4,387
March	9,245	7,755	9,138*	7,429
April	13,160	10,226	8,664	8,907
May	10,266	10,125	8,625	8,659
June	7,262	7,782	7,410	6,753
July	8,474	8,282	6,003	6,341
August	12,958	11,719	9,282	10,149
September	9,921	8,057	9,556	7,889
October	9,196	7,263	6,028	6,883
November	7,784	6,032	5,573	5,702
December	12,785	9,678	10,840	8,061
TOTAL	$109,850	$97,031	$89,686	$84,960

*Introduction of bank credit card.

Operating Data and Analysis—Store 4

Table 21-1 shows the total monthly sales figures for store 4 for the years 1973 through 1976. Total sales show a constant decline over the four-year period. A closer examination of the figures indicates that the high sales months characteristic of the first two years in April, May, August, and December declined considerably in 1975 and 1976. This is contrary to the industry trends in retail clothing for the period. A discussion with the owner produced a number of reasons for the annual decline. Three department stores in or near the shopping center in which store 4 is located remodeled and improved the departments that provide competition for the store. In addition, during this period three new specialty stores that produce direct competition were opened in the neighborhood. The owner also feels that the opening of a large department-discount store and a large grocery store nearby has considerably decreased the pedestrian traffic in the center. A final problem is a large shopping center, which opened in 1975, that draws from part of the same market area as store 4's shopping center. Though all of these factors have occurred, the owner concedes that part of the decline also may be due to managerial error, specifically the failure to develop a significant differential advantage. In hopes of rectifying the problem of declining sales the owner was among the first merchants in the area to adopt a bank credit card.

Credit Operations in the Hindman Stores

Credit programs

Each of the stores offered internally financed credit since starting in business. The internal credit program is relatively standard and includes two types of accounts: thirty-day accounts and ninety-day extended-payment accounts. The thirty-day accounts require no down payment with full payment due on or before the end of the month following the purchase. If full payment is not made within this time period, the account becomes delinquent and a 1.5 percent monthly service charge is added to the balance.

The second type of account is a ninety-day extended payment account. Under this plan the customer pays one fourth of the total amount of the purchase price at the time of the sale. The remaining balance is due in one-third installments on the first day of each month of the three months following the purchase. A charge of 1.5 percent a month is made on the unpaid balance of all ninety-day accounts.

Credit applications

For customers who desire credit, the stores provide a standard credit application, requiring such information as home ownership, employment, personal references, credit references, and bank accounts. All applications are reviewed by the owner who decides if further investigation is necessary before ruling on the request. Often the owner contacts personal and/or credit references by phone to collect all the available pertinent information before ruling on the account and setting the credit limit. The normal limit on ordinary accounts is a maximum balance of 125 dollars outstanding at any time. Although this is an unwritten rule, accounts are handled on a more personal basis, with considerable flexibility in this figure.

The owner does not make use of a credit bureau in checking applications because he feels an account can be personally processed for less than the ninety cents charged by the credit bureau. The owner also feels that personal consideration of the applications is a special service that gives him the opportunity to consider unusual circumstances that might be ignored in an impersonal credit bureau check.

Handling credit sales

At the time of every cash or credit sale, a two-copy sales slip is completed. The slip provides information on the item purchased, the amount of the sale, the name of the customer (for credit sales), and the amount received from the customer. At the end of the day, the information from the accumulated sales slips is transferred to a daily report sheet, which, together with the sales slips, is sent to the bookkeeper. On receiving the package, the bookkeeper verifies the accuracy of the report sheet, posts credit sales to the appropriate ledger cards and credit statements, and prepares the bank deposit.

At the present time, the stores have approximately 2,445 accounts open-to-buy. However, the account file is not regularly purged, and a number of these accounts are no longer active. The management of the stores has made no effort to segregate active from inactive accounts or to develop any measure of the amount of activity in each account. According to the owner, the primary value of such an activity is as a source for direct mail lists. However, he feels the cost of direct mail advertising eliminates it as a promotional tool.

Bank Credit Card Operations

Reasons for adopting the bank plan

According to the owner, the principal reason for adopting the credit plan was to attract additional sales. Another reason for adding the plan is the convenience it provides customers. The owner commented that the bank credit card gives the consumers the opportunity to shop without carrying cash, thus making unplanned purchases easier and therefore more frequent. A final rationale for accepting the credit card is that other stores provide it. In order to be competitive, the store owner feels a complete package of service must be offered to consumers, which includes accepting bank credit cards.

The major disadvantage of the credit card, as seen by the owner, is that its use dilutes the loyalty of the credit buyer toward the store. He commented, "Credit customers have a habit of buying where they have an account due to either better service, recognition, or special service they receive." This objection has been overcome by mentally or intuitively weighing the trade-off between increases in potential customers and sales provided by the credit card against dilution of store loyalty produced by the general acceptability of the card.

Asked how much the plan might dilute store loyalty, the owner stated

I would guess that our account openings may be reduced by 25 percent (because of the bank plan), but the bank credit card brought us additional business. It made it easier for people to shop on a charge plan. Of course, it is impossible to determine how many or how few of the bank credit card customers would open accounts or pay cash if we didn't accept it.

Though the store owner contends that no special effort has been made to encourage the use of credit, employees are given a cash incentive for each credit application taken. Possibly the owner's feelings are revealed in the statement "credit customers are better than cash customers, in a sense, because psychologically they are freer to spend, whether they know it or not."

Promotion of credit

Media promotion of the stores' credit plans is limited to a one-line statement in printed advertisements stating that credit is available. There also is a sign in each of the store's dressing rooms to the same effect. The most expensive promotion is the bonus paid to employees for each completed credit application they secure.

Promotion of the bank plan is equally limited. The only visible notice of the bank plan is the standard window decale advertising the credit card's acceptability in the stores.

The stores do not employ the seasonal promotions—mobiles and stand-up signs—provided by the bank. An employee explained that these are not viewed by the management as merchandising aids but as unnecessary clutter that distracts from the display of clothing.

Handling bank plan sales

The stores do not submit credit sales slips to the bank daily in the manner envisoned by the plan's promoters. Instead of frequently mailing the sales slips to the bank to receive cash for sales, one deposit is made each month. The owner offers two reasons for doing this. First, he does not feel a need for the working capital the bank plan sales could provide since he currently receives the maximum discount on merchandise purchases without resorting to these funds. Secondly, the owner feels that a daily or even weekly submission of credit sales slips would take too much time for the volume of sales involved. Rather than take some fraction of every day to prepare the deposit, he feels it is more efficient to prepare and submit all of the month's bank credit card transactions at once.

Table 21-2 presents total sales divided into cash, internal credit, and bank plan sales. The table indicates that a decline in sales was experienced in both cash and internal credit sales. However, when bank credit card sales are added to internal credit sales, an element of stability appears. In 1975, total credit sales became $32,000, and in 1976, $30,078; a relationship clearly is shown in Table 21-3.

TABLE 21-2

Store 4—cash sales, internal credit sales, and bank plan sales by month, 1973-1976

Month	1973 Cash Sales	1973 Internal Credit Sales	1974 Cash Sales	1974 Internal Credit Sales	1975 Cash Sales	1975 Internal Credit Sales	1975 Bank Plan Sales	1976 Cash Sales	1976 Internal Credit Sales	1976 Bank Plan Sales
January	$ 2,867	$ 1,520	$ 2,813	$ 1,798	$ 1,735	$ 1,661	—	$ 2,364	$ 1,030	$ 406
February	2,606	1,806	3,034	2,467	2,504	2,667	—	2,675	1,293	419
March	6,320	2,925	4,906	2,838	5,965	3,056*	$ 117	4,503	2,365	561
April	9,418	3,742	6,439	3,787	5,600	2,835	229	6,002	2,760	145
May	7,568	2,698	6,618	3,507	6,252	2,210	163	5,441	2,753	465
June	5,599	1,663	5,409	2,373	5,230	1,945	235	4,903	1,167	683
July	5,603	2,871	5,727	2,555	4,093	1,769	141	4,398	1,567	376
August	8,977	3,981	7,599	4,120	5,834	2,999	449	6,303	3,500	346
September	7,094	2,872	4,934	3,123	6,078	2,767	711	5,168	1,907	814
October	6,527	2,669	4,899	2,364	3,771	1,914	343	3,835	2,772	276
November	6,205	1,579	4,553	1,479	3,740	1,349	484	3,737	1,176	789
December	8,415	4,370	6,381	3,297	6,884	3,264	692	5,554	1,861	646
TOTAL	$77,199	$32,696	$63,313	$33,708	$57,686	$28,436	$3,564	$54,883	$24,151	$5,927

*Introduction of bank credit card

188

TABLE 21-3 ▰▰▰▰▰▰▰▰▰▰▰▰▰▰▰▰▰▰▰▰▰▰▰▰▰▰

Store 4—cash and credit sales ratios by year, 1973-1976

Year	Cash Sales / Total Sales	Internal Credit Sales / Total Sales	Total Credit Sales* / Total Sales
1973	70.23%	29.77%	29.77%
1974	65.26	34.74	34.74
1975	64.32	31.71	35.68
1976	64.56	28.43	35.43

*Total credit includes bank credit card sales.

TABLE 21-4 ▰▰▰▰▰▰▰▰▰▰▰▰▰▰▰▰▰▰▰▰▰▰▰▰▰▰

Store 4—number of bank credit plan sales, sales volume, average amount of each sale, and the discount income to the bank, by month, 1975-1976

Year/ Month	Number of Sales	Dollar Volume of Sales	Average Sales	Discount Income to Bank
1975				
March	5	$ 117	$23.31	$ 5.85
April	9	229	25.43	11.40
May	8	163	20.35	8.10
June	14	235	16.80	11.80
July	10	141	14.13	7.10
August	28	449	16.02	22.40
September	29	711	24.53	35.55
October	12	343	28.61	17.15
November	19	484	25.45	24.10
December	30	692	23.08	34.55
TOTAL	164	$3,564	$21.77	$178.00
1976				
January	20	$ 406	$20.31	$ 20.30
February	20	419	20.95	20.95
March	27	561	20.77	28.00
April	10	145	14.49	7.25
May	30	465	15.52	23.25
June	35	683	19.51	34.15
July	19	376	19.78	18.80
August	20	346	16.29	17.25
September	38	814	21.43	40.70
October	9	276	30.68	13.80
November	27	789	29.21	39.45
December	34	646	19.01	32.25
TOTAL	289	$5,926	$20.66	$296.15

Table 21-3 shows that from 1973 to 1974, prior to the adoption of the bank credit card, internal credit sales increased as a proportion of total sales. However, from 1974 to 1975 and 1975 to 1976, internal credit sales showed a decline while total credit sales, including the bank credit card sales, continued to increase. A breakdown of bank credit card sales for store 4 is shown in Table 21-4 by month since the inception of the plan.

Table 21-5 brings together the sales activity of 1975 and 1976 in order to compare bank plan sales with other sales figures. Bank plan sales are a significant portion of total sales in both years, rising 2.34 percent in 1976 to total 6.98 percent of total sales in that year.

TABLE 21-5

Store 4—bank credit plan sales as a percentage of total sales, cash sales, total credit sales and internal credit sales by year, 1975-1976

Year	$\dfrac{\text{BCP Sales}}{\text{Total Sales}}$	$\dfrac{\text{BCP Sales}}{\text{Cash Sales}}$	$\dfrac{\text{BCP Sales}}{\text{Internal Sales}}$	$\dfrac{\text{BCP Sales}}{\text{Total Credit}}$
1975*	4.64%	6.50%	14.76%	12.86%
1976	6.98	10.81	24.54	19.71

*The percentages of 1975 are calculated using the ten months of data that correspond to the presence of the bank plan.

Table 21-6 portrays the role the bank plan has played in the sales decline experienced by store 4. Finally, when bank plan sales are added to internal credit sales, the decline in total credit sales is much more consistent with the changes in total sales and cash sales. Table 21-7 shows the decline in sales from 1975 to 1976 with bank plan sales included and excluded. Thus, if one considers the change in total sales from 1975 to 1976 including bank plan sales, which is what actually occurred, the decline is 5.27 percent. On the other hand, if bank plan sales are deleted from both years, total sales show a decline of 8.23 percent. It is particularly interesting to note the accentuation of the decline in credit sales—from 6.01 percent to 15.07 percent—when bank plan sales are excluded.

Table 21-8 presents a breakdown of returns on bank plan sales showing the number of returns, the amount of returns, and the average return on a monthly basis. Data on internal credit sales returns are not available for comparison. However, Table 21-9 compares bank plan returns with bank plan sales.

In addition to its impact on sales, the cost of the bank credit plan must be considered. Table 21-10 is the result of an analysis of internal credit costs. The comparable costs for bank credit card sales including operating costs and the discount paid to the bank is 5.4 percent of bank credit card sales.

Hindman is faced with a decision about the new credit service. He has several options including dropping the bank credit card completely, adding it to the service package at his other stores, and/or attempting to replace internal credit with the bank plan.

TABLE 21-6

Store 4—yearly percentage change in total sales, cash sales, internal credit sales, total credit sales, and bank plan sales, 1973-76

Year	Total Sales	Cash Sales	Internal Credit Sales	Total* Credit Sales	Bank Plan Sales
1973-74	- 11.66%	- 17.91%	+ 3.10%	+3.10%	—
1974-75	- 7.65	- 8.89	- 15.64	-5.07	—
1975-76	- 5.27	- 4.92	- 15.07	-6.01	+66.30%
TOTAL	-24.58	-31.72	-27.61	-7.98	—

*Total credit includes bank credit plan sales.

TABLE 21-7

Store 4—change in total sales and credit sales from 1975 to 1976 when bank credit plan sales are included and excluded

Year	Total Sales	Cash Sales	Credit Sales	Bank Credit Plan Sales
1975				
with credit card	$89,686	$57,686	$32,000	
without credit card	86,122	57,686	28,436	$3,564
1976				
with credit card	$84,961	$54,858	$30,078	
without credit card	79,034	54,848	24,151	$5,927
Change 1975 to 1976				
with credit card	-5.27%	-4.92%	- 6.01%	
without credit card	-8.23	-4.92	-15.07	

TABLE 21-8 ▬▬▬▬▬▬▬▬▬▬▬▬▬▬▬▬▬▬▬▬▬▬▬▬▬▬▬

Store 4—number of bank credit plan sales returns, amount of returns, and average amount of returns by month, 1975-1976

Year/ Month	Number of Returns	Amount of Returns	Average Return
1975			
March	—	—	—
April	—	—	—
May	—	—	—
June	3	$ 61.95	$20.65
July	1	9.45	9.45
August	—	—	—
September	—	—	—
October	1	21.52	21.52
November	1	47.25	47.25
December	—	—	—
TOTAL	6	$140.17	$23.36
1976			
January	—	—	—
February	—	—	—
March	1	$ 24.15	$24.15
April	1	18.90	18.90
May	—	—	—
June	—	—	—
July	—	—	—
August	—	—	—
September	3	75.60	25.20
October	—	—	—
November	5	57.75	11.55
December	—	—	—
TOTAL	10	$176.40	$17.64

TABLE 21-9 ▬▬▬▬▬▬▬▬▬▬▬▬▬▬▬▬▬▬▬▬▬▬▬▬▬▬▬

Store 4—the number and amount of bank plan sales returns as a percentage of the number and volume of bank plan sales, 1975-1976

	1975	1976
Number of Sales	164	289
Number of Returns	6	10
# Returns/# Sales	3.66%	3.46%
Amount of Sales	$3,564	$5,927
Amount of Returns	$140	$176
Amount Returns/Amount Sales	3.93%	2.97%

TABLE 21-10 ══

Store 4—direct cost of offering internal credit during 1976

Credit Expenses

1. Solicitation of new accounts	$	21.00
2. Checking credit applications		75.18
3. Preparation and issuance of identification cards		253.50
4. Preparation and handling of monthly statements		257.28
5. Receiving correspondence from customers		341.55
6. Contacting and tracing delinquent accounts		190.80
7. Cost of capital invested in accounts receivable (calculated at 7.0%)		223.65
8. Bad debt expense		798.08
TOTAL COST OF CREDIT		$2,161.04

Credit Income

9. Income from services charges	− 222.75
NET COST OF CREDIT	$1,938.29
Total credit sales during 1976	$24,151.00

Direct cost of internal credit as a percentage of internal credit sales at a cost of capital of

7%	8.02%
9	8.29
12	8.69
12	9.87

Discussion Questions

1. Based on the data provided, does the bank credit card plan produce significant benefits for Hindman? Why or why not?

2. The promoters of the bank credit card claim that the plans will
   a) reduce management time in credit
   b) provide increased working capital
   c) offer protection from bad debt losses
   d) result in a lower cost of doing credit business
   e) increase sales
   Has Hindman experienced these benefits?

3. Would you consider the addition of the bank credit card in 1975 a potentially significant differential advantage?

4. What do you recommend Hindman do with the bank credit card plan and why?

Case 22

THE VITESSE CYCLE SHOP—ALTERING THE PRODUCT MIX

THE VITESSE CYCLE SHOP, which opened in Normal, Illinois, on May 15, 1975, focuses primarily on selling and servicing ten-speed bicycles. Although it was originally an offspring of Vitesse, Inc. (located in Madison, Wisconsin), five investors recently bought Vitesse from the parent company. Up to this point, the Madison store had maintained tight control over the Normal store and had assumed that what worked in Madison would work in Normal. The current manager, now a part owner, expressed displeasure at the tight control from Madison. However, the issue of autonomy was resolved when the store was bought; now the store owners have complete discretion concerning their marketing strategies, which allows them to get a fresh start and market the products that match the market's needs.

The Vitesse shop sells predominantly new ten-speed bicycles, although a variety of used bikes are also available. The product mix also consists of the services offered including bicycle repairs. Vitesse's product mix is narrow. The store sells mainly ten-speed bikes and until recently carried only one brand, Stella, a prestige bicycle made in France. For this season the store added two more brands to its line—Viscount, an English bike, and Sekai, a Japanese bike. Viscounts are advertised nationally which should help stimulate brand recognition.

The Viscounts and Sekais help to complement the current product line and add much-needed depth. Vitesse also carries a selection of used bikes (trade-ins) to appeal to customers seeking economical, basic transportation. The store offers bicycle accessories and repair services for all types of bikes. Bicycles bought at Vitesse are repaired at a discount.

To add more depth to the product mix, the shop manager has expressed a desire to acquire two or three more brands, bringing the total to five or six

Source: William M. Pride and O.C. Ferrell, *Marketing—Basic Concepts and Decisions*, 2nd ed. (Boston: Houghton Mifflin Company, 1980), pp. 248–49. Reprinted by permission of Houghton Mifflin Company.

brands. Additional brands would include three- and five-speed bicycles, along with some children's bikes. The manager believes that a multisegment approach is a step toward meeting all customers' needs and increasing the store's sales volume by competing with department stores and discounters.

The manager is negotiating with Schwinn for a dealership, but there is already a local Schwinn dealership in the area. Another alternative is to obtain the Motobecane bike line. This seems to be an ideal choice because of the respectable reputation and brand recognition it offers. Motobecane carries a line of three- and five-speed bicycles. This would help appeal to the groups that may not want or need a ten-speed bike, and at the same time the store's image of quality would be maintained or upgraded. Raleigh was also a possible choice. A Raleigh dealership certainly would benefit Vitesse, because Raleigh is a recognized brand on the American market and because it also offers a line of three- and five-speed bicycles as well as a full line of children's bikes.

At a meeting of Vitesse owners, the following criteria were established for expanding the product mix:

1. The new product mix should stabilize seasonal variations in demand. The peak demand now is in the spring and summer.
2. The new product mix should support the current store image, or a new store image should stress quality products and service.
3. New product lines should attract new market segments.

With these criteria available, there is still some doubt about the direction Vitesse should take in expanding its product mix. There have been suggestions that nonbicycle products are needed to stabilize seasonal demand. Sales and profits need to be increased so that owners can receive an adequate return on their investment.

Questions

1. The most inexpensive new bicycle in the current product mix is a $149 Sekai model. What effect will children's bikes in the $60 to $80 price range have on the store image?

2. Can or should Vitesse compete with discount stores that offer no repair services and sell ten-speed bikes for $70?

3. What do you feel should be done now to the existing product mix to increase sales and profits?

Case 23

ABERCROMBIE AND FITCH

ABERCROMBIE AND FITCH was a relatively high-priced sporting goods and leisure time store. It catered for six decades to presidents and princes as well as to run-of-the-millionaire sportsmen.

David T. Abercrombie made camping goods in a small factory in lower Manhattan and was content to sell to trappers, railroad surveyors, prospectors, and others who worked out-of-doors. However, in 1892, he met Ezra Fitch, a successful but bored lawyer. They became partners and built a store on Broadway where Fitch set out to sell Abercrombie's goods to the public in general and well-heeled sportsmen in particular. After many disagreements over just whom the store should be selling to—Abercrombie's fur trappers or Fitch's monied leisure class—the two, unable to reconcile their positions, parted company, with Abercrombie quitting the business in 1907.

Fitch retired in 1928, but A&F's fame as a marketer of sporting goods to the rich and famous grew steadily. The store outfitted Theodore Roosevelt for safaris, Admiral Richard E. Byrd for his expedition to Antarctica, fisherman Herbert Hoover, golfers Woodrow Wilson and Dwight Eisenhower, and all-around woodsman and outdoorsman, author Ernest Hemingway. Abercrombie and Fitch's stock of firearms and tackle equipment was among the world's largest and finest and its aloof sales staff was made up of technical experts in sporting goods. Their Manhattan store on Madison Avenue was a showcase of such exotic items as $300 miniature antique cannons; $1,200 Yukon dog sleds, and portable store furnaces for heating cabins on yachts. The store at one time even sold chain-mail suits to protect explorers from Indian arrows in South America.

However, during the early 1970s the company began to witness hard times. Losses for the nine-store chain increased steadily over the past six years—from $540,000 on sales of $25.4 million in 1970 to a frightful $1.7

Source: Rom J. Markin, *Marketing* (New York: John Wiley & Sons, 1979, pp. 396–97. Reprinted by permission of John Wiley & Sons.

million in 1976. By late 1976, there was talk of bankruptcy and maybe even closure. To reassure its nervous bankers, Abercrombie's unpaid chairman, Harry G. Haskell, a wealthy sportsman himself and Abecrombie's largest stockholder, brought in an outside manager-consultant to save and revive the firm. The consultant, British-born retailing expert Geoffrey Swaebe, had made his reputation running the Los Angeles May Company, a part of the big St. Louis-based department store chain. He left the May Company in 1972 to freelance his skills among ailing companies. Swaebe, who was being paid $1,000 a day plus expenses, is noted for his ability to restructure management personnel. He planned to extend A&F's appeal beyond the well-heeled sportsmen. Recent managers also tried to do essentially the same things but their efforts mostly succeeded in driving up costs and deepening Abercrombie's debt. The company paid out more than $1 million in interest on loans in 1975.

As participant sports became more and more popular in the United States in the 1950s, Abercrombie opened branches in San Francisco; Troy, Michigan; and Colorado Springs, and it began dealing more in fashion. Other high-priced stores such as Tiffany successfully made the difficult transition to a broader market by combining friendliness with lower-priced items, but A&F apparently did not move far or fast enough. Some affluent but not wealthy customers complained that A&F reminded them of a "stuffy club" which caters to wealthy Midwestern physicians who take four weeks off to shoot ducks in Wyoming or hunt sheep in the Brooks Range of Alaska. Young, affluent skiers, backpackers, and tennis players came into A&F's to admire its conservative, well-stocked departments, but too many of these seemed to buy their gear at cheaper places like Korvette's, Two Guys Stores, and other discount operations catering to the outdoor leisure time market.

Swaebe's efforts unfortunately failed and early in 1978, the staid old firm closed its doors.

Questions

1. Do you believe that the social-economic environment is no longer conducive to a store like Abercrombie & Fitch? Why or why not?

2. What would you have done to change the merchandising strategy of Abercrombie & Fitch?

3. One of the proposals made to save Abercrombie & Fitch was to promote its catalog and mail order sales. Would high-quality, relatively expensive sporting goods items and sporting fashion wear lend themselves to mail order selling? Why or why not?

PART **9**

Retail Price
Management

Case 24

GISTNER FUNERAL HOME

PHIL GISTNER had just returned from the annual convention of his state's association of funeral directors and was reviewing some of his notes from the management sessions:

Death is not as commonplace as it once was. Millions of Americans have never experienced the loss, by death, of someone close to them. Millions of Americans have never been to a funeral, or have even seen a funeral procession, except one which was televised. Millions of Americans have never seen a dead body except on TV, in a movie, on a battlefield, or on a highway. Even where people have been directly involved in the arrangements of a funeral service there is often confusion or doubt about the role of the funeral director and the cost for his services.

Often the place of the casket in the overall funeral service is unclear or undefined. Historically, the funeral director has been a provider of goods and some services. A casket was purchased and all other services provided "free." Today, on the average, the merchandise amounts to only about 20 percent of the total cost of a funeral service.

The casket is not the funeral service, nor is the funeral service the casket. The failure of some funeral directors to accept this fact and explain it to those they serve is in some ways responsible for much of the concern over funeral practices and prices today.

Pricing structures for funeral services at the Gistner Funeral Home had always been based upon a multiple times the wholesale cost of the casket, and Phil was wondering if maybe the time had come to change to a different method of pricing. He was concerned, though, about how customers, the other funeral homes in the area, and his father would react to any such changes.

Source: *Contemporary Cases in Marketing*, 2nd ed., pp. 188–197, by W. Wayne Talarzyk. Copyright © 1979 by The Dryden Press, a division of Holt, Rinehart and Winston, Inc. Reprinted by permission of Holt, Rinehart and Winston.

Background Information

The Gistner Funeral Home was founded in 1906 by George Gistner, Sr., in a small town on the West Coast. George Sr. ran the business with the help of his wife and son until his death in 1947. At that time the funeral home was conducting an average of 75 funeral services a year. Phil joined his father, George Jr., in the operation of business in 1965, at which time the firm was doing about 100 services per year.

Two other funeral homes were operating in the area, one about the same size as Gistner and the other conducting an average of 60 services a year. Both of these homes utilized a pricing system similar to Gistner's, with the price of a funeral service based upon a multiple of the funeral home's cost for the casket. Prices were difficult to compare, since each funeral home represented several different manufacturers of caskets and carried a wide range of casket styles and qualities. Few customers made any attempt to check a competitor's price due to the nature and timing of the purchase decision.

Financial Operations for 1977[1]

In 1977, Gistner Funeral Home conducted 160 services at an average price of $1,210. The average wholesale cost of merchandise sold was $330, broken down into $220 for the casket and $110 for the vault. The costs of the casket and vault were multiplied by an average of 4.5 and 2.0 respectively, to arrive at the selling price. Average variable expenses per funeral were $60. Other relevant financial information for 1977 included: total fixed expenses, $94,000; inventory, $8,000; accounts receivable, $20,000; and fixed assets at market value, $130,000. These figures were relatively consistent with those of the preceding three years. Average national operating expenses for funeral firms are shown in percentages in Exhibit 24-1.

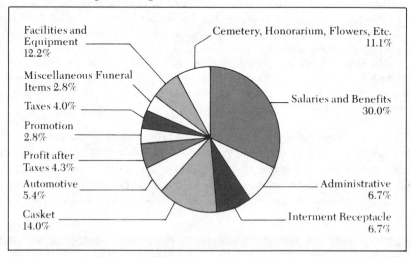

EXHIBIT 24-1

Component breakdown of the funeral director's operations

Source: "A Factual Guide to Funeral Costs," published in the public interest by The Ohio Funeral Directors Association.

Historical Development of Pricing[2]

The pricing policies of the typical funeral firm evolved by historical accident. Funeral directors in the United States originally were casket builders and sellers. Frequently, they were furniture dealers or cabinet makers who began to sell caskets because of their carpentry skills. By 1850, some casket builders had begun to add some services, such as restorative art and livery. Basically, though, they were sellers of caskets until around 1900, when the modern concept of the funeral director became fairly well developed. The funeral director was still judged, however, by the quality of caskets he sold and the breadth of casket selections he offered.

The pricing system used by early funeral directors was obtained by taking three times the cost of the casket. One-third was for the cost of the casket, one-third for the extra services offered by the funeral director, and one-third for overhead and profit. Although the multiplier has changed, even today funeral directors frequently use a multiple pricing system.

Changing Role of the Funeral Director

In the earlier part of this century, when the church, the family, and the neighborhood were all tightly knit groups, they helped the surviving family members adjust to changes in their lives and relationships brought about by a death. All that was required of funeral directors was an adequate casket and a few simple arrangements.

Today, funeral directors serve the living, and their professional reputation rests upon the ability to assist the survivors in this transition process. They are counselors upon whom the survivor must rely.

To operate successfully within the changing environment, a funeral director must provide comfortable facilities, develop sound technical skill for the restorative process and sanitary control, have legal know-how to cut through government and insurance red tape, and possess the psychological knowledge to instill confidence in his judgment during the adjustment process.

Alternative Pricing Methods

In reviewing alternative pricing systems, Phil compiled the following information on the three widely used methods.[3]

Unit pricing

In unit pricing, one price covers all the costs of the funeral except cash advances and optional extras. This method, the most widely used at the present time, is frequently based upon some multiple times the funeral director's cost of the casket. Some funeral homes vary the value of the multiple, using a higher multiple for lower cost caskets than for more expensive ones.

Other funeral directors actually compute their overhead structure and add this to a reasonable markup on a given casket to arrive at the total price unit. The unit price usually includes such items and services as:

1. removal of remains to mortuary.
2. complete preparation and dressing of remains.
3. securing of necessary certificates and permits.
4. use of the mortuary staff.
5. assistance of the mortuary staff.
6. transportation of the remains to the cemetery.
7. fixed amount of additional transportation to cemetery.
8. acknowledgment cards and memorial register.
9. casket selection.

Complete itemized pricing

Complete itemized pricing goes to the other extreme, adding a separate price for each element of the funeral service. Certain states have passed legislation requiring all funeral homes to use this pricing method, thinking that if consumers know what they are paying for, they will be better able to select exactly what they need and want.

This system provides a separate price for each of the following:

1. removal of remains.
2. embalming.
3. dressing, casketing, and cosmetizing.
4. use of chapel.
5. use of other mortuary facilities and equipment.
6. staff assistance.
7. funeral coach.
8. additional vehicles.
9. casket.
10. memorial register.
11. acknowledgment cards.

The list then continues with all other items that are considered extras in other pricing methods.

Professional pricing

The professional pricing system, sometimes called the functional approach, involves charging a separate fee for the professional services of the funeral director rather than just including them with the merchandise he or she sells. Funeral directors charge for their services in the same manner as doctors or lawyers. The casket is then sold separately with a normal markup.

Two to five separate categories may be used with this method. Together, they cover the cost of the funeral except any cash advances or optional extras. Various categories that may be used in different combination are:

1. professional services.
2. preparation for burial.
3. use of facilities and equipment.
4. motor vehicles.
5. cost of the casket.

Possible Need for Change

Based on a national sample of 1,060 respondents, a recent marketing research study found that the majority of consumers would prefer to have more information concerning funeral prices.[4] When offered a choice of the three common methods of pricing funerals, 33.3 percent stated a preference for unit pricing, 16.5 percent preferred professional pricing, and 50.2 percent voiced a preference for itemized pricing. These responses seem consistent with current consumer concepts which have led to public demand for more information on which consumers can make decisions.

In August 1975, the Federal Trade Commission issued a series of proposed rules for the funeral industry, including a specific approach to price disclosures. While it may be some time before a final decision is made regarding the rules proposed by the federal government, certain states have already enacted legislation which requires funeral directors to disclose more price information in their dealings with consumers.

The specific language of the FTC proposal regarding the price list is as follows:

> In connection with the sale or offering for sale of funeral services and/or merchandise to the public, in or affecting commerce as "commerce" is defined in the Federal Trade Commission Act, it is an unfair or deceptive act or practice for any funeral service industry member: To fail to furnish to each customer who inquires in person about the arrangement, purchase, and/or prices of funeral goods or services, prior to any agreement on such arrangement or selection by the customer or to any customer who by telephone or letter requests written price information, a printed or typewritten price list, which the customer may retain, containing the prices (either the retail charge or the price per hour, mile, or other unit of computation) for at least each of the following items:
>
>   (i) Transfer of remains to funeral home.
> (ii) Embalming.
> (iii) Use of facilities for viewing.
> (iv) Use of facilities for funeral service.
>   (v) Casket (a notation that a separate casket price list will be provided before any sales presentation for caskets is made).
> (vi) Hearse.
> (vii) Limousine.
> (viii) Services of funeral director and staff.
> (ix) Outer interment receptacles (if outer interment receptacles are sold, a notation that a separate outer interment receptacle price list will be provided before any sales presentation for such items is made).[5]

Questions

1. What is the economic logic behind the unit pricing system?

2. What are the basic advantages and disadvantages of each pricing system?

3. Do you think customers really understand the pricing systems of funeral homes?

4. How would you go about determining the price charged for a director's professional services and facilities?

5. What are the possible advantages to Gistner in switching to a professional pricing system?

Endnotes

1. The figures in this section have been simplified and adjusted somewhat for ease of calculation and analysis and are, therefore, not representative for the typical funeral home.

2. For a detailed review of the funeral service field, see Roger D. Blackwell, "Price Levels of Funerals: An Analysis of the Effects of Entry Regulation in a Differentiated Oligopoly," unpublished Ph.D. dissertation, Northwestern University, 1966.

3. Portions of these descriptions are adapted from a study done by the Batesville Casket Company entitled "Funeral Directors' Pricing Methods, a Comprehensive National Survey," 1968.

4. From Roger D. Blackwell and W. Wayne Talarzyk, *American Attitudes Toward Death and Funeral Service* (Evanston, IL: The Casket Manufacturers Association, 1974).

5. Extracted from the *Federal Register,* Vol. 40, No. 169, Friday, August 29, 1975, p. 39903.

Case 25

DUDE'S DUDS — PRICING A NEW PRODUCT LINE

DUDE'S DUDS is a large, well-known clothing store chain with more than 400 retail outlets located throughout the United States and Canada. Appealing to the teenage and young adult consumer, the success enjoyed by Dude's Duds is based largely on the firm's ability to market fadish and fashionable merchandise at reasonable and competitive prices. While Dude's Duds stocks a limited selection of national manufacturer's brands (e.g., Levi's and Haggar) to enhance its store image and to generate consumer traffic, the vast majority of each outlet's merchandise consists of the firm's own private retailer brands. To ensure a reliable source of supply for their private labels, Dude's Duds purchased the Fashion-Plus Clothing Company (FPCC) in 1968. At the time of the takeover, FPCC was a well-established national manufacturer of high quality, fashionable apparel. FPCC's product mix consisted of a wide line of both men's and women's wearing apparel.

The recent increase in the popularity and acceptance of western wearing apparel by many diverse consumer groups throughout all market areas of the country prompted Ralph West, the General Merchandise Manager for Dude's Duds, to investigate the possibility of adding a new line of men's western style shirts. Preliminary results of that investigation led Ralph to conclude that such a line would appeal to the consumer group the firm identified as "the swingers"—a consumer market segment that wants fadish and stylish clothing of good quality but whose discretionary income requires certain economic considerations (i.e., affordable prices). As far as Ralph is concerned, the addition of a new line of men's western shirts makes good merchandising sense. However, it will be up to the production people at Fashion-Plus to determine whether the new line is feasible given the price, cost, and profit constraints under which they must produce the product.

While Fashion-Plus is a wholly-owned subsidiary of Dude's Duds, Inc., FPCC's management is responsible for making all production decisions.

This case was prepared by Jon M. Hawes, The University of Akron.

Presently under consideration is Ralph's request for a new line of western shirts. To determine the feasibility of new product lines, Bill Morris (Manager for New Product Development) must collect the necessary information to make a cost and break-even analysis, to project expected profits, and to recommend a suggested retail price as well as a manufacturer's price (the price that Fashion-Plus should charge Dude's Duds). Having spent the last two weeks collecting data, Bill feels he now has the necessary information to make the required evaluations of the new western shirt project. Before proceeding with his analysis, Bill reviews the following information he has collected:

1. Several competitors have introduced similar lines of men's western shirts. Market research indicates that these lines are selling at a brisk pace at competitive retail stores for the following prices:

Retail Selling Prices	Number of Times Observed
$14.00	2
15.00	7
16.00	5
17.00	3

2. Dude's Duds will apply a 40 percent initial mark-up on the retail selling price of shirts.
3. Production costs for the new shirt are estimated to be

Cloth	$2.20 per shirt
Buttons	.05 per shirt
Thread	.05 per shirt
Direct labor	20 minutes per shirt
Shipping weight	2 pounds per packaged shirt

4. Basic marketing costs for introducing the new line of shirts are estimated to be $300,000 the first year if a penetration pricing policy is used or $340,000 if a skimming pricing policy is employed.
5. Being a large company, FPCC has fifteen production facilities strategically located throughout the USA. Last year, the average round trip distance from FPCC production facilities to Dude's Duds outlets was 225 miles. Current plans are to produce the new line of shirts at each of FPCC's production facilities.
6. An examination of FPCC's annual report reveals the following information:

Managerial salaries	$ 1,500,000
Rent and utilities expense	1,200,000
Transportation costs (1,250,000 miles)	750,000
Depreciation on plant and equipment	1,300,000

Other overhead	2,000,000
Direct labor costs (2,000,000 hours)	8,000,000
Total company sales	45,000,000
Average order size	1,000 pounds

7. The Kurt Behrens Market Research Corporation was hired to develop a sales forecast for the new line of western shirts. Their research findings estimate that if a skimming pricing policy were used, Dude's Duds could expect to sell approximately 110,000 to 130,000 shirts. Under a penetration-type pricing policy, the Behrens organization estimates a unit sales volume of approximately 130,000 to 150,000 shirts.

The Problem

Assume that Bill Morris was unexpectedly called out of town and he has asked you to prepare the analysis and written report on the feasibility of the project and then to make a recommendation for the pricing strategy he should use. At a minimum, your analysis should include a cost analysis (variable cost per shirt, fixed cost allocation for the line, and total cost per shirt), a break-even analysis in units and dollars, a determination of the manufacturer's price and suggested retail price, and a statement as to expected profit the company can derive from the new line.

Case 26
EXECUTIVE INN, INC.

EARLY IN 1979, Mr. Charles Rabb, manager of the Executive Inn, had just completed reading a new book on pricing. As he leaned back in his chair, he pondered on some pricing principles that the book's author had expounded. To be sure that he had the principles correctly in his mind, he reopened the book and reread the principles:

The correct pricing of a product line should follow three principles:

1. Each product should be priced correctly in relation to all other products in the line. Specifically, perceptively noticeable differences in the products should be equivalent to perceived value differences.
2. The highest and lowest price in the product line have a special complementary relation to other products in the line and should be priced so as to facilitate desired buyer perceptions.
3. Price differentials between products in the product line should get wider as price increases over the product line. This principle follows the behavioral finding that price perception follows a logarithmic scale rather than an arithmetic or linear scale.[1]

Mr. Rabb realized that his director of marketing and sales had completed a study of room sales several weeks ago and he asked his secretary to get a copy of the report for him to read that evening.

History of the Hotel

The Executive Inn is a 900-room hotel located in a major city in the southeastern United States. The hotel first opened for business in the spring

Adapted from Kent B. Monroe, "Executive Inn, Inc.," *Marketing Management: Strategies & Cases*, ed. M. Wayne DeLozier and Arch G. Woodside (Columbus, Ohio: Charles E. Merrill Publishing Company, 1978), pp. 282–86.

of 1969, and since that time has had an average room occupancy of 80 percent. Room occupancy had peaked at 87 percent in 1976. Part of the decline in the past two years was due to a number of new hotels that had been opened in the past few years. Indeed, about 1,500 new hotel rooms had become available in 1977. Another 500-room hotel was under construction three blocks away, with an expected occupancy date of mid-1980.

Over the past seven years, the hotel had been successful in attracting a major portion of its room business from traveling business and sales people. The hotel was located close to the downtown business district, and travelers had immediate access to the airport expressway. The drive to the airport took about fifteen minutes in normal traffic. Also, the hotel was about five blocks away from the state university. Parents, alumni, and friends of the university have found the hotel a convenient place to stay when coming to sports, cultural, and other events on the campus. Although its location was not as attractive for tourists, many tourists stayed in the hotel when visiting the city.

The Marketing and Sales Director's Report

That evening, Mr. Rabb read the report of the marketing and sales director. The report was organized into three parts: analysis of room demand, a comparison of the supply of rooms with room demand, and a ranking of rooms according to noticeable physical attributes.

	Room Price	
Single Occupancy	Double Occupancy	Number of Rooms
$16.00	$19.50	30
16.50	20.00	40
17.00	20.50	30
17.50	21.00	300
18.00	21.50	200
18.50	22.00	50
19.00	22.50	30
19.50	23.00	30
20.00	23.50	60
21.00	24.50	10
22.00	25.50	10
24.00	27.50	25
26.00	29.50	10
27.00	30.50	5
27.50	31.00	5
28.00	31.50	10
29.00	32.50	5
29.50	33.00	20
30.00	33.50	5
32.00	35.50	15
35.00	38.50	10

EXHIBIT 26-1

Executive Inn, Inc. price and room classification schedule

Room Price	Average Percentage Paying Price	Cumulative Percentage
$16.00	5.0%	5.0%
16.50	4.0	9.0
17.00	8.0	17.0
17.50	8.0	25.0
18.00	10.0	35.0
18.50	20.0	55.0
19.00	10.0	65.0
19.50	8.0	73.0
20.00	7.0	80.0
21.00	5.0	85.0
22.00	5.0	90.0
24.00	3.0	93.0
26.00	1.0	94.0
27.00	1.0	95.0
27.50	0.5	95.5
28.00	0.5	96.0
29.00	1.0	97.0
29.50	1.0	98.0
30.00	0.5	98.5
32.00	1.0	99.5
35.00	0.5	100.0

EXHIBIT 26-2 ====================================

Executive Inn, Inc. sample occupancy data (single rate)

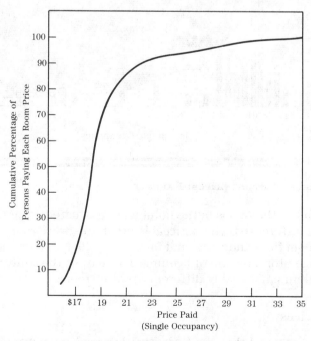

EXHIBIT 26-3 ====================================

Room demand curve: Executive Inn, Inc.

The report's first exhibit shows that the hotel had 900 rooms and twenty-one different single and double occupancy room rates. (See Exhibit 26-1.) The director had taken two samples of fourteen days each, recording the number of persons paying each single room rate on each day. These data were converted into the average percentage of persons paying each rate, as shown in Exhibit 26-2. From Exhibit 26-2 a demand curve was developed that shows the cumulative percentage of persons versus the rate paid, shown in Exhibit 26-3.

The director then assumed that if 5 percent of the guests occupied a $16 room, then 5 percent of 900, or 45 rooms, was the demand for a $16 room. Using this reasoning, he developed Exhibit 26-4.

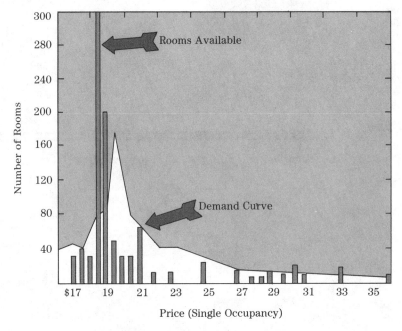

EXHIBIT 26-4

Room demand at current prices: Executive Inn, Inc.

Finally, all of the rooms in the hotel were evaluated according to factors of noticeable differences. The noticeable attributes were room size, location in terms of room floor and view, and facilities available: television, air conditioning, refrigerator, and size of bedding. This part of the study revealed that the hotel had nine noticeably different types of rooms.

Room prices

Mr. Rabb believed that the Executive Inn was not following the pricing principles he had just read about and he decided to ask the marketing and sales director to recommend a new pricing schedule. Currently, the prices were competitive with other hotels in the city, but Mr. Rabb was concerned that the current pricing schedule was too complex and probably was not correct for his market.

Questions for Discussion

1. What is wrong with the current pricing scheme used by Executive Inn, Inc.? Explain.
2. Using the pricing principles discussed in the case, develop a pricing strategy for Executive Inn, Inc.
3. How will the opening of additional rooms among competitors affect the Executive Inn's pricing strategy? Explain.

Endnotes

1. Kent B. Monroe, *Making Profitable Pricing Decisions* (New York: McGraw-Hill Book Company, 1979).

PART **10**

Retail Promotion
Management

Case 27

J.B. WHITE— ITS ADVERTISING OBJECTIVES, STRATEGY, AND MEDIA

J.B. WHITE was founded in 1874 by an adventurous young Irishman, James Bryce White, who ran away from home at the age of sixteen and went to work in a New York City dry goods store. While working at the store, he kept hearing about the golden opportunities in the South from two visiting merchants from Augusta, Georgia. So White moved to Augusta and worked in a local store for six years. Through frugal living, he was able to save enough money to open his own store with the help of a partner. Later, he bought out his partner and established the J.B. White Store. After thirty years of successful operation, White retired in 1904 and sold his store to the Claflin Company. The new management operated the store until 1914 when it was bought by its present parent organization, the Mercantile Chain.

Under Mercantile management, a branch of White's was opened in Columbia, South Carolina on Main Street in 1949. Another White's store was opened in Richland Mall in 1961 and was very profitable until the mid-1970's. The downtown store was closed in 1965 and in 1970 White's opened a large unit in the Dutch Square Shopping Mall which also has been, and still is, very profitable. However, with the opening of the regional shopping center Columbia Mall in 1977, followed in early 1978 with the new Woodhill Mall, department store retailing has become very competitive in metropolitan Columbia. Consequently, success and survival depends more than ever on good management. Astute buying and merchandising are essential as is efficient advertising and sales promotion.

The Mercantile Organization

The Mercantile Chain operates seventy-eight department stores in downtown and suburban areas in eighteen states and in Ontario, Canada.

This case was prepared by Steven J. Shaw, University of South Carolina.

Mercantile does not open units in large metropolitan areas, but instead prefers to locate in intermediate-sized cities like Columbia and Augusta. The stores carry both national and house brands in a wide variety of items. Emphasis is placed on a high degree of service since the stores cater to middle- and upper-income groups.

By the end of 1978, Mercantile expects an annual sales volume of about $900 million with sales increasing 10 percent or more each year thereafter. They rank fiftieth in size among retailers in the United States. Mercantile follows a policy of decentralized management, with local managers running the stores. This policy of autonomy of unit management makes it possible for store managers to tailor merchandise, personnel, and advertising to the special needs of the local markets. In addition to store managers, each unit may have a superintendent of operations and personnel, an office manager, a credit manager, and a display and advertising manager. Some of the larger stores have fashion coordinators and public relations managers. The buying staff in a store ranges from twelve to forty buyers with merchandise managers over related departments.

Advertising plans and items for specific ads emanate from the buying staff with the help of the advertising manager. The store manager reviews advertising plans and suggests changes. Buyers decide what to advertise on the basis of the folowing criteria:

1. Is the product in high demand?
2. Is it competitively priced?
3. Does the store have sufficient quantities of the item?
4. What is the item's sales potential?
5. Will the product either promote immediate business or enhance store image?
6. Is there another item that would do better either in pulling in traffic or in promoting store image?

Budgeting For Advertising at White's

To determine the number of dollars that should be spent on advertising for the coming year, store management uses a combination of the following methods: (1) the percent of sales method, (2) the objective and task method, and (3) the competitive parity method.

Percent-of-sales method

Like most other large stores, White's uses the percentage-of-sales method as a convenient measuring stick to guard against over-spending. To keep prices competitive, store management has to keep an eye on all operating costs which tend to keep rising. Departmental buyers and merchandise managers are under great pressure to increase sales and to improve or at least sustain profits. Consequently, they always discover some new or timely merchandise that might sell better if advertised. And either the vendor or the chain's buying office has on hand statistics which show the improved sales results through advertising in other stores in the same or other regions. If not kept under tight control, departmental advertising budgets might get way out of line.

When worthwhile, specific objectives for the year might justify a reasonable increase in advertising outlay and the store manager can authorize the additional expenditure. For example, due to the extremely competitive retail environment of the 1977-1978 period, it was necessary to increase advertising expenditures for the Columbia area stores by more than one percent for 1979.

Objective-and-task approach

To take advantage of new opportunities and to make adjustments for negative environmental threats that come into play each year, White's management carefully plans its advertising strategy in advance.

Some specific objectives that tend to be of a recurring nature are (1) to meet or exceed last year's sales figures while at the same time keep the same over-all markup/markdown ratio, (2) to reduce or eliminate inventories in departments when sales turnover figures show that customers are losing interest in certain items, and (3) to get out of end-of-season goods through drastic markdowns.

Exhibit 27–1 lists in detail some of the more general objectives of White's advertising program. This exhibit suggests that the store can seek new customers through several different strategies. Thus, during one year the store might try to expand its geographical trading area by advertising in weekly newspapers in towns such as Camden, Newberry, and Orangeburg. In another year new customers could be sought by either opening new departments or by introducing new merchandise lines.

EXHIBIT 27-1

A checklist of White's advertising objectives

1. To seek new customers by
   a. attracting new target groups to the store.
   b. expanding the geographical trading area of the store.
   c. introducing the store's new departments to customers.
   d. introducing new merchandise lines, brand name products, and services to customers and others in the trading area as the store diversifies operations.

2. To sell more merchandise and services to present customers by
   a. increasing their pride in being a customer of the store and reinforcing a feeling of "oneness" with the store and its personnel.
   b. continuously reestablishing customers' confidence in the store and building their self image by reassuring them of their good judgment in being a regular customer.
   c. keeping customers aware of improvements in and additions to the store's merchandise, services, personnel, and policies.

3. To increase the stability of store operations by
   a. leveling out fluctuations in sales volume over time, enabling the store to minimize expenses associated with peak-season overloads and slack season dearths of business.

EXHIBIT 27-1 (continued)

   b. stabilizing the merchandise and service demands of customers, prices, and
      operating procedures so that the store can operate in the most economical way.
4. To perform a service for customers and prospective customers by
   a. providing information that saves them time, effort, confusion, and money.
   b. providing information on the use, maintenance, and repair of merchandise sold;
      this serves both to create goodwill, which benefits the store's future sales, and to
      generate business for service departments.
5. To make the store a community personality by
   a. explaining candidly store policies that affect the community as a whole.
   b. providing information on civic affairs.
   c. performing various public services.
   d. taking notice of popular holidays and important local and national events.
6. To influence the morale and effectiveness of employees by
   a. building pride, understanding, and empathy among employees, management,
      customers, and the community at large.
   b. saving employees' time and energy by informing customers about merchandise
      and store policies.
   c. increasing total customer traffic through the store, enabling more salespersons to
      personally reach more customers and prospective customers.
7. To reinforce the impact of other promotional efforts by
   a. paving the way for acceptance of sales solicitation by mail.
   b. following up locally on customer demand created by manufacturers' advertising.
   c. capitalizing on the opportunities offered by manufacturers' cooperative adver-
      tising.
   d. reinforcing in-store promotions by glamourization of the events.

After all requests and objectives are translated in a tentative master
advertising plan, a total cost estimate is calculated. If the total dollar figure is
too high in relation to planned sales, management and staff review each ad
item to determine where cutbacks can be made.

Competitive parity

However, White's management has to watch closely the advertising
strategy and tactics of principal competitors like Tapp's, another department
store in Columbia. And as mentioned previously, during the 1977-1978 period
the competitive situation in the greater Columbia area was unusually intense.
Consequently, top management decided that White's must spend a higher
percentage of sales than usual.

White's Advertising Philosophy

Leonard Fisk, vice president of marketing at Mercantile, addressed the
store managers, superintendents of operations and personnel office managers,
display and advertising managers, and other key personnel from the greater
Columbia area White's stores. In his talk, he made the following comments:

A quality department store like White's is a place where customers come for excitement and fulfillment of a need. Shopping should give a customer an emotional lift—a revival from sagging spirits. A store that is successful in accomplishing these objectives is alive, young, bouncing with exciting merchandise in exciting settings. All departments should work together to make an enticing presentation of the store and its merchandise.

The first of these elements is advertising. Advertising's job is to pull customer traffic into the store. According to the Mercantile store experience, the most successful advertising for building store traffic is advertising that dares to be different, that stimulates the imagination, that arouses curiosity, that surprises, entertains, and informs the consumer.

Once a customer enters the store, the interior displays, point-of-purchase displays, signs, the merchandise itself, and the service, attitude, and knowledge of sales personnel all work together to make the final sale. But first advertising must get traffic into the store.

Advertising that dares to be different gets noticed and gets results. Certain ads are perfectly safe, such as the two-column ad on inexpensive jersey dresses, or the one-half-off dress sale. These and similar ads are utterly defendable. All one has to do is point to the results. For example, a buyer can point out, "See, fifty dresses were sold today." Who can argue with success?

However, the truth is, these promotions are *not* the ones that pay off. Any store that depends on "advertised items" for its daily volume will die of starvation. And, an ad that sells just a jersey dress is no success, no matter how many are sold. It is not a success if it fails to sell something much more important—our store.

Even worse, it can have a negative effect. If a store runs nothing but cheap jersey dresses and one-half-off dress sales, the picture the customer gets of the store's fashion importance is "cheap jersey dresses and one-half-off dress sales."

Yet, the store may have a fine collection of better fashions. One day, someone authorizes a full page on one high-fashion dress. The newspaper space costs much more than the dress so there is no way, seemingly, to recover this advertising expense.

One ad doesn't make a reputation, but assume that the ad was so magnificent that it persuaded hundreds of women that this is a real fashion store. They may never want the dress that was advertised, but no matter. The ad wasn't run to sell that dress. The ad had an entirely different purpose—to sell customers on the fact that this is a fashion store; and when they want fashion, this is where to look for it!

While it is true that fashion advertising does not get immediate results, it does increase the overall sales picture by lifting the image of the store in the minds of the consumers. That is, when a storewide sale event is run, the customer feels she is receiving *much more* than she would from a store that runs nothing but cheap dresses and one-half-price sales. Fashion-institutional advertising must be considered an *investment* that pays by giving added impetus to sale advertising, even though it is by subtle means.

Dramatic, authoritative, exciting fashion advertising reinforces customer confidence in the store. A consistent, well-executed, year 'round fashion advertising presentation communicates that the store knows what it is talking about and that it knows its merchandise. Great institutional advertising that reports on community events, tells of the store's personnel, services, policies, observes certain national holidays, or simply thanks the customer for his or her business creates a feeling of goodwill, pride, confidence, and a desire to do business with the store among consumers. It also has the double effect of boosting the morale of sales personnel by building pride in their store and what it stands for. This attitude carries over to the customers on the floor, hence increasing repeat business.

A sound program of fashion and institutional advertising romances the store, its merchandise, and its personnel and thus woos the customer to shop at the store. It not only boosts the image of the store, but of its merchandise as well in terms of quality, not price, for prices speak for themselves.

Once the commitment is made to run fashion advertising and institutional advertising, item-price-sale advertising must be analyzed carefully and the waste trimmed out to allow for the extra expense incurred by the fashion ads. The end result will be fewer item ads, which will require a great deal of selectivity on the part of department managers. Only the great sellers or volume items should be run again and again, while the "slow movers" fall by the wayside. New items should be tried, but certainly no more than twice with no appreciable results. Even proven sellers should be planned each month to reasonably assure the department of increasing its sales volume of a year ago, taking into consideration external factors.

Later in his talk, Mr. Fisk discussed the topic of retail advertising, its role, how the various media should be used, and his views on retail advertising as an investment.

Newspapers

As with most large retailers serving an extensive metropolitan market, the newspaper is the backbone of White's advertising. The superiority of the newspaper over other media is evidenced by the many advantages it offers the advertiser. First, the local newspaper offers White's the opportunity of reaching a large percentage of its customers at a comparatively low cost. For instance, the *Columbia State* has a paid circulation of 102,000 homes. But its readership is probably three or four times this number because its pages carry something of interest to every member of the family, such as home economics and fashions for the housewife, financial and business news for the men of the family, sports pages for the sports-minded, and comics and puzzles for the children.

Another advantage of the newspaper over other media is that it allows customers the opportunity of comparing prices, shopping values, and other differences between competitive retailers. Also, the newspaper offers the retail advertiser flexibility and speed. It is published every day and makes it possible for a store to take quick action. A typical case arises when a fashion buyer returns from the market with a new style. Copy and illustration can be quickly prepared by the store's advertising staff and sent to the newspaper on the same day. The next day a proof of the complete advertisement comes back to the store. Corrections can be telephoned to the newspaper and the finished advertisement can appear in the evening *Columbia Record* or in the next morning's edition of the *State*, or both. Here, the newspaper performs a function impossible in any other medium. Very often such speed in advertising preparation is matched by speed in actual sales of the advertised article. Frequently, the item will begin to sell within an hour after the papers are in the homes and on the street. Thus, a newspaper also offers the retail advertiser a quick check on the success of his advertising.

With the tempo of retailing today, the speed of newspaper advertising response has become a necessary part of store operation. The daily publication of newspapers makes it possible for a store to tie its advertising to current events, such as the forecast of an impending storm or the first freeze of the year.

Television

A quality department store is a place where hundreds, even thousands, of people walk in every day with stars in their eyes. Each comes in with a tiny spark of anticipation, a secret joy. A living store is a living experience, and living people come there to live in another world for a fragment of time. They want to dream a little, to be excited and stimulated, and to see and learn.

So, what does White's give this dreamer of dreams, this gal with stars in her eyes? How does management communicate to her that the store is alive, exciting, and colorful? Is it through items of gray lined up in little boxes on a newspaper page? She's after ideas. She's after life and moments of excitement.

The most exciting way White's can advertise to her is on television—if it is done properly. Television has limitless scope. It has power. It brings all of the color, motion, emotion, and faculties of life into the home.

Most retailers take the attitude of "we have to try television" and somebody does a few commercials. That's a sure waste of advertising money. Television is no longer experimental. It is here, it is now, and it works. Television should not be compared with newspaper advertising. Television is another world. It's entertainment. It's a medium that can transcend any other medium of communication available to the large store.

A store must create the commercial with a twist! The unusual idea, the surprise element, the sudden flash of excitement that makes the brief moment on the tube something to see and remember.

Generally, sales results are not immediate. A store at times may get an avalanche of sales from a TV commercial, but usually this does not happen. Generation of instant customer response is not the main purpose of White's television advertising. A lasting contribution to store image is the principal objective. The main product sold is the store as a place to shop and television, with its almost total penetration of homes in the metropolitan area, will help to sell that product.

Before using television, the retail advertiser must carefully consider the following: (1) geographic area, (2) coverage, (3) ratings of each station, (4) costs, (5) what TV can say to people that cannot be said through other media, and (6) can TV say it better. The advertiser must budget a long range plan for TV, prepare campaigns, and let them run their full course.

The following are what I consider to be points of a good TV commercial:

1. It is not a talkathon. Television is primarily theatrical and pictorial. If the intended idea cannot be conveyed in one short sentence, then it should not be attempted at all.
2. It is simple and clear to the point. Since the viewer is in a relaxed state of mind, the message should not be complicated.
3. It is short. The message should take no more than thirty seconds. It should not be dragged out to sixty seconds.
4. It is entertaining and interesting.
5. It identifies the store and product clearly. A singing commercial is not necessary. Each commercial should be different and tell a different story.
6. If it is a single item, then price should be mentioned.
7. It reflects the store's overall image and ties in with its other advertising.

On the subject of *radio*, radio is different from newspaper and television advertising in that it is nonvisual. It must reach and stimulate the listener's imagination through carefully chosen words. Despite the advertiser's inability to see and to be seen by his audience, radio advertising is a highly personal form of communication, particularly when the program is broadcast by a person who becomes known as the "voice of the store."

The commuting hours are generally the peak listening hours, and radio reaches most automobile drivers exceptionally well as they can drive and listen simultaneously. Radio is also a good companion to people spending time at home reading or relaxing. It is person-to-person communication. A radio listener is less likely to tune out the store's commercial or walk away from it to raid the refrigerator, since the commercial is not sandwiched in between segments of a show as it is on TV.

There are many local radio stations and each may cater to a different audience. In Columbia, White's can reach different segments of its customers through the use of several stations with complementary audiences. The strategy is to match the merchandise to the principal audience of each radio station used.

The per minute cost of advertising is much lower over radio than television. A retailer can take advantage of the relatively low cost and combine it with an advertising schedule that is designed to reach the target market groups in which he is interested.

Media mix

While newspapers, television, and radio are different and one medium may be more effective than another under a given situation, White's blends them together into a promotional mix. When a major promotional campaign is undertaken, one medium can reinforce another. Skillful supplementation of newspaper messages with those of television and radio can maximize the flow of information from the store to its customers and result in a much greater sales volume. While these three media carry the brunt of White's advertising, direct mail, car and bus cards, circulars, and catalogs can be used effectively during major promotional campaigns.

Advertising is an investment

While many stores look upon advertising as a business expense, White's tries to look at it as an investment. Advertising has a cumulative effect. Done when business is good, it lays the groundwork for future business. Done only when the store needs sales, it may be advertising that is too little and too late. Historical studies show that stores that have the most liberal advertising policies and are willing to invest the most dollars for advertising are able to ward off the effects of recession and to rebound from it faster than those with more restricted policies.

Advertising waste—seven deadly Cs

1. Color. Any attempt to depict merchandise realistically with less than full color is usually a waste of money.
2. Co-op advertising. The use of co-op advertising for a store as distinctive as White's has limits. If the ad looks like the manufacturer's, store advertising funds have been wasted, even though it's only 50 percent.
3. Contracts. Contracts are always written in favor of the media. The store must run ads that reach its target markets, and anything else is wasted. If White's is trying to reach the working women, driving times on radio and prime time on TV are the best purchases. Although the cost per spot is more, the cost per potential customer is less.

4. Consistency. Change for the sake of change is a waste of money. Store advertising must not confuse the customer. She is used to the ads the way they are, so any changes must be evolutionary, not revolutionary. But change is good, as long as it is evolved just enough to keep catching the eye. However, a stubborn insistence in consistency is another waste of money.

5. Cuteness. Cuteness is an occupational hazard. A little pun in the headline or a play on words may be misconstrued by customers. The copywriter is saying in his ad, ''see how good I am'' rather than ''see how good our merchandise is.'' The advertisement must give facts and radiate sincerity.

6. Competition. Spending too much time contemplating the competition can result in too much advertising similarity. Creative people can be overwhelmed by too intense a study of the competitor's advertising. It seems that everything has already been done. It has. Better to be underwhelmed than overwhelmed. Competitors trying to stare each other down tend to become more and more alike and thus lose individuality.

7. Cost. The advertising department should not skimp on production. Expenses bear watching, but poor production quality loses reader interest and quickly whittles away the store image. If potential customers become disinterested in the selling messages, the store's quality image begins to slip and so do sales.

Questions for Discussion

1. In what ways does the Mercantile Chain differ from a chain like K-Mart? List and describe briefly as many differences as you can.

2. Two criteria used by buyers in the Mercantile organization to determine what merchandise to advertise are (1) is the product in high demand, and (2) what is the item's sales potential. Distinguish between these two criteria. What other criteria would you suggest that Mercantile consider? Why?

3. Study the checklist of White's advertising objectives given in Exhibit 27–1. Which of the seven advertising objectives should be given the highest priority during the present fiercely competitive times? Explain.

4. From a study of White's advertising philosophy, do you feel that store management places too much emphasis on fashion and institutional advertising? Explain your position.

5. Pick out two items of merchandise that would be particularly suited for promotion using a combination of newspapers, television, and radio. Defend your choices.

6. Would White's accounting department view advertising as a current expenditure or as an investment? Explain. Can future effectiveness of current advertising be measured? If so, how? Explain.

WORTHINGTON DEPARTMENT STORES

WORTHINGTON DEPARTMENT STORES was a national chain, with centralized purchasing in New York City. Each store was under the control of a general manager, to whom the various merchandise division heads reported. Department managers, who were under the divisional managers, were judged on both sales volume and maintained margin. The individual Worthington Stores priced to the level of local competition rather than on a national basis. It was felt that this procedure would ensure that Worthington's customers would receive quality merchandise at comparable prices in any given area.

Centralized buying permitted private brand labeling on many of the items Worthington's sold, particularly their extensive lines of appliances. Worthington contracted directly with many manufacturers to produce items with an appropriate private Worthington brand label, including their vacuum cleaners.

The Worthington policy of customer satisfaction was a critical ingredient in its promotional strategy. The original policy of unconditional refunds to any dissatisfied customers had been strictly adhered to over the years as an important part of its advertising programs. Many customers expressed the belief that you could never really get a "bargain" at Worthington Stores, compared with discount-store prices on comparable goods, but at least you could buy with absolute confidence.

In a major Southern city, one department of one of the larger Worthington Stores was being harassed by what the divisional manager thought was unfair and unethical competition. The store policy of pricing at the level of local competition did not include price competition with discount stores. Worthington had relied upon the insulative effect of its private labels on appliances to protect it from price comparison from discount outlets featuring national brands.

This case was prepared by Prof. Barry J. Hersker, Florida Atlantic University. Reproduced with permission.

The department in question was household appliances, including vacuum cleaners. Worthington Stores carried several price ranges of cannister and upright vacuum models, but the Worthington Swift-Clean cannister model, including attachments, was its best seller, with a retail price of just under $50. It also was the lowest-priced model in its vacuum cleaner line.

Mr. Randolph Osker was the department manager whose merchandise included the Worthington Swift-Clean vacuum cleaner. He noted that its sales were definitely off, and he attributed this sales decline to intensive local discount competition.

Several local retail firms, some having questionable character and ethics, had engaged in a "bait and switch" promotional strategy. They advertised heavily that they would sell a "like new" reconditioned vacuum for $19.95, and asked customers to telephone their requests for a free home demonstration. Mr. Osker believed that this competition was hurting his department at the Worthington Store, and he personally answered several of the advertisements for a "free home demonstration" of the $19.95 vacuum cleaner. In each instance, he discovered that a salesman would arrive at his home, demonstrate an obsolete and inferior vacuum, and then attempt to "trade up" the customer with a demonstration of a new, more expensive machine. The approach was definitely "hard sell," and indeed the $19.95 vacuum was—in his estimation—a "come on," which no prudent customer would probably actually purchase. The intensive promotion of these inferior machines had caused several department stores to announce price reductions on several nationally advertised cleaners, and this problem compounded the already difficult situation in which Mr. Osker found himself.

Mr. Osker had met several times with Mr. Fred Hodge, his divisional manager, to plan a competitive strategy for his department to follow. Mr. Hodge appeared reluctant to advise Mr. Osker to cut the price on the Swift-Clean, since they both knew it already represented a quality product at a reasonable price, in the best tradition of the Worthington reputation. In addition, of course, price reductions would adversely affect both maintained margins and store profits. Still, they felt some action should be forthcoming.

Both Mr. Osker and Mr. Hodge decided to seek approval from the store manager, Mr. Martin Stern, for a bold and unconventional strategy in behalf of the vacuum cleaner department at this Worthington Store. Both Mr. Hodge and Mr. Osker were in agreement that unconventional action was justified under the circumstances, and began by thoroughly briefing Mr. Stern on the serious competitive problem which confronted the department. After this was done, they then explained their plan to Mr. Stern in detail, and asked for his approval or rejection. The plan was as follows:

Mr. Osker had carefully shopped the used vacuum cleaner market, in an effort to purchase a cannister model with certain distinctive features. He and Mr. Hodge described the cleaner to Mr. Stern in the following manner. Mr. Osker did most of the explaining at first.

"Well, the cleaner had to have some physical similarity to our Swift-Clean—that is, it should look like it belongs in our line. Then, it had to be in sufficiently good condition to look new once it has been reconditioned and repainted. But, it couldn't be too fancy—almost no chrome or frills. Just a plain and undistinguished product."

Mr. Hodge interjected, "Except for one important factor—the refurbished vacuum will have to photograph well—but that shouldn't be too difficult. The machine must look much better in print than in the flesh—so to speak."

"Fred, I think I know what you're leading up to," said Mr. Stern.

"We figured you would. The major product characteristic we saved for last," Mr. Hodge continued. "The vacuum cleaner must not work too well. I'm sure Mr. Osker's used machine will fit the bill perfectly. It almost can be guaranteed not to pick up anything. In fact, this is even more dramatic because it sounds like it's working hard—it even shows a few sparks for an added effect!" said Mr. Hodge, with some degree of humor in his voice. "Then, we simply put on the Worthington decal plate, and we've got ourselves a fighting brand! We advertise the phantom machine as a special at $19.95—not often, mind you, but only when competitive strategy necessitates. The customers come to the store to see the bargain, and, of course, we demonstrate both the fighting brand and the Swift-Clean."

"And, of course," Mr. Osker added, "the Swift-Clean will appear to be the marvel of the century compared to the phantom vacuum."

"How do you explain this strategy to your sales clerks?" asked Mr. Stern. "Would they cooperate, and how would they react?"

"I'm sure that will be no problem—they're good boys, all of them, and they are just as concerned as we are about the position we're being forced into."

"Fred, what do you think? After all, aren't we above 'bait and switch' tactics?" asked Mr. Stern.

"Martin, I hate this kind of thing as much as you do, but I honestly think we've got to retaliate in this competitive situation. In fact, under the circumstances, we are really acting in the customer's best interest."

"How's that, Fred? And, is this in Worthington's best interest in the long run? We've got a reputation to protect!"

"Mr. Stern, I personally guarantee that no one is going to be cheated," said Mr. Osker. "The Swift-Clean is an excellent product, and this temporary tactic will permit us to steer our customers to it. The alternative is we do nothing, and the Worthington customer ends up buying from someone else, and he probably buys an inferior product."

"There is some truth in that, Mr. Osker, but how are you going to handle any complications? I mean, suppose someone really wants the phantom? Suppose someone demands it?" asked Mr. Stern.

"Well, first we don't permit mail or phone orders. Thus, we are sure every prospect gets a demonstration. This alone will deter most customers from seriously considering the phantom."

"And for those who don't discourage so easily?"

"Well, we certainly won't actually sell the phantom in any event. As a last resort, we explain that the model is out of stock and simply back-order the cleaner. If need be, we can offer an inducement to substitute the Swift-Clean, after some reasonable point of time."

"Mr. Osker, that is all well and good—but how thoroughly have you considered this thing? You say no customer can be hurt by your tactics. O.K. I do have faith in the ability of any half-trained clerk to 'sell' the Swift-Clean's advantages over the inferior phantom cleaner. *But,* what if someone demands the phantom and demands that he receive a quality product which doesn't exist at a price which is also nonexistent, and flatly rejects a 'back-order' explanation as to why he cannot be served within a reasonable period of time? What then, Mr. Osker?"

"Well, I certainly could not advocate any deviation from our dedicated policy of complete customer satisfaction," said Mr. Osker, after a few seconds pause. "I understand the risks I am asking us to assume. Perhaps these are not risks, sir. Perhaps they are obligations."

"Mr. Osker, please make your point," said Mr. Stern.

"Well, I am serving two interests. First, Worthington's and second, my customers'. You—and I mean that in the most respectful and plural connotation—have established standards by which to judge my performance. I will guarantee that I will improve my maintained margin and my record for satisfied customers. If, indeed, any customer is really dissatisfied, I am quite willing to reduce the price of the Swift-Clean to $19.95 to satisfy him."

"Mr. Osker, you always had the opportunity to reduce the price, if Mr. Hodge agreed. It's your department."

"I don't want to cut the price across-the-board to counter false competition. The Swift-Clean already is one of the best values we offer. I prefer to reduce the price selectively—correction, *highly* selectively—to fulfill our obligations to satisfied customers. But massive sales and bargains are not, in my judgment, indicated here."

"Fred, both you and Randy probably are fully aware of the many considerations that enter into a proposal of this kind. I appreciate your candid and frank proposal. Let me deliberate on this in the context of all things concerned. I'd like to set up an appointment for us to speak again on this next week."

Questions

1. Should Mr. Stern approve the Osker-Hodge proposal?

2. If not, what should Mr. Osker do to meet the "bait and switch" promotional strategy of his competitors?

Case 29

CROMER'S PHARMACY — DEVELOPING AN EFFECTIVE ADVERTISING PROGRAM

JULIUS CROMER is a long-term resident and businessman in Smithfield, South Carolina. He knows everyone and everybody in the town of Smithfield. As a boy he always wanted to be a doctor, but his parents could not afford the tuition and books for a higher education. Although he was salutorian of his high school class, Julius did not go to college, but instead joined the Army in 1949 "to get his education." While in the Army, Julius tried to follow his first true love of medicine as closely as he could. Since he had no college education as a doctor, he decided to do what he considered to be the best next thing—become a medic.

After the Army's initial training in medicine, he was sent immediately to the Korean War where he distinguished himself by saving the lives of three men who had been severely wounded in combat. The citation read, "Lt. Julius T. Cromer, through heroics becoming an Army officer, did administer to and comfort fellow officers who sustained severe injuries in the line of duty. Lt. Cromer, a highly-trained medic, saved the lives of his comrades. His heroic deeds are hereby acknowledged and highly commended in this citation."

Julius was astounded by this recognition and believed that he had "stumbled" into the award by being at the right place at the right time. Modestly, he accepted the award and continued to serve his country and his fellow human beings.

In 1953 Cromer was honorably discharged from the Army and began thinking about his future. With his G.I. Bill, Cromer took the opportunity to apply to and later accept admission to the School of Pharmacy at the University of North Carolina. Julius believed that pharmacy would give him the necessary training for entering medical school. Although he excelled in his field, his aspirations as a medical student went "out the window" when his mother became severely ill and had to be placed in a nursing home. Being an only child, it became Julius' responsibility to care for and finance his mother's

This case was prepared by Sarah B. Wise, University of South Carolina.

"last days." Therefore, Julius decided to forego medical school for a while and make enough money to support himself and his mother's nursing home costs.

The only thing Julius felt he could do was to return to Smithfield, his birthplace and home, and take up his father's business in pharmacy. Although highly educated in the field of pharmacy, Julius knew very little about running a business. His retailing experience was limited to sweeping out his dad's store six nights a week and counting inventory. Nevertheless, Julius was determined to make a go of it.

As a devoted son, Julius sustained the costs of his mother's nursing home until she died in 1958. A beautiful funeral was held in which most of the townspeople participated. The Cromers were well known throughout the town of Smithfield and the County of Smithfield.

Cromer's Pharmacy prospered throughout the 1960's and into the mid-1970's. But as the town grew into a city, additional pharmacies located within the "old town" and its suburbs. Julius began to feel the effects of competition. The "good ole boys" had died, and a new breed of people had entered the town.

Cromer's Present Situation

Cromer's Pharmacy had prospered for forty years and Julius was faced with declining sales and profits. Exhibit 29–1 shows Cromer's 1980 sales by item and for total sales. The total figure represents a 10 percent decline from the previous year.

Item	Sales ($)
Prescriptions	$191,418
OTC products	61,649
Hair products	20,429
Shaving products	3,616
Dental products	8,483
Cosmetics/fragrances	25,419
Sundries	22,534
Magazines and newspapers	19,498
Stationery	12,101
Photo products	40,258
Tobacco products	27,773
Candy and gum	11,355
All other	37,013
TOTAL	$481,546

EXHIBIT 29-1

1980 sales by item for Cromer's Pharmacy

Because competition from chain pharmacy retailers were adversely affecting his business, Julius decided after long and hard thinking to invest in a major advertising campaign. His competitors, it appeared, had been successful in mounting an advertising offensive. He realized he could not survive any longer on word-of-mouth advertising.

Julius knew very little about advertising or how to go about it. He knew what local media were available and began to consider which ones he should use. The local newspaper was *The Courier* and had been in existence for over one hundred years. *The Post* was the state's largest newspaper and was delivered locally. Three local radio stations, WCIO, WPUK, and WCIG, were the primary stations that local residents listened to. Finally, there were two local television stations, WCOD and WTIS, which commanded 90 percent of the local viewing audience. Julius realized that there were other options such as billboards, direct mail, specialty advertising, handbills, and other forms of advertising that he could use. However, he did not know whether to mount a print campaign, a broadcast campaign, or a combination of both.

Bob Wise, a close friend and retired advertising executive, gave Julius the following advice:

> To make a wise decision about your investment in advertising, you must analyze your customer mix and your market area. Some of the basic questions which you must ask yourself are
>
> 1. Who are the potential customers?
>   a. What are their income levels?
>   b. What are the age levels of the customers?
> 2. Where are the customers located?
>   a. What distance must the customer travel?
>   b. How do recent energy costs affect the customers?
> 3. What type of advertisement will reach these potential customers?
>   a. Will they respond to print media?
>   b. Will they respond to broadcast media?
>   c. Will they respond to a combination of print and broadcast media?
>
> After answering these questions, you then must determine the budget within which to operate. Ask yourself whether you should develop your budget on the basis of a certain percentage of projected sales, a percentage of past sales, an "all you can afford" approach, or "match the budget of competitors" approach.
>
> After you have determined the size of your budget, you then must select the appropriate media to use. In doing this, you should consider the relative advantages and disadvantages of each medium. Further, you must consider how frequently you want to advertise and when. You also must decide what types of media are most appropriate for your business. Will the local radio station reach a larger percentage of your customers? Should you advertise every day, every week? How much should you allocate for each month? Can you plan your advertising to the seasonal patterns of the store, to the store's special days, and to special events of the community? Also consider the use of cooperative advertising.

In addition to these comments, Bob gave Julius a summary report of statistics which his advertising agency had collected in the past year, just prior to his retirement. Tables 29–1 through 29–12 provide this information.

TABLE 29-1 ═══════════════════════════════════════

Average amount spent on RX's last time purchased in a drugstore (Smithfield)

Singles/young couples	$ 8.22
Young parents	8.47
Middle/older parents	9.03
Old/retired couples/sole survivor	11.20
Under $14,000	10.60
$14,000 to $24,900	9.17
$25,000 to $34,900	8.22
Over $35,000	9.23
Average shopper	9.17

TABLE 29-2 ═══════════════════════════════════════

Average amount spent on OTC's last time purchased in a drugstore (Smithfield)

Singles/young couples	$5.49
Young parents	5.17
Middle/older parents	5.47
Old/retired couples/sole survivor	6.19
Under $14,000	5.93
$14,000 to $24,900	5.51
$25,000 to $34,900	5.48
Over $35,000	6.49
Average shopper	5.73

TABLE 29-3 ═══════════════════════════════════════

Average amount spent on sundries last time purchased in a drugstore (Smithfield)

Singles/young couples	$ 7.20
Young parents	7.05
Middle/older parents	6.65
Old/retired couples/sole survivor	9.07
Under $14,000	6.69
$14,000 to $24,900	7.32
$25,000 to $34,900	8.17
Over $35,000	13.02
Average shopper	8.01

TABLE 29-4 ▬▬▬▬▬▬▬▬▬▬▬▬▬▬▬▬▬▬▬▬▬▬▬▬▬▬▬

Frequency of shopping in a drugstore during a one-month period (Smithfield)

	None	1-3	4-6	7-9	10+	Mean
				Days		
Over $35,000	2%	41%	32%	7%	18%	5.0%
$25,000 to $34,900	5	43	45	2	5	3.8
$14,000 to $24,900	8	38	35	4	15	4.5
Under $14,000	6	50	34	4	6	3.7
Old/retired couple/sole survivor	4	55	31	1	9	3.7
Middle/older parent	3	40	38	4	15	4.7
Young parent	7	34	36	5	18	4.9
Single/young couple	10	46	27	5	12	4.0

TABLE 29-5 ▬▬▬▬▬▬▬▬▬▬▬▬▬▬▬▬▬▬▬▬▬▬▬▬▬▬▬

Consumers' most important criteria in choosing a retail pharmacy (classified by consumers' age groups)

Criteria	Age Groups		
	18-30 years	31-50 years	Over 50 years
Price	20.0%	25.0%	27.1%
Pharmacist	12.5	22.0	28.2
Professional services	2.5	12.3	6.5
Physician's recommendation	8.0	2.0	0.0
Quality of merchandise	15.0	8.7	13.2
Store location	31.0	21.0	20.0
Other factors	11.0	9.0	5.0
TOTALS	100.0%	100.0%	100.0%

TABLE 29-6

Rate schedule for The Courier* (simplified retail advertising rate schedule)

Non-Contract Rate and Volume Contract Rates

Non-Contract Rate	Volume Contract Space	125"	250"	500"	1000"	2500"	5000"	10,000"	15,000"	20,000"	25,000"
	Volume Discount**	10%	15%	18%	20%	22%	24%	26%	28%	30%	32%
4.05	Daily	3.645	3.483	3.321	3.24	3.159	3.078	2.997	2.916	2.835	2.754
4.50	Sunday	4.05	3.87	3.69	3.60	3.51	3.42	3.33	3.24	3.15	3.06

Frequency Contract Rates

Number contract inches	1"	1"	1"	2"	2"	2"	3"	5"
Times Weekly	1	3	7	1	3	7	1	1
Frequency Discount**	10%	20%	22%	14%	22%	24%	18%	20%
Daily	3.645	3.24	3.159	3.483	3.159	3.078	3.321	3.24
Sunday	4.05	3.60	3.51	3.87	3.41	3.42	3.69	3.60

*All retail advertising billed at non-contract rate. Payment is due the 15th day of the month following publication, and the contract discount will be earned only if payment is made during this period.

**Represents the percentage discount off non-contract rates.

TABLE 29-7

Rate schedule for The Post* (simplified retail advertising rate schedule)

Non-Contract Rate and Volume Contract Rates

Non-Contract Rate	Volume Contract Space	125"	250"	500"	1000"	2500"	5000"	10,000"	15,000"	20,000"	25,000"
	Volume Discount**	10%	14%	18%	20%	22%	24%	26%	28%	30%	32%
8.05	Daily	7.245	6.923	6.601	6.44	6.279	6.118	5.957	5.796	5.635	5.474
8.50	Sunday	7.65	7.31	6.97	6.80	6.63	6.46	6.29	6.12	5.95	5.78

Frequency Contract Rates

Number contract inches	1"	1"	1"	2"	2"	2"	3"	3"	3"	5"
Times Weekly	1	3	7	1	3	7	1	3	7	1
Frequency Discount**	10%	20%	22%	14%	22%	24%	18%	22%	24%	20%
Daily	7.245	6.44	6.279	6.923	6.279	6.118	6.601	6.279	6.118	6.44
Sunday	7.65	6.80	6.63	7.31	6.63	6.46	6.97	6.63	6.46	6.80

*All retail advertising billed at non-contract rate. Payment is due the 15th day of the month following publication, and the contract discount will be earned only if payment is made during this period.

**Represents the percentage discount off non-contract rates.

239

TABLE 29-8

WCIO radio retail ratecard* (simplified rate card)

Total Audience Package Plans

	1-51 Weeks			52 Weeks		
	10X	20X	30X	10X	20X	30X
60 Seconds	$12 each $120/week	$11 each $220/week	$10 each $300/week	$10 each $200/week	$9 each $180/week	$8 each $240/week
30 Seconds	$9 each $90/week	$8 each $160/week	$7 each $210/week	$7 each $70/week	$6 each $120/week	$5 each $150/week

"Prime Time" Package Plans

	1-51 Weeks			52 Weeks		
	10X	20X	30X	10X	20X	30X
60 Seconds	$15 each $150/week	$14 each $280/week	$13 each $390/week	$12 each $120/week	$11 each $220/week	$10 each $300/week
30 Seconds	$11 each $110/week	$10 each $200/week	$9 each $270/week	$9 each $90/week	$8 each $160/week	$7 each $210/week

All Other Times (AOT) Packages

	3X	6X	10X	20X
60 Seconds	$6 each	$5 each	$4 each	$3 each
30 Seconds	$5 each	$4 each	$3 each	$2 each

*Rabitron Radio Survey
Adults 18+
Monday thru Sunday/6 am - midnight

Station	CUME Persons
WCIO	42,900

(Contemporary/talk show)

TABLE 29-9

WPUK radio retail ratecard* (simplified rate card)

Total Audience Package Plans

	1–51 Weeks			*52 Weeks*		
	10X	20X	30X	10X	20X	30X
60 Seconds	$11 each $110/week	$10 each $200/week	$9 each $270/week	$9 each $90/week	$8 each $160/week	$7 each $210/week
30 Seconds	$8 each $80/week	$7 each $140/week	$6 each $180/week	$6 each $60/week	$5 each $100/week	$4 each $120/week

"Prime Time" Package Plans

	1–51 Weeks			*52 Weeks*		
	10X	20X	30X	10X	20X	30X
60 Seconds	$14 each $140/week	$13 each $260/week	$12 each $360/week	$11 each $110/week	$10 each $200/week	$9 each $270/week
30 Seconds	$10 each $100/week	$9 each $180/week	$8 each $240/week	$8 each $80/week	$7 each $140/week	$6 each $180/week

All Other Times (AOT) Packages

	3X	6X	10X	20X
60 Seconds	$5 each	$4 each	$3 each	$2 each
30 Seconds	$4 each	$3 each	$2 each	$1 each

*Rabitron Radio Survey
Adults 18+
Monday thru Sunday/6 am - midnight

Station	CUME Persons
WPUK (Country and Western)	39,900

TABLE 29-10

WCIG radio retail ratecard* (simplified rate card)

Total Audience Package Plans

	1-51 Weeks			52 Weeks		
	10X	20X	30X	10X	20X	30X
60 Seconds	$7 each $70/week	$6 each $120/week	$5 each $150/week	$6 each $60/week	$5 each $100/week	$4 each $120/week
30 Seconds	$5 each $50/week	$4 each $80/week	$3 each $90/week	$4 each $40/week	$3 each $60/week	$2.50 each $75/week

"Prime Time" Package Plans

	1-51 Weeks			52 Weeks		
	10X	20X	30X	10X	20X	30X
60 Seconds	$10 each $110/week	$9 each $180/week	$8 each $240/week	$7 each $70/week	$6 each $120/week	$5 each $150/week
30 Seconds	$6 each $60/week	$5 each $100/week	$4 each $120/week	$4 each $40/week	$3 each $60/week	$2.50 each $75/week

All Other Times (AOT) Packages

	3X	6X	10X
60 Seconds	$4 each	$3 each	$2 each
30 Seconds	$3 each	$2 each	$1 each

*Rabitron Radio Survey
Adults 18+
Monday thru Sunday/6 am - midnight

Station	CUME Persons
WCIG (Soul)	27,400

TABLE 29-11

WCOD-TV rate card* (simplified rate card)

Day/Time		30 Seconds	Day/Time		30 Seconds
Monday-Friday			*Friday*		
7 am	- 8 am	$ 30.00	8 pm	- 9 pm	$325.00
8 am	- 9 am	40.00	9 pm	- 10 pm	700.00
9 am	- 10 am	55.00	10 pm	- 11 pm	700.00
10 am	- 11 am	45.00			
11 am	- 1 pm	50.00	*Saturday*		
1 pm	- 4 pm	45.00	6 am	- 6:30 am	50.00
4 pm	- 5 pm	55.00	6:30 am	- 7 am	50.00
5 pm	- 6 pm	60.00	7 am	- 12:30 pm	65.00
6 pm	- 7 pm	70.00	12:30 pm	- 1:30 pm	65.00
7 pm	- 7:30 pm	110.00	1:30 pm	- 2:30 pm	65.00
7:30 pm	- 8 pm	140.00	2:30 pm	- 4:30 pm	65.00
11 pm	- 11:30 pm	85.00	4:30 pm	- 6 pm	65.00
11:30 pm	- cc	40.00	6 pm	- 7 pm	70.00
			7 pm	- 8 pm	110.00
Monday			8 pm	- 9 pm	240.00
8 pm	- 9 pm	225.00	9 pm	- 11 pm	240.00
9 pm	- 10 pm	275.00	11 pm	- 11:30 pm	75.00
10 pm	- 11 pm	225.00	11:30 pm	- cc	45.00
Tuesday			*Sunday*		
8 pm	- 9 pm	240.00	6 am	- 9 am	50.00
9 pm	- 11 pm	240.00	9 am	- 10:30 am	70.00
			10:30 am	- 12 noon	50.00
Wednesday			12 noon	- 1 pm	60.00
8 pm	- 9 pm	240.00	1 pm	- 6 pm	80.00
9 pm	- 11 pm	240.00	6 pm	- 6:30 pm	80.00
			6:30 pm	- 7 pm	110.00
Thursday			7 pm	- 8 pm	700.00
8 pm	- 9 pm	240.00	8 pm	- 9 pm	325.00
9 pm	- 10 pm	240.00	9 pm	- 10 pm	325.00
10 pm	- 11 pm	275.00	10 pm	- 11 pm	325.00
			11 pm	- 11:15 pm	45.00
			11:15 pm	- cc	45.00

*Note: Major sports and specials take special rates.
          60 seconds: twice the applicable 30-second rate.
          10 seconds: 50% of the applicable 30-second rate.

TABLE 29-12 ▬▬▬▬▬▬▬▬▬▬▬▬▬▬▬▬▬▬▬▬▬▬▬▬

WTIS-TV rate card* (simplified rate card)

Day/Time			30 Seconds	Day/Time			30 Seconds
Monday-Friday				*Friday*			
7 am	-	8 am	$ 25.00	8 pm	-	9 pm	$300.00
8 am	-	9 am	45.00	9 pm	-	10 pm	550.00
9 am	-	10 am	50.00	10 pm	-	11 pm	750.00
10 am	-	11 am	50.00				
11 am	-	1 pm	55.00	*Saturday*			
1 pm	-	4 pm	40.00	6 am	-	6:30 am	40.00
4 pm	-	5 pm	50.00	6:30 am	-	7 am	40.00
5 pm	-	6 pm	65.00	7 am	-	12:30 pm	60.00
6 pm	-	7 pm	75.00	12:30 pm	-	1:30 pm	70.00
7 pm	-	7:30 pm	125.00	1:30 pm	-	2:30 pm	70.00
7:30 pm	-	8 pm	135.00	2:30 pm	-	4:30 pm	70.00
11 pm	-	11:30 pm	70.00	4:30 pm	-	6 pm	85.00
11:30 pm	-	cc	35.00	6 pm	-	7 pm	140.00
				7 pm	-	8 pm	180.00
Monday				8 pm	-	9 pm	260.00
8 pm	-	9 pm	250.00	9 pm	-	11 pm	230.00
9 pm	-	10 pm	250.00	11 pm	-	11:30 pm	90.00
10 pm	-	11 pm	290.00	11:30 pm	-	cc	40.00
Tuesday				*Sunday*			
8 pm	-	9 pm	220.00	6 am	-	9 am	40.00
9 pm	-	11 pm	260.00	9 am	-	10:30 am	60.00
				10:30 am	-	12 noon	40.00
Wednesday				12 noon	-	1 pm	60.00
8 pm	-	9 pm	220.00	1 pm	-	6 pm	70.00
9 pm	-	11 pm	260.00	6 pm	-	6:30 pm	80.00
				6:30 pm	-	7 pm	140.00
Thursday				7 pm	-	8 pm	300.00
8 pm	-	9 pm	200.00	8 pm	-	9 pm	425.00
9 pm	-	10 pm	220.00	9 pm	-	10 pm	375.00
10 pm	-	11 pm	240.00	10 pm	-	11 pm	375.00
				11 pm	-	11:15 pm	40.00
				11:15 pm	-	cc	40.00

*Note: Major sports and specials take special rates.
        60 seconds: twice the applicable 30-second rate.
        10 seconds: 50% of the applicable 30-second rate.

For Discussion

1. List the advantages and disadvantages of the various types of print media.

2. List the advantages and disadvantages of various types of broadcast media.

3. Develop a budget for Mr. Cromer. Justify your figures and method. Indicate the approximate percentage of your budget you would allocate for each medium by month. Defend.

PART **11**

Retail Financial Management

Case 30

THE STYLE SHOP— AM I A TOUGH GUY?

A FRIEND OF MINE recently said that 1975 is going to be the year of the tough guys, and that's right. It's for the guys and gals who care enough to put everything they've got into what they're doing, and do their best. It's not the year for sitting around and letting everyone else do it for them. It's a good year for challenge and productivity because there is still money there, and there are still people who are ready to spend it. It's up to the tough guys, to the ones who merit being the ones with whom that money is spent![1]

Dorothy Barton, sitting at her desk in the small office just off the Style Shop sales floor, ponders this quotation which happens to catch her eye as she leafs through the latest edition of the *Dallas Fashion Retailer*.

Nineteen seventy-four was a rough year in the women's ready-to-wear business as it was in many businesses. It was particularly rough, however, for the attractive, energetic Style Shop owner. Wife and mother of four teenage daughters, Mrs. Barton saw her sales fall 12.5 percent from 1973 to 1974; but more significantly, her net profit plunged 62.5 percent over the same time period. Untold hours were spent on the sales floor catering to her customer's eye for quality and fashion; in the office appealing to manufacturers to ship the next season's orders even though the current ones were yet to be paid; and at the Dallas Apparel Mart buying just the fashions she hoped would fit the needs and desires of her customers. At the same time, she was spending many hours each week in an effort to help her husband get his infant construction business off the ground.

This case was prepared by Janelle C. Ashley, Stephen F. Austin State University. It was prepared as a basis for class discussion rather than to illustrate either effective or ineffective handling of an administration situation. Presented at a Case Workshop and distributed by the Intercollegiate Case Clearing House, Soldiers Field, Boston, MA 02163. All rights reserved to the contributors. Printed in USA. Copyright by Janelle C. Ashley, 1975.

She remembered hearing one "expert" say, "This is not a time for pessimism, nor a time for optimism. This is a time for realism." And an economic prognosticator had indicated that he saw a good future in the industry, despite the economic slowdown. Buyers, he noted, are working a little more cautiously right now. They are still buying—just looking at things a little more carefully.

"What is 'realism' for me?" she asked herself. "Am I one of the tough guys who can stick it out and 'merit being the one with whom that money is spent?'"

Company History and Development

The Style Shop opened its doors on February 12, 1954 at 121 South First Street, Lufkin, Texas. A city of approximately 12,000, Lufkin had a need at that time for a first-rate women's specialty shop. The Style Shop filled that need. With an emphasis on quality merchandise and friendly service, the Style Shop owners immediately established a reputation as "the place to go" for fashionable wearing apparel for all occasions.

Helen Barton and Dana Young founded the original partnership. Mrs. Barton, owning 65 percent of the business, brought with her the financial acumen gained in part from 25 years experience as accountant with a local automobile dealership. Mrs. Young complemented this knowhow with over 20 years experience in retail selling—both buying and selling. Due to ill health, Mrs. Young was forced to leave the business after four years of profitable operation. Mrs. Barton bought the remaining 35 percent, therefore, and operated the specialty shop as a single proprietorship until July of 1969.

Dorothy Barton, daughter-in-law of Helen Barton, began with the Style Shop as a part-time accountant in March 1962. As her children entered school, she assumed more responsibility at the store and started work on a full-time basis. She worked not only in the financial area, but also in the buying and selling phase as well.

By the mid-60s, the Style Shop owner began to feel that she was reaching a saturation point in her present location. Sales had continued to climb steadily, but there was no room to expand. Established businesses were located on either side and above the Style Shop location. The severe space constraints made it impossible to display the merchandise effectively; and customer service areas were sorely inadequate.

The opportunity for expansion came in 1968 when a totally enclosed, air-conditioned mall was put in the planning stages. The Angelina Mall, located at the intersection of Highway 59 and Loop 287 in Lufkin, rests as the hub of a trade area extending over a radius of more than 100 miles. The only centers comparable to the Angelina Mall at the time were as distant as Houston to the south and Dallas to the north.

After a great deal of consultation and planning, Helen Barton and her new partner, Dorothy Barton, made the move to the air-conditioned mall in July 1969. The Style Shop, with a floor space of 3,183 square feet, joined 16 other retail operations including a major discount chain store, two full-line department stores, and several specialty shops. On the same plot are located a twin cinema and a Texaco service station with a new and modern Holiday Inn across the highway intersection and a new and growing junior college less than a mile down the highway.

The two partners, Helen and Dorothy Barton, shared a 50-50 ownership in the Style Shop commencing on the date the new shop was opened. According to the partnership agreement, however, it was contemplated that Dorothy Barton "shall from time to time hereafter assume greater responsibility in the management of such business...however, this process shall in no way affect the ownership or rights of Helen Barton in the assets and profits of the business." Between 1970 and 1972 the senior Mrs. Barton did in fact assume less and less responsibility in the management of the business. She worked none in 1973, and in January of 1974, Dorothy Barton purchased the 50 percent of the business belonging to her mother-in-law and proceeded to operate the business as a single proprietorship.

The City and Its Potential

With a population of 25,812, Lufkin is in 1975 a small, but rapidly growing city located in central East Texas, midway between the Angelina and Neches Rivers; 166 miles southeast of Dallas; and 120 miles northeast of Houston. Approximate population breakdown is 72 percent white, 28 percent Negro, 97 percent American born.

The county seat of Angelina County (population 51,600), Lufkin and the county have over 62 industrial manufacturing plants. The manufacturing payroll is over $60,000,000 annually going to industrial employees numbering over 8,000. The largest plants include oil field equipment, newsprint, trailers, gears, malleable iron and steel castings, dairy products, furniture, plywood plants, and lumber mills.

Approximately 7,600 families reside in the city of Lufkin with 15,700 families in Angelina County. Per household income averages $10,000 for the city and $9,056 for the county. Lufkin annual retail sales amount to $67,748,000 with the county reporting $101,863,000. Five banks in Lufkin and in the county carry over $140,000,000 in deposits.

Serving the Lufkin area are two newspapers (one daily), three radio stations and a television station. Transportation facilities include air, rail, and six motor freight lines.

The Style Shop Up to 1974

Personnel

The Style Shop employs four full-time clerks, one alteration lady and a maid. One former employee and the teenage daughter of Mrs. Barton are frequently called in for part-time work during peak seasons. Mrs. Flo Gates has been with the shop ten years. She works as a clerk and floor manager and accompanies Mrs. Barton to market. The other three clerks have been with the Style Shop from one to three years each. Personnel turnover and apathy have been problems in the past, but Mrs. Barton is quite pleased with her present work force.

Policies

The Style Shop operates with no formal, written policies. Personnel are paid wages and benefits comparable to other workers in similar capacities in the city. They enjoy a great deal of freedom in their work, flexibility in hours of work, and a 20 percent discount on all merchandise purchased in the shop.

Competition

Lufkin has an average number of retail outlets carrying ladies ready-to-wear for cities its size. Several department stores and other specialty shops carry some of the same lines as does the Style Shop, but they are all comparable in price. The Style Shop does handle several exclusive lines in Lufkin, however, and enjoys the reputation of being the most prestigious women's shop in town. Its major competition is a similar, but larger, specialty shop complete with a fashion shoe department in neighboring Nacogdoches, 19 miles away.

Inventory control

The Style Shop uses the services of Santoro Management Consultants, Inc. of Dallas, Texas for inventory control. I.B.M. inventory management reports are received each month broken down into 23 departmental groupings. These reports show beginning retail inventory for the month plus purchases for the month and year to date. Sales are broken into monthly and year to date figures with percentage change also indicated. The summary next itemizes mark downs for the month and year to date. Initial mark up percent for the current and past year is followed by maintained mark up percent also for the current and past year. Ending inventory is given at both cost and retail complete with percent change. Finally, the monthly report shows the month's supply on hand, department percent to total sales and department percent to total inventory. Provision is also made to indicate merchandise on order at the end of the month at retail and an adjusted open to buy column at both retail and cost. In February, Santoro prepares an ''Actual Fall and Winter'' summary sales report and in August an ''Actual Spring and Summer'' summary sales report. Each of these two includes a ''Projected Sales and Inventory'' breakdown for the ensuing period.

Financial position

It is often quite difficult and sometimes next to impossible to evaluate the ''true'' financial position of a single proprietorship or a partnership due to the peculiarities that are either allowed or tolerated in accounting practices for these forms of ownership. This is evident in looking at the following five-year summary Statements of Income and Financial Condition plus the complete statements for 1974 of the Style Shop. Key business ratios (median) for the "Women's Ready-to-Wear Stores" are also given for comparative purposes. (See Tables 30–1 through 30–5.)

TABLE 30-1

Consolidated Statement of Income (dollars)

Item	Year				
	1970	1971	1972	1973	1974
Sales	200,845.43	213,368.15	216,927.31	217,969.59	190,821.85
Cost of Sales	132,838.30	133,527.91	131,900.84	138,427.14	121,689.74
Gross Profit	68,007.13	79,840.24	85,026.47	79,542.45	69,132.11
Expenses	60,727.46	70,051.29	67,151.58	69,696.93	65,438.20
Net Profit	7,279.67	9,788.95	17,874.89	9,845.52	3,693.91

TABLE 30-2

Consolidated Statement of Financial Condition (dollars)

Item	Year				
	1970	1971	1972	1973	1974
Curr. Assets	38,524.93	70,015.11	66,749.78	58,530.44	68,458.34
Inventory	23,039.00	37,971.00	33,803.00	36,923.00	35,228.00
Fixed Assets	7,314.58	86,504.94	83,924.45	80,534.06	63,943.67
Total Assets	45,839.51	156,520.05	150,674.23	139,064.50	132,402.01
Curr. Liab.	35,892.81	19,586.45	20,161.93	31,587.57	55,552.70
Lg.-Tm. Liab.	none	39,042.90	33,680.07	26,841.76	20,003.45
Total Liab.	35,892.81	58,629.35	53,842.00	58,429.33	75,556.15
Net Worth	9,946.70	97,890.70	96,832.23	80,635.17	56,845.86

TABLE 30-3 ═══

Statement Of Income
Style Shop
Year Ended December 31, 1974

Sales		$190,821.85
Cost of Sales:		
Beginning Inventory	$ 36,923.00	
Purchases	119,994.74	
	156,917.74	
Ending Inventory	35,228.00	121,689.74
GROSS PROFIT		$ 69,132.11
Expenses:		
Advertising	$ 3,034.63	
Auto Expense	1,509.63	
Bad Debts	(439.83)	
Depreciation	1,580.49	
Freight, Express, Delivery	2,545.90	
Heat, Light, Power, and Water	1,847.96	
Insurance	1,431.80	
Interest	4,064.25	
Legal and Accounting	2,034.74	
Rent	11,220.40	
Repairs	528.98	
Salary	26,227.69	
Supplies	5,138.11	
Tax—Payroll	1,656.18	
—Other	604.62	
Telephone	784.67	
Dues and Subscriptions	601.89	
Market and Travel	1,066.09	65,438.20
NET PROFIT		$ 3,693.91

TABLE 30-4 ▰▰▰▰▰▰▰▰▰▰▰▰▰▰▰▰▰▰▰▰▰▰

Consolidated Statement Of Financial Condition
Style Shop
December 31, 1974

ASSETS

Current Assets:

Cash on Hand and Banks	$ 4,923.92
Accounts Receivable	21,306.42
Inventory	35,228.00
Cash Value—Life Insurance	7,000.00
Total Current Assets	$ 68,458.34

Fixed Assets:

Furniture and Fixtures and Leasehold Improvements	$27,749.94	
Less: Allowance for depr.	9,806.27	17,943.67
Auto and Truck		9,500.00
Real Estate		20,000.00
Furniture		10,000.00
Boat and Motor		2,000.00
Office Equipment		2,500.00
Jewelry		2,000.00
Total Fixed Assets		$ 63,943.67
TOTAL ASSETS		$132,402.01

LIABILITIES AND CAPITAL

Current Liabilities:

Accounts Payable	$ 30,413.12
Accrued Payroll Tax	825.64
Accrued Sales Tax	1,193.94
Note Payable—Due in one year	9,420.00
Note Payable—Lot	10,700.00
Note Payable—Auto	3,000.00
Total Current Liabilities	$ 55,552.70
Note Payable—Due after one year	20,003.45
TOTAL LIABILITIES	$ 75,556.15
Net Worth	56,845.86
TOTAL LIABILITIES AND CAPITAL	$132,402.01

TABLE 30-5

Key business ratios for women's ready-to-wear stores*

Ratio / Year	$\dfrac{CA}{CL}$	$\dfrac{NP}{NS}$	$\dfrac{NP}{NW}$	$\dfrac{NP}{NWC}$	$\dfrac{NS}{NW}$	$\dfrac{NS}{NWC}$	$\dfrac{NS}{INV}$	$\dfrac{FA}{NW}$	$\dfrac{CL}{NW}$	$\dfrac{TL}{NW}$	$\dfrac{INV}{NWC}$	$\dfrac{CL}{INV}$	$\dfrac{LTL}{NWC}$
1974	2.65	2.05	8.92	11.43	3.82	4.61	6.7	18.3	49.4	98.5	73.0	84.6	30.1
1973	2.81	2.30	8.53	10.96	3.96	4.92	6.7	18.2	49.2	100.1	72.3	87.2	33.2
1972	2.51	1.81	6.68	8.64	3.95	4.73	6.6	18.6	51.0	104.0	76.7	87.0	29.8
1971	2.38	1.86	7.14	9.98	3.76	4.90	6.7	17.5	54.5	124.1	71.1	93.9	34.0
1970	2.50	2.18	8.73	10.92	3.78	4.49	6.1	14.7	56.5	125.8	78.3	86.6	30.8

Key:
CA — Current Assets
CL — Current Liabilities
NP — Net Profit
NS — Net Sales
NW — Net Worth
NWC — Net Working Capital
INV — Inventory
FA — Fixed Assets
TL — Total Liabilities
LTL — Long Term Liabilities

*Collection period not computed. Necessary information as to the division between cash sales and credit sales was available in too few cases to obtain an average collection period usable as a broad guide.

Source: *Dun's Review and Modern Industry*, September issues, 1970–1974. Key added.

Two explanatory footnotes should be added to these statements. The jump in fixed assets between 1970 and 1971 and the subsequent changes are due in large part to the inclusion of personal real estate on the partnership books. The long-term liability initiated in 1971 is an S.B.A. loan. Caught in a period of declining sales (due in part to the controversy over skirt length and women's pantsuits) and rapidly rising expenses in the new mall location, the Style Shop owners found themselves in that proverbial "financial bind" in late 1969 and 1970. They needed additional funds both for working capital and fixed investments. Since a big jump in sales was anticipated in the new location, additional working capital was necessary to purchase the required inventory. The new tenants also desired fixed-asset money to purchase display fixtures for their new store. This money they obtained through a local bank in the form of a Small Business Administration-insured loan.

The Style Shop, 1975?

"Certainly there is no longer an arbiter of the length of a skirt or the acceptance of pantsuits," Mrs. Barton muses. "The economic picture is looking brighter. The experts tell us there will be more disposable personal income and a lower rate of inflation. Yet this is a time for 'realism.' Am I a 'tough guy?' "

Questions for Discussion

1. What key issues must ultimately be resolved by Mrs. Dorothy Barton?
2. What have been Mrs. Barton's (1) business objectives, (2) personal objectives, (3) business strategies? Do you see any conflict or inconsistency in the above?
3. Evaluate the position and performance of the Style Shop as a firm. What comparisons with other data are useful? What limitations are involved in your evaluation?
4. Estimate the market potential for the Style Shop on the basis of the Lufkin statistical data.
5. Determine the approximate value of the Style Shop. What alternative assumptions do you use for this purpose?
6. What strategic alternatives should Mrs. Barton consider? Review the opportunity and risk involved in each alternative. Compare with objectives.
7. Recommend a plan of action for Mrs. Barton, based on the above analysis.

Endnotes

1. "Merchandisers Must Provide Leadership," *Dallas Fashion Retailer*, June 1975, p. 17.

Case 31

THE STYLE SHOP—A CASE OF OPTIMISM

WE SHOULD HAVE OUR WRITEOFFS behind us, and 1979 is going to be a record year. Even increased payroll costs, fuel, and other operating costs will not keep us from producing a profit," declared President Perry Allgood in his March 1979 cover letter to the 1978 *Annual Report* for Lynn's Stores, Inc. "A year of progress," he called 1978 evidenced by net earnings of $21,646.00 or 30¢ per share, as compared to $6,448.00 or 9¢ per share achieved in 1977. "The 1978 figures reflected an 11.95¢ return on stockholders' equity," enthused the optimistic president.

Optimism was not the tenor of the times in 1979 for most businesses and individuals, however. The *Wall Street Journal* regularly reported on the declines in the leading economic indicators, public and private employment agencies noted that companies were tending to run much leaner, the price of gold continued to surge upwards of $325 an ounce, and the ravages of inflation endured to plague the wary consumer.

Tracing the comments from *Dun's* included in their reports on "Key Business Ratios for Retailing," one found in the September 1977 issue, "Retailers in '76 chalked up their first year of clear-cut improvements at the cash register since '73."[1] In September of 1978 reporting on the year 1977, *Dun's* pointed out,

> Despite all of last year's economic uncertainties, the retailers clearly outdid their 1976 performance. Of the 22 major categories of retailing, no fewer than sixteen showed gains in net profits as a proportion of net sales. The only losers: discount stores, gas service stations, lawn and garden supply stores, variety stores,

---

This case was prepared by Janelle C. Ashley and Robert H. Solomon, Stephen F. Austin State University. The research and written case information were presented at a Case Research Symposium and were evaluated by the Case Research Association's Editorial Board. Distributed by the Case Research Association. All rights reserved to the authors and the Case Research Association. Permission to reprint granted by the Case Research Association.

women's ready-to-wear outlets and stores selling paint, glass and wallpaper...So far 1978 has been a baffling year—for retailers as well as for economists and government planners. First, a fierce winter and the coal strike threw every economic indicator out of whack. While the Administration has succeeded in bringing unemployment down by several pegs since the first quarter, inflation continues to ravage the economy. Surveys of consumer confidence swing from low to high and back without any continuity. All in all, it is a very uncertain climate in which to do business.[2]

But industry sources in the fall of 1979 representing the industry of one of Lynn's newest acquisitions spoke in a vein more like that of Allgood. A *Women's Wear Daily* survey produced the following lead: "Top retailers are predicting a strong start for fall accessories business, despite all-time high prices for key items such as gold jewelry and leather handbags."[3] And if capital expansion is any positive indicator, the Dallas Apparel Mart opened its new 500,000-square foot fifth and sixth floor addition at the women's and children's mid-winter apparel market, August 25–30, 1979. The grand opening of the seven-story 1,200,000-square foot Atlanta Apparel Mart in the center of downtown Atlanta, a $41 million project, was timed to coincide with the women's apparel and accessories spring market, November 3–7, 1979.

In terms of advice, James J. Cohn offered the following:

> Merchants, in planning fall, have adopted a more cautious position with a sensitivity to current economic conditions. The aggressive retailer who keeps his stocks lean, assortments right and open-to-buy available will be able to take full advantage of opportunities that can appear in an economic pause.
>
> While it's proper to work on defensive measures in a slowed economy, insure your merchandisers also are working on offensive steps and positive opportunities.
>
> Included here would be energy shops to include heaters, robes, body comforters and blankets, along with physical fitness concepts to include jogging, warmup suits, and sporting goods.
>
> The times call for flexibility. Spend less effort putting out fires and more time lighting them.[4]

Company History and Development

An entrepreneur in the truest sense of the word, Perry Allgood moved from his position as buyer for Perry Brothers, Inc., a regional variety chain based in Lufkin, Texas, to president and chairman of the board of his own brainchild, Lynn's Stores, Inc. Allgood had served the Perry chain in various capacities for 22 years. In just a few short years, the new corporation grew from its original small chain of variety and discount stores to what might be called a mini-conglomerate.

As Exhibit 31–1 indicates, Allgood evidenced a strong customer orientation in his organization. Lynn's Variety Stores—numbering four—originally included several less profitable locations which were spun off. Lynn's—The Toy Store operation Allgood considers his "gold mine." Holland Sales Co. Inc., a wholesale company, serviced in part, not only the stores in the variety chain, but independents as well including other variety stores, mom-and-pop grocery stores, convenience stores, marina operations, and the like.

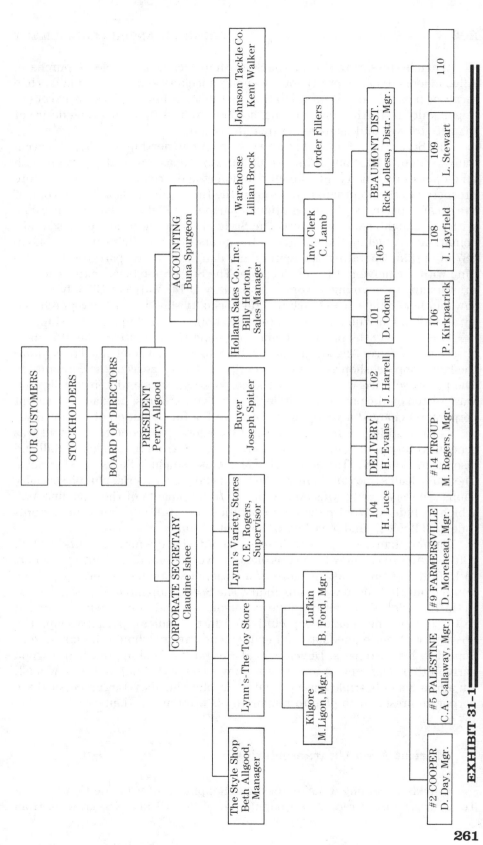

EXHIBIT 31-1

Organizational chart for Lynn's Variety Stores

When in the spring of 1977 The Style Shop became available for purchase, Allgood looked on the prestigious women's specialty shop situated in a prime location near his toy shop operating in the Angelina Mall as an excellent opportunity to further diversify his holdings and fulfill a long-time desire of his wife to own and manage her own dress shop.

The Style Shop, founded as a two-woman partnership in 1954, was originally located at 121 South First Street, Lufkin, Texas. Through the years with an emphasis on quality merchandise and personal, friendly service, the store prospered to the point where it outgrew the first location. In July 1969 one of the original partners (the other original partner had left the business in 1958) with her daughter-in-law moved The Style Shop to the totally enclosed, air-conditioned Angelina Mall located at the intersection of Highway 59 and Loop 287 in Lufkin. Operating as a mother and daughter-in-law partnership beginning with the move to the new location, The Style Shop became the sole proprietorship of the younger woman in January 1974. Mid-year 1975, however, saw another change in ownership of the specialty shop when it was purchased by an individual who again operated the shop as a single proprietorship.

After 22 months of owning and managing the operation, the 1975 purchaser sold to Perry Allgood and his Lynn's Stores, Inc. who planned to organize the ladies apparel shop as a separate entity under the aegis of the corporation. The purphase price was borne by the corporation, thus an interest obligation was created on the part of The Style Shop to Lynn's Stores, Inc.; and the parent corporation charged a yearly administrative fee for operation of the facility.

For the spring of 1980 a new totally enclosed, air-conditioned mall was scheduled for opening directly across Highway 59 from the Angelina Mall and also facing Loop 287. The new Lufkin Mall was to include Sears, J.C. Penneys, The Fair, Beall's (moving from the Angelina Mall), a cafeteria, plus 65 specialty shops. The Style Shop was one of the 25 to 30 tenants of the Angelina Mall which included a Woolco discount operation, two full-line department stores (one was Beall's), and a variety of specialty shops.

Rather than feeling apprehensive about the opening of Lufkin Mall, Allgood viewed the new facility as one that would tend to pull out-of-towners to Lufkin and thus make it more of a regional shopping center. Though he pointed out that there was a possibility The Style Shop might lose some walk-in traffic, Allgood saw his clientele as persons and individuals who responded to the one-on-one relationship cultivated in the ladies' specialty shop. The possibility of more adequate and convenient parking should, he noted, also appeal to his customers. Developers of the Lufkin Mall approached Allgood early in their planning to urge him to move The Style Shop to the new mall. An approximately triple lease commitment plus the above arguments led the corporate president to plan to remain in his present location.

Market Area Characteristics

Quickly becoming a major regional shopping center of the Central East Texas area, Lufkin recorded a population of 30,273 in 1978, growing from

23,049 in 1970 and 19,600 in 1960. Angelina County (of which Lufkin is the county seat) showed 58,803 residents in 1978. Approximate population breakdown was 83 percent white, 17 percent non-white, and 2 percent persons of Spanish surname. An estimated 165,000 persons resided within a 30-mile radius of the Central East Texas city, located midway between the Angelina and Neches River, 166 miles southeast of Dallas, and 120 miles northeast of Houston.

Sixty-two industrial manufacturing plants produced a payroll over $100 million annually, going to employees numbering over 8,000. The largest plants included oil field equipment, newsprint, trailers, dairy products, furniture, malleable iron and steel castings, gears, plywood plants, and lumber.

Households in Lufkin (1977) numbered 9,046 with 19,575 for the county. Estimated income per household for that year was $17,157 for the city and $15,607 for the county. Retail sales (also 1977) were recorded at $148,736,767 for the city and $201,566,381 for Angelina County. Five financial institutions in the city carried over $312 million in deposits and advertised plant financial assistance. The Lufkin Industrial Foundation offered 200 acres of land available for industrial properties with other private tracts also available ranging from 500 to 600 acres.

Lufkin boasted a commissioner-manager type of city government complete with planning commission, industrial plan approval, and zoning regulation. They considered their radius of labor-drawing area to be 50 miles with an estimated 14,774 males and 7,713 females available in the county labor force. With only one work stoppage in the previous five years, Lufkin graduated approximately 700 students from high school each year and recorded an unemployment rate of only 4.4 percent. Texas is a "right-to-work" state.

Home of the annual Southern Hushpuppy Olympics—which attracted such notables as Mrs. Lillian Carter—Lufkin touted excellent community, educational, medical, and recreational facilities. The area was served by two newspapers (one daily), four radio stations (both AM and FM), and a full-service television station. Transportation facilities included air, rail, bus, and seven motor freight lines.

The Style Shop Up to 1978

Personnel

Beth Allgood, wife of Perry Allgood, served as manager of The Style Shop. Working for her were one part-time and two full-time salesladies. One of the salesladies had worked for The Style Shop for approximately 15 years and served in effect as floor manager, often accompanying Mrs. Allgood to market. An alterations lady was employed for four days per week, and the accountant for Lynn's Stores, Inc. worked on the premises of The Style Shop two days per week.

Policies

The Style Shop operated with no formal, written policies. Personnel were paid wages and benefits comparable to other workers in similar capacities in the city including 80 percent paid on their hospitalization policy, a one-week vacation after one year of service, a two-week vacation after five years of service, and a small life insurance policy. Personnel enjoyed a great deal of freedom in their work, flexibility in hours of work, and a 15 percent discount on all merchandise purchased in the shop. The Style Shop opened its doors at 9:30 each morning and remained open until 9 p.m. on Thursdays and Fridays. The remaining days they closed at 6 p.m. The 9 p.m. closings were always extended to every day beginning the day after Thanksgiving each year and continuing until after Christmas. Beginning in 1980, all stores in the Angelina Mall planned to remain open until 9 p.m. each evening.

Competition

Lufkin had an average number of retail outlets carrying ladies ready-to-wear for cities its size. Several department stores and other specialty shops carried some of the same lines as did The Style Shop, but they were all comparable in price. The Style Shop did handle several exclusive lines in Lufkin, however, and enjoyed the reputation of being the most prestigious women's shop in town. Its major competition was a similar, but larger, specialty shop complete with a fashion shoe department in neighboring Nacogdoches, 19 miles away.

Financial position

With complete accounting statements for The Style Shop for only one full year of operation as a division of Lynn's Stores, Inc., comparisons are rather difficult to make if not completely meaningless. It is often instructive, however, to consider the various means used in presenting financial data and the implications for "bottomline" figures because of the variations. Tables 31-1 and 31-2 offer quasi-comparable data for years 1974-1978 footnoting the various periods of ownership and the fact that sales figures for 1975 and 1977 were for less than a 12-month period.

Tables 31-3 and 31-4 present the complete statements of income and financial condition for the first full year of operation of The Style Shop under the ownership of Lynn's Stores, Inc. To place these statements in their proper context, Exhibits 31-2 and 31-3 offer the consolidated statements of financial condition and income and retained earnings for Lynn's Stores, Inc. and Subsidiary which were included as a part of the corporation's 1978 *Annual Report.*

For comparative purposes, Table 31-5 shows how the statement of income appeared for The Style Shop in 1976 while operated as a sole proprietorship by the owner prior to Allgood. The corresponding statement of Financial condition was not available. Again for comparative purposes, Tables 31-6 and 31-7 offer complete statements of income and financial condition for 1974, the last complete year in which the specialty shop was operated as a sole proprietorship by the daughter-in-law of one of the original founders. Key business ratios (median) for the "Women's Ready-to-Wear Stores" are also given in Table 31-8 to serve as a basis for industry comparisons.

The Style Shop, 1980

"Though all of the figures are not yet in and I'm not in a position, therefore, to document my prediction of March 1978, I'll stand by that prediction and say again, '1979 is going to be a record year.' This will be true not only for Lynn's Stores, Inc., but for The Style Shop as well!" Perry Allgood, despite the often dire economic predictions, stood by his optimistic forecast, and planned to follow the advice of James Cohn by spending "less effort putting out fires and more time lighting them."

Was Mr. Allgood's optimism justified?

Endnotes

1. "Ratios of Retailing," *Dun's*, September 1977, p. 80.
2. "Ratios of Retailing," *Dun's*, September 1978, p. 124.
3. "Stores Say Fall Accessories Are Hot, Despite High Prices," *Women's Wear Daily*, August 17, 1979, p. 1.
4. James J. Cohn, "Independent Thinking," *Fashion Showcase*, August Market, 1979, p. 2E.

TABLE 31-1

Consolidated Statement of Income (dollars)

Item	Year				
	1974 *	1975 *	1976 *	1977 *	1978 *
Sales	190,821.85	128,469.25[1]	289,887.67	165,191.56[2]	264,566.02
Cost of Sales	121,689.74	**	168,597.94	**	165,406.06
Gross Profit	69,132.11	**	121,289.73	**	99,159.96
Expenses	65,438.20	**	76,625.63	**	114,087.79
Net Profit	3,693.91	**	44,664.10	(13,858.12)	(14,927.83)

[1]For six months *only* ending December 31, 1975.

[2]For eight months *only* ending December 31, 1977.

*1974 - Owned and managed complete year as sole proprietorship by daughter-in-law of original founder of The Style Shop.
*1975 - Sold July 1, 1975.
*1976 - Owned and managed complete year as sole proprietorship by 1975 purchaser.
*1977 - Sold May 1, 1977.
*1978 - Owned and managed complete year by Lynn's Stores, Inc.

**Comparable data not available.

TABLE 31-2 ━━━━━━━━━━━━━━━━━━━━━━━━━━━━━━━━━━━━━━

Consolidated Statement of Financial Condition (dollars)

Item	Year				
	1974 *	1975 *	1976 *	1977 *	1978 *
Curr. Assets	68,458.34	**	**	120,014.42	107,501.30
Inventory	35,228.00	**	**	86,449.40	73,873.09
Fixed Assets	63,943.67	**	**	47,927.38	42,122.25
Total Assets	132,402.01	**	**	167,941.80	149,623.55
Curr. Liab.	55,552.70	**	**	36,106.75	21,537.47
Lg.-Tm. Liab.	20,003.45	**	**	145,693.57	142,435.08
Total Liab.	75,556.15	**	**	167,941.80[1]	149,623.55[2]
Net Worth	56,845.86	**	**	N/A	N/A

[1] Current and long-term liabilities do not add to this figure as $13,858.52 loss has not been deducted.

[2] Current and long-term liabilities do not add to this figure as $14,349.00 loss has not been deducted.

*1974 - Owned and managed complete year as sole proprietorship by daughter-in-law of original founder of
    The Style Shop.
*1975 - Sold July 1, 1975.
*1976 - Owned and managed complete year as sole proprietorship by 1975 purchaser.
*1977 - Sold May 1, 1977.
*1978 - Owned and managed complete year by Lynn's Stores, Inc.

**Comparable data not available.

TABLE 31-3 ═══════════════════════════════════

Lynn's, The Style Shop
Statement Of Income
Year Ended December 31, 1978

SALES		$264,566.02
Service Charges		578.83
Cost of Sales		165,406.06
GROSS PROFIT		$ 99,738.79
EXPENSES:		
Advertising	$ 3,914.80	
Administrative	13,265.22	
Bad Debts	319.70	
Depreciation	6,501.88	
Dues and Subscriptions	626.82	
Donations	14.00	
Freight and Postage	1,336.52	
Insurance	601.00	
Interest	8,263.00	
Legal and Accounting	3,110.95	
Miscellaneous	580.11	
Contract Labor	844.10	
Refunds	568.74	
Service Charges	595.05	
Rent	15,061.98	
Repairs	1,008.72	
Salaries	41,760.40	
Supplies	6,032.86	
Taxes—Payroll	3,129.73	
Taxes—Property	382.49	
United Way	76.05	
Telephone	934.23	
Travel	1,968.23	
Utilities	3,202.77	
Cash Short (over)	(11.56)	
Total Expenses		$114,087.79
NET INCOME (LOSS)		$ (14,349.00)

TABLE 31-4 ▬▬▬▬▬▬▬▬▬▬▬▬▬▬▬▬▬▬▬▬▬▬▬▬▬▬▬▬▬▬▬▬▬▬▬▬

Lynn's, The Style Shop
Statement Of Financial Condition
Year Ended December 31, 1978

ASSETS

Current Assets:

Cash on Hand and in Bank		$ 3,100.00
Inventory at Cost		73,873.09
Accounts Receivable		30,528.21
Total Current Assets		107,501.30

Fixed Assets:

Equipment	$52,404.13	
Less: Depreciation Allowance	10,281.88	
Total Fixed Assets		42,122.25
TOTAL ASSETS		$149,623.55

LIABILITIES

Current Liabilities:

Accounts Payable	$ 16,137.47
Accrued Expenses	5,400.00
Total Current Liabilities	$ 21,537.47

Long-term Liabilities:

Long-term Notes Payable	600.00
Due to Lynn's Stores	141,835.08
Total Long-term Liabilities	$142,435.08
YTD Profit—(Loss)	(14,349.00)
TOTAL LIABILITIES	$149,623.55

TABLE 31-5

The Style Shop
Statement Of Income
Year Ended December 31, 1976

SALES		$290,305.08
Less: Returns and Adjustments		417.41
Total Gross Sales		$289,887.67
COST OF GOODS SOLD		
Inventory, January 1, 1976	$ 37,846.55	
Purchases	221,318.04	
Freight and Express	816.42	
	$259,981.01	
Less: Inventory, 12/31/76	91,383.07	
Total Cost of Goods Sold		168,597.94
GROSS PROFIT		$121,289.73
STORE AND ADMINISTRATIVE EXPENSE		
Rent	$ 9,790.00	
Salaries—Store	32,337.44	
Advertising	2,947.68	
Store Utilities and Telephone	5,767.39	
Store Supplies	5,943.18	
Office Supplies	1,409.05	
Insurance and Bond	2,705.30	
Taxes	2,251.51	
Legal, Audit and Professional	2,697.50	
Repairs	610.31	
Alterations and Cleaning	313.30	
Credit Card Fees	1,232.50	
Credit Report Expense	210.00	
Dues	165.00	
Marketing Expense	4,438.06	
Entertainment	966.25	
Style Show Expense	453.48	
Business Car Expense	1,857.43	
Miscellaneous Expense	530.25	
Total Store and Adm. Expense		76,625.63
TOTAL OPERATING INCOME		$ 44,664.10

TABLE 31-6

The Style Shop
Statement Of Income
Year Ended December 31, 1974

SALES		$190,821.85
Cost of Sales:		
Beginning Inventory	$ 36,923.00	
Purchases	119,994.74	
	$156,917.74	
Ending Inventory	35,228.00	121,689.74
GROSS PROFIT		$ 69,132.11
Expenses:		
Advertising	$ 3,034.63	
Auto Expense	1,509.63	
Bad Debts	(439.83)	
Depreciation	1,580.49	
Freight, Express, Delivery	2,545.90	
Heat, Light, Power, and Water	1,847.96	
Insurance	1,431.80	
Interest	4,064.25	
Legal and Accounting	2,034.74	
Rent	11,220.40	
Repairs	528.98	
Salary	26,227.69	
Supplies	5,138.11	
Tax—Payroll	1,656.18	
—Other	604.62	
Telephone	784.67	
Dues and Subscriptions	601.89	
Market and Travel	1,066.09	65,438.20
NET PROFIT		$ 3,693.91

TABLE 31-7

The Style Shop
Consolidated Statement Of Financial Condition
December 31, 1974

ASSETS

Current Assets:

Cash on Hand and Banks		$ 4,923.92
Accounts Receivable		21,306.42
Inventory		35,228.00
Cash Value—Life Insurance		7,000.00
Total Current Assets		$ 68,458.34

Fixed Assets:

Furniture and Fixtures and Leasehold Improvements	$27,749.94	
Less: Depreciation Allowance	9,806.27	17,943.67
Auto and Truck		9,500.00
Real Estate		20,000.00
Furniture		10,000.00
Boat and Motor		2,000.00
Office Equipment		2,500.00
Jewelry		2,000.00
Total Fixed Assets		$ 63,943.67
TOTAL ASSETS		$132,402.01

LIABILITIES AND CAPITAL

Current Liabilities:

Accounts Payable	$ 30,413.12
Accrued Payroll Tax	825.64
Accrued Sales Tax	1,193.94
Note Payable—Due in one year	9,420.00
Note Payable—Lot	10,700.00
Note Payable—Auto	3,000.00
Total Current Liabilities	$ 55,552.70
Note Payable—Due after one year	20,003.45
TOTAL LIABILITIES	$ 75,556.15
Net Worth	56,845.86
TOTAL LIABILITIES AND CAPITAL	$132,402.01

TABLE 31-8
Key business ratios for women's ready-to-wear stores*

Ratio / Year	$\frac{CA}{CL}$	$\frac{NP}{NS}$	$\frac{NP}{NW}$	$\frac{NP}{NWC}$	$\frac{NS}{NW}$	$\frac{NS}{NWC}$	$\frac{NS}{INV}$	$\frac{FA}{NW}$	$\frac{CL}{NW}$	$\frac{TL}{NW}$	$\frac{INV}{NWC}$	$\frac{CL}{INV}$	$\frac{LTL}{NWC}$
1974	2.52	1.77	6.93	7.48	4.31	5.02	6.4	18.9	52.4	132.8	80.9	88.3	36.5
1975	2.68	1.82	6.68	7.31	3.89	4.62	7.1	29.4	49.6	109.4	72.5	84.6	32.3
1976	2.76	2.37	7.83	9.77	3.40	4.12	5.8	18.7	45.9	82.8	75.1	76.8	33.3
1977	2.63	2.13	6.82	10.16	3.83	4.54	6.1	20.8	59.1	103.7	72.8	74.6	28.3
1978**	3.32	5.00	18.77	21.73	3.42	3.86	4.5	19.8	34.0	52.0	87.8	50.0	56.6

Key: CA — Current Assets
CL — Current Liabilities
NP — Net Profit
NS — Net Sales
NW — Net Worth

NWC — Net Working Capital
INV — Inventory
FA — Fixed Assets
TL — Total Liabilities
LTL — Long Term Liabilities

*Collection period not computed. Necessary information as to the division between cash sales and credit sales was available in too few cases to obtain an average collection period usable as a broad guide.

**"Reflecting operations in 1978, the fourteen ratios for each of the industries are based this year on data from 400,000 companies, compared with 12,000 in previous samples. With this broader base, the number of SIC's has been expanded from 125 in prior reports to 800. Due to the heavy increase in the number of companies in the data sample, comparisons with past years' ratios are obviously invalid." (*Dun's*, October, 1979, p. 140.)

Source: *Dun's*, September issues, 1976–1978; October issues, 1975 and 1979. Key added.

Consolidated Statement Of Income And Retained Earnings
Lynn's Stores, Inc. And Subsidiary

	FOR THE YEAR ENDED DECEMBER 31,	
	1978	1977
Net sales	$1,743,597.77	$1,576,588.50
Other income	21,782.06	19,713.00
TOTAL INCOME	$1,765,379.83	$1,596,301.50
Cost and Expenses:		
Cost of goods sold	$1,119,753.03	$1,017,735.40
Operating expenses	492,722.83	425,779.30
Administrative expenses	63,106.13	96,190.60
Interest expense	34,968.42	27,728.20
Depreciation expense	33,182.61	22,370.90
Income tax		9.00
TOTAL COSTS AND EXPENSES	$1,743,733.02	$1,589,813.40
NET INCOME	21,646.81	6,488.10
Retained earnings - Beginning of period	45,650.47	39,162.30
Retained earnings - End of period	$ 67,297.28	$ 45,650.40
Income per share based on number of shares outstanding at end of year	$ .30	$ .09

EXHIBIT 31-2

Consolidated Statement Of Financial Condition
Lynn's Stores, Inc. And Subsidiary

	DECEMBER 31,	
	1978	1977

ASSETS

	1978	1977
Current Assets:		
Cash	$ 37,544.68	$ 42,544.47
Accounts receivable	48,429.14	39,470.95
Inventory - At lower of cost or market	438,526.66	429,769.35
Prepaid expenses	3,147.41	6,471.02
TOTAL CURRENT ASSETS	$527,647.89	$518,255.79
Property and equipment - At cost less accumulated depreciation	146,262.69	145,289.60
Investments - At cost	1,000.00	—0—
TOTAL ASSETS	$674,910.58	$663,545.39

LIABILITIES AND STOCKHOLDER'S EQUITY

	1978	1977
Current Liabilities:		
Accounts payable	$102,244.70	$ 85,947.39
Accrued expenses	5,887.27	8,779.47
Notes and mortgages payable - Portion due in one year	58,181.72	26,864.55
TOTAL CURRENT LIABILITIES	$166,313.69	$121,591.41
Notes and mortgages payable in over one year	$299,793.44	$360,797.34
Stockholder's Equity:		
Capital stock - 1,000,000 shares at 1.00 par value authorized, 71,000 and 70,000 shares issued and outstanding as of December 31, 1978 and 1977	$ 71,000.00	$ 70,000.00
Paid-in capital	70,506.17	65,506.17
Retained earnings	67,297.28	45,650.47
TOTAL STOCKHOLDER'S EQUITY	$208,803.45	$181,156.64
TOTAL LIABILITIES AND STOCKHOLDER'S EQUITY	$674,910.58	$663,545.39

EXHIBIT 31-3

Case 32

SAM'S ENTERPRISES — A PROBLEM OF RISK MANAGEMENT

SAM PARKINSON is a young, energetic, sociable man who enjoys his work, his family, and his sporting activities. He is ambitious, intelligent, and supportive of community functions.

Sam, a pharmacist by training, has a pharmacy which is located in a neighborhood shopping center. Other stores in the center include a chain supermarket, a local hardware store, a barber shop, a dry cleaning establishment, and a branch bank. Sam's place of business is at the end of the shopping center in a freestanding location.

Sam's product-line mix is basically limited to pharmaceutical and related items. The major departments are prescription drugs, nonprescription drugs, health and beauty aids, tobacco products, a magazine and book department, a small gift and stationery department, and a lunch counter and soda fountain combination. While Sam's prices are slightly higher than most drugstore chains, he emphasizes personal services such as home delivery, personal credit, medical income tax statements, and basic nonmedical advice on drug products. He has experienced constant and increasing growth over the five-year period he has been in business and expects this trend to continue. With this success he has increasingly developed an awareness of the pervasiveness of risk and has become concerned with how to deal with it.

Most people describe Sam as a "comer," moderately successful, and innovative. At age thirty-two, he is in good health, is married, and has two small children ages three and one. He owns his own home (equity $25,000 and mortgage $60,000), two cars, a boat and motor, and a motorcycle. He also owns his store building (equity $20,000 and mortgage $40,000) and employs one additional registered pharmacist. Sam also employs two other full-time workers in the pharmacy, both of whom handle cash transactions. He owns a small delivery truck which he uses principally in connection with his drug store and other business activities.

This case was prepared by Jewell Watson, University of Arkansas at Little Rock.

Sam invests in real property. He already owns a fully-occupied apartment building which has eight family units. His mortgage on this building is $80,000. He expects rental income to cover all payments on his mortgage plus a reserve for the upkeep of the building. He does not engage in construction.

Sam has opened a small laboratory and has a patent on a lotion that he has already begun to produce. He has enough of this product in his leased warehouse to provide him with $25,000 profit when it is sold. He cannot put it on the market, however, for two months. Furthermore, he has to rely upon one source for one of the ingredients of the lotion. If fire or some other peril were to close down his supplier, he would have to suspend operation of his laboratory.

Sam intends to use both public and contract inland carriers to transport his merchandise. He does not sell in foreign markets, although this may be a future consideration. He employs enough people to come under the purview of Workmen's Compensation laws.

Sam is an avid golfer. On his last outing he hit the governor of the state on the head with a drive from the tee at the seventh hole. He also engages in other sports which presents the possibility of causing personal injury or property damage to others.

For Discussion

1. Comment upon the major techniques for handling risks.

2. Identify the major exposures to loss which confront Sam in both his personal and business activities.

3. Suggest ways for dealing with Sam's risks. In commenting upon insurance needs, be specific as to types of coverage to meet his needs.

4. Contact a local insurance agent to help you solve Sam's insurance needs. Write a brief report on the agent's suggested insurance plan and then critique it.